THE NICOMACHEAN ETHICS

ARISTOTLE (384–322 BC), with Plato one of the two greatest philosophers of antiquity, and in the view of many the greatest philosopher of all time, lived and taught in Athens for most of his career. He began as a pupil of Plato, and for some time acted as tutor to Alexander the Great. He left writings on a prodigious variety of subjects, covering the whole field of knowledge from biology and astronomy to rhetoric and literary criticism, from political theory to the most abstract reaches of philosophy. He wrote two treatises on ethics, called *Eudemian* and *Nicomachean* after their first editors, his pupil Eudemus and his son Nicomachus. *The Nicomachean Ethics* was probably written later, in Aristotle's fifties and sixties, when he was head of the Lyceum, the school he founded in Athens.

SIR DAVID ROSS (1877–1971) was Provost of Oriel College and Deputy Professor of Moral Philosophy at Oxford. He acted as General Editor of the complete Oxford Translation of Aristotle, of which the present translation forms part.

J. L. ACKRILL is Professor of the History of Philosophy at Oxford, and a Fellow of Brasenose College.

J. O. URMSON was until 1979 Fellow and Tutor in Philosophy at Corpus Christi College, Oxford.

OXFORD WORLD'S CLASSICS

For over 100 years Oxford World's Classics have brought readers closer to the world's great literature. Now with over 700 titles—from the 4,000-year-old myths of Mesopotamia to the twentieth century's greatest novels—the series makes available lesser-known as well as celebrated writing.

The pocket-sized hardbacks of the early years contained introductions by Virginia Woolf, T. S. Eliot, Graham Greene, and other literary figures which enriched the experience of reading. Today the series is recognized for its fine scholarship and reliability in texts that span world literature, drama and poetry, religion, philosophy and politics. Each edition includes perceptive commentary and essential background information to meet the changing needs of readers.

OXFORD WORLD'S CLASSICS

ARISTOTLE

The Nicomachean Ethics

Translated with an Introduction by
DAVID ROSS

Revised by
J. L. ACKRILL *and* J. O. URMSON

OXFORD
UNIVERSITY PRESS

OXFORD
UNIVERSITY PRESS

Great Clarendon Street, Oxford OX2 6DP

Oxford University Press is a department of the University of Oxford.
It furthers the University's objective of excellence in research, scholarship,
and education by publishing worldwide in

Oxford New York

Athens Auckland Bangkok Bogotá Buenos Aires Calcutta
Cape Town Chennai Dar es Salaam Delhi Florence Hong Kong Istanbul
Karachi Kuala Lumpur Madrid Melbourne Mexico City Mumbai
Nairobi Paris São Paulo Singapore Taipei Tokyo Toronto Warsaw

with associated companies in Berlin Ibadan

Oxford is a registered trade mark of Oxford University Press
in the UK and in certain other countries

Published in the United States
by Oxford University Press Inc., New York

British Library Cataloguing in Publication Data

Data available

Library of Congress Cataloging in Publication Data

Data available

ISBN 0–19–283407–X

9 10 8

Printed in Great Britain by
Clays Ltd, St Ives plc

INTRODUCTION

THE corpus of Aristotle's works contains two treatises
bearing the name *Ethics*—the *Nicomachean* and the
Eudemian. At one time the latter was believed to be the
work not of Aristotle but of his pupil Eudemus, but
more recent research has shown that the *Eudemian
Ethics* belongs to a stage of Aristotle's thought in which
he stood nearer to Plato and to his own early Dialogues
than he did when he wrote the *Nicomachean Ethics*. This
being so, the titles are probably to be explained by the
fact that the two works were edited respectively by
Eudemus and by Aristotle's son Nicomachus. The later
of the two should probably be assigned to the latest
period of Aristotle's life, the period of his headship of
the Lyceum, i.e. to his fifties or sixties.

The plan of the work is not altogether simple. The
first four books form a natural sequence. Bk. 1 deals
with the nature of the good for man, and finishes with
a division of the faculties of man, in which Aristotle
distinguishes a faculty which forms plans and a faculty
which carries them out; goodness is accordingly divided into intellectual excellence and moral excellence.
Bks. 2–4 are concerned with moral excellence; bk. 2.
1–3.5 gives a general account of it, and 3.6 to the end of
4 discusses particular moral virtues in detail. Bks. 5–7
are according to the ancient tradition common to the
Eudemian and the *Nicomachean Ethics*; which would
mean that, while the two main works represent an
earlier and a later course of lectures, this part was left
unchanged. Bk. 5 discusses one of the two cardinal virtues not dealt with in bks. 2–4—justice. Bk. 6 discusses
the various forms of intellectual excellence. 7.1–10
discusses two conditions which lie between virtue and

vice—continence and incontinence. 7. 11–14 is a discussion of pleasure. Bks. 8 and 9, on friendship, do not form an essential part of a treatise on ethics, and certainly so full a treatment of it seems out of place; it is not improbable that these two were originally a separate treatise. Bk. 10, on *eudaimonia* or well-being, forms a fitting conclusion to the work, but some embarrassment is caused by the fact that chs. 1–5 form a second discussion of pleasure, in part duplicating and in part differing from that in bk. 7; it is natural to suppose that the treatment in bk. 7 belongs to the earlier and that in bk. 10 to the later of the two courses already mentioned.

Though the general plan is fairly simple, it will be seen that it has defects. Aristotle cannot have meant the work to appear in its present form; we must suppose that Nicomachus did not wish to omit anything that had a bearing in any way on ethics, and that that accounts for the present form of the work.

Aristotle regards human life as consisting of the pursuit of ends, and his main object is to discover the nature of the end or ends at which man ought to aim—though he does not always distinguish this from the question what the ends are at which men actually do aim. He describes the end as being *eudaimonia*, and this word is usually translated 'happiness'. The translation is not altogether satisfactory. Happiness is a state of feeling, but he makes it clear that by *eudaimonia* he means a certain kind of activity (carrying feeling, no doubt, with it), not a kind of feeling. Wordsworth asks:

> *Who is the happy warrior? Who is he*
> *That every man in arms would wish to be?*

and Aristotle is similarly bent on discovering what is the most enviable life. There are, he says, three popular views about the nature of this life. One is that it is the life of pleasure; but the life which aims at pleasure, regardless of the source from which it is derived, is worthy of beasts rather than of men. The political life aims at honour, but honour depends more on him who gives it than on him who gets it. The life of money-making cannot be regarded as an end in itself. There remains a fourth life, the contemplative life; and here he sounds the note which resounds in the final book. Meantime he lays down two conditions—that the end of human life must be something chosen for its own sake, and something that is itself satisfying, needing no supplement beyond itself. He seeks to get further light on its nature by asking what the typical function of man, the function that only man has, must be. The life of nutrition and growth is shared by the plants. The life of sense-perception is shared by the animals. What remains is the life of the rational element in us. Thus human good turns out to be 'activity of soul in the sense either of being obedient to a rational principle or of apprehending such a principle'; in other words, either good moral activity or good intellectual activity. It is 'activity of soul in accordance with virtue, or, if there be more than one virtue, in accordance with the best and most complete'—to which Aristotle adds 'in a complete life', since activity for a short time does not constitute a satisfactory end.

The remainder of the first book is occupied mainly with an attempt to show that the account just given of the end for man is in accord with views commonly held, either by the many or by the wise. In ch. 13 he returns to a matter already mentioned. Since he has defined *eudaimonia* as an activity of soul in accordance with virtue, he turns to the discussion of virtue. He returns to his distinction between the rational and the irrational element in the soul. He had divided the rational element into two parts—that which obeys such a principle and that which discovers one for itself. He now divides the irrational element into two parts. The first is that which acts independently of any such principle; this is that by which animals and plants live and grow. The other is that which, while it may follow a rational principle, may also disobey it. This is in fact the faculty of desire. Thus one and the same faculty is at one time called by Aristotle rational and at another irrational. It is irrational, in the sense that it does not grasp a principle—it is reason that does that; it is rational, in the sense that it can accept such a principle when presented to it by reason—though it can also refuse to accept such a principle and may act irrationally. This leads Aristotle to divide virtue, or excellence, into two kinds, intellectual excellence and moral excellence, which is the excellence of this semi-rational faculty of desire.

The consideration of virtue is continued in bk. 2. Just as men become builders by building, they become just by doing just acts, and temperate by doing temperate acts: 'states of character arise out of like activities'. And activities which produce excellence are those in which both excess and defect are avoided. Virtue has, too, an essential connexion with pleasure and pain; it is not by indifference to these, but by taking pleasure in the right things and to the right degree, that men become virtuous.

There is some difficulty, he admits, in the saying that it is by doing virtuous acts that we become virtuous; it might be said that to do just acts we must already be just. But Aristotle points out that acts which are such as a just man would do are not just acts unless they are done *as* the just man would do them—that it is possible to do acts which are on the outside precisely those that a just man would do, but to do them without the knowledge that they are just, or without the desire to do them because they are just, or without having the firm character that a just man has.

He turns next to the question what kind of thing virtue is—a passion, a faculty, or a state of character, and has no difficulty in showing that it is a state of character. It remains to say what sort of state of character it is. It is an intermediate state, but that does not mean that it is always equidistant between the two possible extremes; what must be sought is 'the mean relatively to us'; the act must be done at the right times, with reference to the right objects, towards the right people, with the right motive, and in the right way. 'Virtue is a state of character concerned with choice, lying in a mean, i.e. the mean relatively to us, this being determined by a rational principle, i.e. by that principle by which the man of practical wisdom would determine it.' That is Aristotle's definition of virtue. At the same time (he points out) in respect of excellence it is an extreme. There is, of course, no mean or excess or deficiency of vice, nor any excess or deficiency of virtue.

Aristotle proceeds to fill in the detail of the doctrine of the mean. Courage is a mean with regard to feelings of fear and confidence, temperance a mean with regard to pleasures and pains. Similarly liberality, munificence (liberality on a large scale), proper pride, good temper are means; and he adds four intermediate states for which there are no recognized names—the intermediates between boastfulness and mock modesty, between boorishness and buffoonery, between obsequiousness and quarrelsomeness, between bashfulness and shamelessness; he also recognizes what is really a false opposition, between envy and spite. He adds, too, that sometimes a virtue leans rather towards one extreme than towards the other—courage towards rashness, liberality towards generosity—and that no rules to guide us in choosing how to act virtuously can be laid down in advance: 'the decision depends on perception of the individual circumstances'.

In bk. 3 Aristotle turns to discuss the conditions of responsibility for actions. He first lays it down that virtue is displayed only in those passions and actions that are voluntary, and proceeds to consider the conditions under which action is *in*voluntary. It is so if it is done either under compulsion or in ignorance. It may be debated, he says, whether things done from fear of greater evils or for some noble object are voluntary. He admits that such actions have an element of the involuntary, but maintains that they are in fact voluntary, since at the moment of action the doer wills to do them. His definition of compulsion is strict; actions are involuntary only when the cause is in external circumstances and the agent contributes nothing. With regard to ignorance, he distinguishes between actions done in ignorance and those done by reason of ignorance, and identifies the former with actions done in ignorance of the general principles of right action, and the latter with those done by reason of ignorance of the particular circumstances; and he pronounces that it is only ignorance of the latter kind that makes an action involuntary and frees the doer from liability: 'the voluntary is that of which the moving principle is in the agent himself, he being aware of the particular circumstances'. Thus acts done by reason of anger or appetite are not rightly called involuntary.

While knowledge of the circumstances and absence

of compulsion are the necessary preconditions of voluntary action, Aristotle now proceeds to something which he considers to discriminate characters better than actions do, namely choice, which he defines as the adoption of action decided on after deliberation. He points out that we deliberate not about ends but about means, and he indicates the nature of deliberation by comparing it with the process of discovering the solution of a geometrical problem. The problem being to construct a certain kind of figure, we ask what we must first have constructed in order to do this, and so on until we come to a figure which we can construct on the basis of knowledge we already have. So too before acting we consider what we want to bring about, and ask what we must bring about to bring that about, and what we must bring about to bring *that* about . . . until we come to something we can bring about here and now: 'what is last in the order of analysis is first in the order of becoming'. Choice is the adoption of an action arrived at by such a process.

From bk. 3, ch. 5, to the end of bk. 4 Aristotle is occupied with a detailed account of the virtues and vices that have been named in bk. 2. He starts with two of the four cardinal virtues recognized by the Greeks, courage and temperance; in accordance with the principle he has already laid down, he describes each virtue as a mean between extremes. Courage he describes as a mean in respect of feelings of fear and confidence. This is, at first sight, surprising; one is inclined to say that it is simply the control of natural feelings of fear. But he is in fact right in holding that there is a feeling, less common than fear, but equally needing control, the enjoyment of danger for danger's sake. There is less to be said for his treatment of temperance as a mean; at least, instinctive shrinking from bodily pleasures is probably less common than the enjoyment of danger. Of all the virtues, the one his description of which is least congenial to modern feeling is *megalopsychia*—impossible to translate but with 'pride' as perhaps its nearest equivalent. His difficulty in dealing with it is partly accounted for by a fact which he notes elsewhere, that in the Greek notion of *megalopsychia* two different things, resentment of injury and indifference to fortune, are combined.

To justice Aristotle devotes the whole of bk. 5. He begins with a distinction between universal justice and particular justice. Universal justice is coextensive with virtue, but in speaking of virtuous acts as 'just' in this sense we are emphasizing a particular aspect of them, that they are acts in which the rights of others are given due consideration. He passes rapidly to 'particular justice', the justice which is only one virtue among others. This is the justice which is opposed to all acts the motive of which is the specific desire of gain in honour, wealth, or safety. Within particular justice Aristotle distinguishes two species. One is that which is manifested in distribution of 'honour or money or the other things that fall to be divided among those who have a share in the constitution'. It used to be said that *we* regard ourselves rather as taxpayers than as shareholders in the state, but it may be that the welfare state has brought us nearer to the Greek way of thinking, which is Aristotle's way of thinking. Public property, such as the land of a new colony, was often distributed between the citizens, and public assistance to the needy was also recognized. Aristotle has also in mind the distribution of profits to partners in proportion to what they have put into their business. By distribution of honours he means the distribution of office in accordance with the 'hypothesis' of the particular state that free status, wealth, noble birth, or virtue is to be the standard. The arithmetical formula is simple: if a person A bears a certain ratio to person B in merit (according to the standard of merit in the state to which they belong), the task of the distributor is to divide the whole good available for distribution, into two parts C and D which are in the same ratio, and assign C to A, and D to B.

The other kind of 'particular justice' is rectificatory justice. This is the justice administered in civil cases; it is concerned not with the punishment of wrongdoing, but with restitution. The two persons concerned are treated as equally deserving. The good originally enjoyed by one party is represented by the line AA', that of the other by the line CC' (= AA'). The second party has deprived the first of a good which, as being what that party has lost, is called AE, and as being what the other party has gained is called DC. Thus the new positions of the two parties are represented by AA'−AE and CC'+DC. The task of the judge is simply to transfer DC to the injured party. There is here no question of a proportion; there is just an arithmetical progression; the new position of each party (BB', which = AA' = CC') is half-way between the gainful position DC' and the lossful position EA'. (See p. 116.)

Aristotle now proceeds to yet another form of justice. The Pythagoreans had defined justice as reciprocity. This does not apply, Aristotle observes, either to distributive or to remedial justice, but there is a third kind of 'particular justice', viz. justice in exchange, or commercial justice, to which it does apply. Reciprocity is necessary if the State is to be held together, for it is held together by exchange of services, and people will not exchange services unless they get as good as they give. But simple reciprocity will not do; for the exchanging parties are of unequal worth in respect of efficiency.

Their products must be brought into an equation before exchange takes place. What is to be the unit? It must be demand. But A, whose product B wants, may not want B's product, or not want it when B wants A's. To avoid the fluctuation in demand which this would cause, money, which is 'a conventional representative of demand', 'a guarantee that if you do not want something in exchange now, you can get it when you want it', has been introduced. Money is itself subject to fluctuation in value, but less so than most goods. Now if we know that a house is worth five minae and a bed one mina, we know that a house is worth five beds, so that if 'cross-conjunction' takes place accordingly, five beds exchanging for one house, justice will be done. This analysis, one of the earliest efforts in political economy, has been generally recognized as an important example of Aristotle's analytic genius.

Two other matters in bk. 5 are specially worthy of notice. One is Aristotle's statement about the degrees of responsibility. When an injury done by one person to another takes place contrary to reasonable expectation, it is a misadventure. When it is not contrary to reasonable expectation, but does not imply vice, it is a mistake (what our law calls negligence). When it is done with knowledge but not after deliberation, it is an act of injustice but does not imply that the doer is a wicked man. When it is done by deliberate choice, the doer is a wicked man. The other matter is Aristotle's distinction between justice and equity. He recognizes that it is impossible for lawgivers to foresee all the circumstances that may arise and to provide for them by law, and he therefore holds that there should be a power of taking any unusual circumstance into account and deciding accordingly. 'This is the nature of the equitable, a correction of law where it is defective owing to its generality'—which he compares to 'the leaden rule used in making the Lesbian moulding, a rule which adapts itself to the shape of the stone'. The distinction drawn in our legal system between justice and equity owes its precise form to a variety of historical facts, but is to a large extent derived from Aristotle's conception, transmitted through the Roman lawyers.

Bk. 6 is devoted to the study of the various excellences of intellect, and at first sight this might seem irrelevant to a work on ethics, i.e. on conduct. Aristotle offers two reasons why it is relevant. One is that he has defined the virtuous man as acting in accordance with the right rule, and that the framing of this rule is an intellectual operation. The other is that he has defined the end of life as consisting in 'virtuous activity of soul, or, if there be more than one virtue, in accordance with the best and most perfect'; he has therefore to ask which of these excellences is the best—whether it is a moral or an intellectual excellence, and what particular excellence it is. There are, he says, five states of mind by which we reach truth, and whose names imply that they are infallible. These are science, art, practical wisdom, intuitive reason, theoretical wisdom; of these the first, fourth, and fifth are concerned with knowledge alone, the second and third with practice also. By science Aristotle means the act of drawing correct inferences from premisses known to be true. By art he means the kind of knowledge which enables us to make useful or beautiful things; and in his usage of the term 'art' he is more often thinking of the making of useful than of the making of beautiful things. By practical wisdom he means the power of deliberating how a state of being which will satisfy us is to be brought into existence. The lack of such wisdom is an intellectual, not a moral, condition, but he points out that vice has the power of making such wisdom impossible for a man, by destroying the first principle, the major premiss of the practical syllogism, which tells us what the true ends of life are.

Intuitive reason is the complement to the excellence called science which Aristotle has already named. *That* was the power of drawing correct conclusions; *this* is the power by which we know the premisses from which these conclusions are drawn. Finally, theoretical wisdom is the union of these two things, science and intuitive reason. Of it he says that it is as much superior to practical wisdom as its objects, such as the heavenly bodies, are superior to man, whose good is the object of practical wisdom. Theoretical wisdom must be understood as including all the divisions of 'wisdom' recognized in the *Metaphysics*—metaphysics, mathematics, and natural science.

The later chapters of bk. 6 throw further light on Aristotle's conception of practical wisdom. He says that it coincides with political knowledge, though it must be defined differently. This means that the same quality of mind which will enable a man to see his own duties aright would enable him to see how the life of the community can best be carried on. This might seem a very questionable view. But if we realize that by practical wisdom he means not merely a knowledge of the generally accepted rules of morality, but also an intelligent understanding of the reasons for them, his view may not seem so paradoxical.

Having distinguished these five faculties, Aristotle says later that they converge to the same point. In particular, his account begins to bring practical wisdom nearer to intuitive reason. Practical wisdom being concerned with particular actions, it is better, he says, to know the conclusion of the practical syllogism without the major premiss, than the latter without the former. In other words, he recognizes a secondary kind of practical wisdom which knows the right thing to do without reaching it by a deliberative analysis. Indeed he even approximates this secondary kind of practical wisdom to the act of sensory perception, thereby emphasizing its direct, non-ratiocinative character. The book ends with two important remarks. One is that, while the instinctive virtues can exist in isolation from one another, the moral virtues cannot, since each moral virtue implies practical wisdom and practical wisdom implies all the moral virtues. The other is that, while practical wisdom determines which studies are to be pursued in a state, it is issuing commands not *to* theoretical wisdom but in its interests; it is inferior, not superior, to theoretical reason. This is an anticipation of what is said more fully in bk. 10 about the superiority of the theoretical life.

Bk. 7 has two quite distinct though connected parts. One is a discussion of two states intermediate between virtue and vice; the other is a discussion of the nature of pleasure. The connexion is that the two states referred to are attitudes towards pleasure. He starts by distinguishing three degrees of badness (incontinence, vice, bestiality) and three degrees of goodness (continence, virtue, 'heroic and divine virtue'). He has little to say of the extreme types, bestiality and superhuman virtue, or saintliness; of bestiality he says that it is found chiefly among barbarians (he is thinking of such things as cannibalism), but may occur in civilized man as a result of disease or mutilation. He says nothing more of superhuman virtue, and it is probably only a love of symmetry that induces him to bring it in at all. His discussion of incontinence is very interesting, because it shows him proceeding, not infallibly but very carefully, by stages towards his final account. The first stage is to point out the difference between actual knowledge of the right and potential knowledge of it, having it at the back of one's mind. This takes us some way towards his solution, but is defective through not distinguishing between the various items of knowledge involved in knowing one's duty. The second stage consists in drawing this distinction. You may be knowing the major premiss, e.g. that 'Dry food is good for men', but not knowing a necessary minor premiss, such as 'This food is dry'. You may even be knowing a minor premiss, such as 'Food of a certain kind is dry'. But you may not know the final minor premiss, 'This food is of that kind', and you may in consequence act incontinently. The defect of this second solution is that in making incontinence depend on ignorance of a non-moral fact it would, according to the doctrine of bk. 3, make the action involuntary. According to that doctrine, if the incontinent act is voluntary (as it clearly is), the ignorance involved must either be ignorance of the *major* premiss, or be due to something for which the agent is to blame, so that, though he acts in ignorance, he acts not on account of ignorance but on account of a moral fault. Aristotle adopts the second alternative. For the third stage of his discussion is a refinement on the distinction between potentiality and actuality: a man asleep, mad, or drunk is removed by two stages from actual knowledge; he must first awake, become sane, or become sober, and then he has still to pass from potential to actual knowledge. Now the condition of the incontinent man is in fact akin to this; passion changes the bodily state just as sleep, madness, or drunkenness does. The fourth stage of the discussion is a refinement on the second, as the third is on the first.

You may have a major premiss which says 'Nothing that is *x* should be tasted', but the minor premiss you may not know, or may know only in the sense in which a drunken man may be said to know 'the verses of Empedocles'; and you may have also the major premiss 'Everything that is sweet is pleasant', and the minor premiss 'This is sweet', and you may have a desire for what is pleasant. Then you will take the sweet food.

This situation may in fact exist. But the explanation will account only for one of the types of incontinence which Aristotle later distinguishes—for impetuosity, but not for weakness. It says nothing of a moral struggle: the minor premiss of the moral syllogism and its conclusion 'I ought not to do this' have never been present, or have been already suppressed by appetite. But elsewhere Aristotle shows himself fully aware of the possibility of moral struggle, and aware that incontinence is sometimes due not to absence of knowledge but to weakness of will.

The other main points dealt with in this part of bk. 7 consist in naming the pleasures and pains with which incontinence is concerned and in distinguishing between incontinence (a weakness in face of pleasure) and softness (a weakness in face of the pain due to unfulfilled desire for pleasure).

This naturally leads Aristotle to a general discussion of pleasure. He has in mind three views: (1) the view of the Platonist Speusippus that no pleasure is good, (2) the view expressed in Plato's *Philebus* that most pleasures are bad, and (3) the view also expressed there, that even if all pleasures were good, pleasure could not be the supreme good. These are all views in varying degrees adverse to pleasure. Aristotle's main contention is that pleasure is *a* good, which he infers from the facts that pain is admittedly an evil, and that pleasure is opposed to pain just in that respect in which pain is an evil. Even if most pleasures were bad, he urges, well-being must be the unimpeded activity either of all our faculties or of some of them, and this is pleasure, so that, as far as this objection is concerned, pleasure might even be the *summum bonum*. The general view is, he maintains, right in treating pleasure as at least an element in well-being, for well-being, being perfect activity, must be unimpeded; it is nonsense to say that good men are happy on the rack. Even the fact that all animals pursue pleasure is a sign of its being in some sense the *summum bonum*. Even bodily pleasures must be good in some sense, since the opposite pains are admittedly bad. But things which thus assuage a want are only indirectly pleasant; it is the activity which remains healthy that affords the cure and gives the pleasure. The things that are naturally pleasant are those that stimulate activity of a given nature. If our nature were simple and free from opposites, we could find enjoyment in a single unchanging pleasure, and such an experience is the experience of God, whose activity involves no change, but is 'activity of immobility'.

Aristotle will return to the subject of pleasure in bk. 10; and if bk. 7 is, as ancient tradition says, common to the *Eudemian* and the *Nicomachean Ethics*, and the *Nicomachean Ethics* is, as modern research shows, the later of the two, the view of pleasure in bk. 10 must be Aristotle's more mature view.

In bk. 8 we are suddenly, and with very little explanation, introduced to the subject of friendship, which occupies this and the next book. These books stand in no vital relation to the rest of the work, and one is left with the suspicion that they may have been originally a separate treatise, which faulty editing has included in the *Ethics*. There is much that is interesting in these two books, but we may be pardoned for omitting them in this general sketch.

In bk. 10 Aristotle returns to the subject of pleasure. So far, he has been defending pleasure against excessive attacks. He now proceeds to define his view not only as against extreme opponents of pleasure, but also as against the view of Eudoxus, who regarded it as the only good. Pleasure is, Aristotle says, like seeing, complete at each moment of its existence; it does not become any better by lasting longer. Therefore it cannot be a transition, since all transition takes time, aims at certain ends, and is complete only in the whole time which it occupies, or in the moment of attainment. Each part of a movement is incomplete, and differs in kind from the others and from the whole; this is so, even in a comparatively homogeneous movement like walking. Pleasure, on the other hand, is complete in each moment. So far, Aristotle confirms the point he has made in bk. 7, that the objections to pleasure based on the view that it is a transition break down. If it were a transition, we should, while we are enjoying it, be restless until we reached the state to which it leads; it is in fact complete in each moment of its duration.

The activity of any of our senses, he continues, is necessarily pleasant, and so is the activity of thought; and the pleasure perfects the activity. It is like the bloom of youth, something that supervenes on the activity and, being itself desirable, makes the activity more desirable. It makes little difference whether we say that we desire activity *qua* pleasant, or pleasure *qua* accompanying activity. Since activities differ in kind, the pleasures that complete them differ in kind. We do things worse when alien pleasures interfere; they have much the same effect as pains arising out of the activity in hand. And as activities differ in goodness, their proper pleasures differ accordingly. Which pleasures, then, are the true human pleasures? Those which complete the function or functions proper to man.

And so Aristotle comes to his final question: What is *eudaimonia*, well-being, the end of man? We have learnt from bk. 1 that well-being must be not a state or a disposition but an activity, and one desirable for its own sake. The things that are desired for their own sake are good activities, and amusement. Amusement cannot be the end of life; for it is valued not for its own sake but as a relaxation which fits us for serious activity. Well-being, then, must consist in good activity. We know from bk. 6 that intellectual and moral excellence are distinct, and that both theoretical and practical wisdom are good in themselves, since they are exercises of different faculties, and that they are not merely means to well-being, but actually constitute well-being. But we have also learnt that theoretical wisdom is superior to practical, and that the latter derives some, at least, of its value from its tendency to produce the former. Contemplation is, then, for Aristotle, the main ingredient in well-being. He has not, so far, made it clear whether moral action is also included in well-being. In bk. 10 we read that well-being must be activity in accordance with the excellence of the best part of us; and this is reason. Theoretical activity is the best activity of which we are capable; it is what we can do most continuously; it brings pleasures of wonderful purity and stability; it is less dependent than moral activity, since moral activity needs other men as its objects; it, unlike practical activities, is loved for itself; it is the life we ascribe to the gods. But we cannot live that life and that alone; we have not only reason, but also bodies and irrational elements of soul. We ought, nevertheless, not to follow those who say that, being men, we should mind human things; we should, so far as we can, make ourselves immortal by living the life of that element in us which is most truly ourself.

He who lives thus is, Aristotle says, the happiest man. But he is not the only happy man. The life of moral virtue and practical wisdom, concerned with the feelings springing from our bodily nature, is the life of the composite being which man is, and gives us 'human well-being'. Aristotle assigns two roles to the moral life. It is a secondary form of well-being, one forced upon us by the fact that we are not all reason and cannot always be living the contemplative life. And, secondly, it helps to bring the contemplative life into being; the practical wisdom of the statesman provides by legislation for the pursuit of philosophy and science, and the moral action of the individual provides for it by keeping the passions in subjection.

This is Aristotle's final conclusion. But in the course of his treatment of ethics he has often spoken of good moral activity as being an end in itself: the brave man, for instance, is described as acting 'for the sake of the noble', i.e. because of the inherent nobility of his act.

One naturally asks what, exactly, Aristotle means by the contemplative life. In the *Metaphysics* he includes under it metaphysics, mathematics, and apparently also the study of nature, and in the *De Partibus Animalium* he puts the study of nature very high. It has often been conjectured that the contemplation of beauty and religious contemplation also come under his conception of the contemplative life; but the *Poetics* hardly supports that view with regard to the arts, and the tone of the tenth book of the *Nicomachean Ethics* is less religious than that of the *Eudemian Ethics*, where he describes man's chief end as being 'to serve and contemplate God'.

W. D. ROSS

1953

TRANSLATOR'S PREFACE

THE text of this translation is taken, with a very few slight alterations, from the Oxford edition of *The Works of Aristotle Translated into English* (Volume IX), by permission of the Jowett Trustees. The notes are based on those in that edition, with the omission or simplification of certain technicalities. The translation is based on Bywater's text, and I have departed from it only occasionally, where there seemed to be a good deal to be gained by doing so.

There is considerable difficulty in translating terms which are just crystallizing from the fluidity of everyday speech into technical meanings; and in my treatment of such words as λόγος or ἀρχή I cannot hope to please everybody. Any attempt to render such a term always by a single English equivalent would produce the most uncouth result, and would be in principle wrong. I have tried, however, to limit my renderings of such terms to a reasonably small number of alternatives, so that the thread of identical significance may not be entirely lost.

W. D. ROSS

1954

NOTE ON THE REVISION

THE translation by Sir David Ross of the *Nicomachean Ethics* in Volume IX of the Oxford Translation of Aristotle was revised by J. O. Urmson in 1973, and his revisions were incorporated into the 1975 impression of that volume. Another revision of the greater part of the *Nicomachean Ethics*, by J. L. Ackrill, was published in his *Aristotle's Ethics* (London, 1973). Though the two revisions were independently prepared for publication, they had a common origin in preparations jointly made by the two revisers for a B.Phil. class on Aristotle's ethics which they gave in Oxford in Michaelmas Term 1970. For this paperback reissue of the World's Classics version of Ross's translation changes have been made in all the places where Mr. Urmson made changes (in a great many of these places Professor Ackrill had also made changes, though not always in exactly the same way, and in a few instances his wording has been adopted), and also in several of the places where Professor Ackrill alone had made an alteration. Both revisers have approved all the changes in the present version, which include a few in passages not previously altered by either.

The policy adopted by the two revisers was virtually identical. Each made only minor changes, and only where Ross's translation seemed probably wrong, or likely seriously to mislead a Greekless reader; and each made a number of verbal alterations in order to increase the consistency of translation of some key terms. Neither ventured to change Ross's translation of the central terminology, though, as Mr. Urmson pointed out, 'the reader should be aware that the Greek text reads more like compressed lecture notes than like a literary work. Translation often involves interpretation.' In general, Ross's considered interpretations were left unchanged, even where the revisers were inclined to take another view.

Mr. Urmson offered a few comments on some of the key English terms systematically employed by Ross, and Professor Ackrill, remarking that 'An English word used in a translation often corresponds only partly to the Greek word it renders', printed a list showing Ross's normal renderings of certain important Greek terms, and alternatives that are used or that might be used. The comments and list that follow represent a conflation of these aids to the reader.

Virtue. The Greek word traditionally translated as 'virtue' (*aretē*) has not the specifically moral connotation that 'virtue' has acquired in modern English. 'Excellence', which is sometimes used by Ross, is less liable to mislead. Thus moral virtue will be excellence of character, and intellectual virtue excellence of intellect or intelligence.

Vice. For similar reasons, 'fault', 'defect', or 'flaw' might be more natural modern English for *kakia* than 'vice'. Thus a failure to appreciate bodily pleasures in moderation will be a fault of character rather than a moral vice, and inability to reason a fault of intellect rather than an intellectual vice.

Desire, wish, appetite. Ross consistently uses 'desire' to translate *orexis*, Aristotle's generic term for any form of appetition, 'wish' to translate *boulēsis*, the term for rational appetition of the good, and 'appetite' to translate *epithumia*, the term for any non-rational appetition of the pleasant.

Voluntary, involuntary, willingly, unwillingly. In the Greek there is but a single pair of opposed terms, *hekousion* and *akousion*. 'Intended' or 'intentional' are possible alternatives to 'voluntary', and 'unintended', 'contrary to intention' or 'unintentional' to 'involuntary'.

Continence, incontinence. The reader may find 'self-control' and 'lack of self-control' (or 'weakness') preferable to these traditional translations of *enkrateia* and *akrasia*.

Habit, habituate. 'Custom' and 'accustom' might be better. Aristotle has not a mere automatic response in mind.

Courage. Ross regularly has 'courage' as the noun and 'brave' as the corresponding adjective. 'Bravery', or even 'valour', might be better, since Aristotle has in mind fearlessness (within reason), pre-eminently on the battlefield.

Pain. The Greek word so translated (*lupē*) covers all adverse emotional reactions, including dislike, boredom, grief, and distress. For 'pleasures and pains' one could often read 'likes and dislikes'. Similarly 'painful' (*lupēron*) in the translation often means 'unpleasant'.

Movement. This traditional translation covers a wide variety of changes, of which locomotion (1174^a 29) is only one type.

Happiness. The word *eudaimonia* is used to refer to whatever life is most desirable and satisfying. The word 'happiness' has not quite the same force. In particular, *eudaimonia* is not a state of feeling or enjoyment or content.

Rational principle, rational ground, rule, argument, reasoning, course of reasoning. Such renderings as these are used by Ross for *logos* (*orthos logos* he always renders 'right rule'). The word is often translated 'reason', but normally in Aristotle it stands not for the faculty of reason, but for something grasped by reason.

Normal rendering(s)	*Alternatives and comments*	*Greek*
noble, fine, beautiful	sometimes simply 'good'	*kalon*
state of mind, state of character	really just 'state' (relatively permanent disposition)	*hexis*
final, complete, perfect		*teleion*
the means to the end	literally 'things related to the end'	*ta pros to telos*
action, conduct	this may refer to what is done or to the doing of it	*prāxis*
perception, sensation		*aisthēsis*
passion, emotion, feeling		*pathos*
process, coming into being	literally 'becoming'	*genesis*
knowledge, science	branch of knowledge (covers arts and crafts)	*epistēmē*
it is thought that, it seems	often used to report what everyone thinks, without any suggestion that they may be wrong	*dokei*
choice, purpose, intention		*prohairesis*
product, function, work		*ergon*

CONTENTS

BOOK I. THE GOOD FOR MAN

BOOK II. MORAL VIRTUE

BOOK III. MORAL VIRTUE (*cont.*)

BOOK IV. MORAL VIRTUE (*cont.*)

BOOK VIII. FRIENDSHIP

BOOK X. PLEASURE, HAPPINESS

BOOK I · THE GOOD FOR MAN

◆◆

SUBJECT OF OUR INQUIRY

All human activities aim at some good: some goods subordinate to others

1. EVERY art and every inquiry, and similarly every action and pursuit, is thought to aim at some good; and for this reason the good has rightly been declared[1] to be that at which all things aim. But a certain difference is found among ends; some are activities, others are products apart from the activities that produce them. Where there are ends apart from the actions, it is the nature of the products to be better than the activities. Now, as there are many actions, arts, and sciences, their ends also are many; the end of the medical art is health, that of shipbuilding a vessel, that of strategy victory, that of economics wealth. But where such arts fall under a single capacity—as bridle-making and the other arts concerned with the equipment of horses fall under the art of riding, and this and every military action under strategy, in the same way other arts fall under yet others—in all of these the ends of the master arts are to be preferred to all the subordinate ends; for it is for the sake of the former that the latter are pursued. It makes no difference whether the activities themselves are the ends of the actions, or something else apart from the activities, as in the case of the sciences just mentioned.

The science of the good for man is politics

2. If, then, there is some end of the things we do, which we desire for its own sake (everything else being desired

---

[1] Perhaps by Eudoxus; cf. 1172ᵇ9.

for the sake of this), and if we do not choose everything
for the sake of something else (for at that rate the process
would go on to infinity, so that our desire would be
empty and vain), clearly this must be the good and the
chief good. Will not the knowledge of it, then, have a
great influence on life? Shall we not, like archers who
have a mark to aim at, be more likely to hit upon what
is right? If so, we must try, in outline at least, to determine what it is, and of which of the sciences or capacities it is the object. It would seem to belong to the most
authoritative art and that which is most truly the
master art. And politics appears to be of this nature;
for it is this that ordains which of the sciences should be
studied in a state, | and which each class of citizens
should learn and up to what point they should learn
them; and we see even the most highly esteemed of
capacities to fall under this, e.g. strategy, economics,
rhetoric; now, since politics uses the rest of the sciences,
and since, again, it legislates as to what we are to
do and what we are to abstain from, the end of this
science must include those of the others, so that this
end must be the good for man. For even if the end is
the same for a single man and for a state, that of the
state seems at all events something greater and more
complete whether to attain or to preserve; though it
is worth while to attain the end merely for one man,
it is finer and more godlike to attain it for a nation or
for city-states. These, then, are the ends at which our
inquiry aims, since it is political science, in one sense
of that term.

NATURE OF THE SCIENCE

*We must not expect more precision than the subject-matter ad-
mits of. The student should have reached years of discretion*

3. Our discussion will be adequate if it has as much

clearness as the subject-matter admits of, for precision is not to be sought for alike in all discussions, any more than in all the products of the crafts. Now fine and just actions, which political science investigates, exhibit much variety and fluctuation, so that they may be thought to exist only by convention, and not by nature. And goods exhibit a similar fluctuation because they bring harm to many people; for before now men have been undone by reason of their wealth, and others by reason of their courage. We must be content, then, in speaking of such subjects and with such premisses to indicate the truth roughly and in outline, and in speaking about things which are only for the most part true, and with premisses of the same kind, to reach conclusions that are no better. In the same spirit, therefore, should each type of statement be *received*; for it is the mark of an educated man to look for precision in each class of things just so far as the nature of the subject admits; it is evidently equally foolish to accept probable reasoning from a mathematician and to demand from a rhetorician demonstrative proofs.

Now each man judges well the things he knows, and of these he is a good judge. And so the man who has been educated in a subject is a good judge of that subject, | and the man who has received an all-round education is a good judge in general. Hence a young man is not a proper hearer of lectures on political science;[1] for he is inexperienced in the actions that occur in life, but its discussions start from these and are about these; and, further, since he tends to follow his passions, his study will be vain and unprofitable, because the end aimed at is not knowledge but action. And it makes no difference

---

[1] Cf.   'Young men, whom Aristotle thought
Unfit to hear moral philosophy.'
(*Troilus and Cressida*, II. ii. 166 f.)

whether he is young in years or youthful in character;
the defect does not depend on time, but on his living,
and pursuing each successive object, as passion directs.
For to such persons, as to the incontinent, knowledge
brings no profit; but to those who desire and act in accordance with a rational principle[1] knowledge about
such matters will be of great benefit.

These remarks about the student, the sort of treatment to be expected, and the purpose of the inquiry,
may be taken as our preface.

WHAT IS THE GOOD FOR MAN?

*It is generally agreed to be happiness, but there are various
views as to what happiness is. What is required at the start
is an unreasoned conviction about the facts, such as is produced by a good upbringing*

4. Let us resume our inquiry and state, in view of the
fact that all knowledge and every pursuit aims at some
good, what it is that we say political science aims at and
what is the highest of all goods achievable by action.

---

[1] Of all the words of common occurrence in the *Ethics*, the hardest to
translate is λόγος. Till recently the accepted translation was 'reason'.
But it is, I think, quite clear that normally λόγος in Aristotle does not
stand for the faculty of reason, but for something grasped by reason, or
perhaps sometimes for an operation of reason. Its connexion with reason
is so close as to make 'irrational' the most natural translation of ἄλογος.
But for λόγος I have used, according to the shade of meaning upper-
most in each context, such renderings as 'rational principle', 'rational
ground', 'rule' (ὀρθὸς λόγος I always render 'right rule'), 'argument',
'reasoning', 'course of reasoning'. The connexion between reason and
its object is for Aristotle so close that not infrequently λόγος occurs where
strict logic would require him to be naming the faculty of reason, and it
is possible that in some of the latest passages of his works in which λόγος
occurs it has come to mean 'reason'—which it certainly had come to
mean, not much later in the history of philosophy.

The meaning of λόγος in Aristotle was discussed by Professor J. L.
Stocks in *Journal of Philology*, xxxiii (1914), 182–94, *Classical Quarterly*,
viii (1914), 9–12, and by Professor J. Cook Wilson in *Classical Review*,
xxvii (1913), 113–17.

Verbally there is very general agreement; for both the
general run of men and people of superior refinement
say that it is happiness, and identify living well and
faring well with being happy; but with regard to what
happiness is they differ, and the many do not give the
same account as the wise. For the former think it is
some plain and obvious thing, like pleasure, wealth, or
honour; they differ, however, from one another—and
often even the same man identifies it with different
things, with health when he is ill, with wealth when he
is poor; but, conscious of their ignorance, they admire
those who proclaim some great thing that is above
their comprehension. Now some[1] thought that apart
from these many goods there is another which is good
in itself and causes the goodness of all these as well.
To examine all the opinions that have been held
were perhaps somewhat fruitless; enough to examine
those that are most prevalent or that seem to be
arguable.

Let us not fail to notice, however, that there is a
difference between arguments from and those to the
first principles. For Plato, too, was right in raising this
question and asking, as he used to do, 'Are we on the
way from or to the first principles?' There is a differ-
ence, as there is|in a race-course between the course
from the judges to the turning-point and the way back.
For, while we must begin with what is evident, things
are evident in two ways—some to us, some without
qualification. Presumably, then, *we* must begin with
things evident to *us*. Hence any one who is to listen
intelligently to lectures about what is noble and just
and, generally, about the subjects of political science
must have been brought up in good habits. For the
fact is a starting-point, and if this is sufficiently plain

---

[1] The Platonic School; cf. ch. 6.

to him, he will not need the reason as well; and the man who has been well brought up has or can easily get starting-points. And as for him who neither has nor can get them, let him hear the words of Hesiod:

Far best is he who knows all things himself;
Good, he that hearkens when men counsel right;
But he who neither knows, nor lays to heart
Another's wisdom, is a useless wight.

Discussion of the popular views that the good is pleasure, honour, wealth; a fourth kind of life, that of contemplation, deferred for future discussion

5. Let us, however, resume our discussion from the point at which we digressed.[1] To judge from the lives that men lead, most men, and men of the most vulgar type, seem (not without some ground) to identify the good, or happiness, with pleasure; which is the reason why they love the life of enjoyment. For there are, we may say, three prominent types of life—that just mentioned, the political, and thirdly the contemplative life. Now the mass of mankind are evidently quite slavish in their tastes, preferring a life suitable to beasts, but they get some ground for their view from the fact that many of those in high places share the tastes of Sardanapallus. A consideration of the prominent types of life shows that people of superior refinement and of active disposition identify happiness with honour; for this is, roughly speaking, the end of the political life. But it seems too superficial to be what we are looking for, since it is thought to depend on those who bestow honour rather than on him who receives it, but the good we divine to be something of one's own and not easily taken from one. Further, men seem to pursue

[1] ᵃ30.

honour in order that they may be assured of their
merit; at least it is by men of practical wisdom that
they seek to be honoured, and among those who know
them, and on the ground of their virtue; clearly, then,
according to them, at any rate, virtue is better. And
perhaps one might even suppose this to be, rather than
honour, the end of the political life. But even this
appears somewhat incomplete; for possession of
virtue seems actually compatible with being asleep, or
with lifelong inactivity, and, further, with the greatest
sufferings and misfortunes; | but a man who was
living so no one would call happy, unless he were
maintaining a thesis at all costs. But enough of this;
for the subject has been sufficiently treated even in the
popular discussions. Third comes the contemplative
life, which we shall consider later.[1]

The life of money-making is one undertaken under
compulsion, and wealth is evidently not the good we
are seeking; for it is merely useful and for the sake of
something else. And so one might rather take the afore-
named objects to be ends; for they are loved for themselves. But it is evident that not even these are ends;
yet many arguments have been wasted on the support
of them. Let us leave this subject, then.

*Discussion of the philosophical view that there is an Idea of
good*

6. We had perhaps better consider the universal good
and discuss thoroughly what is meant by it, although
such an inquiry is made an uphill one by the fact that
the Forms have been introduced by friends of our own.
Yet it would perhaps be thought to be better, indeed to
be our duty, for the sake of maintaining the truth even
to destroy what touches us closely, especially as we are

[1] 1177ᵃ12–1178ᵃ8, 1178ᵃ22–1179ᵃ32.

philosophers or lovers of wisdom; for, while both are dear, piety requires us to honour truth above our friends.

The men who introduced this doctrine did not posit Ideas of classes within which they recognized priority and posteriority (which is the reason why they did not maintain the existence of an Idea embracing all numbers); but the term 'good' is used both in the category of substance and in that of quality and in that of relation, and that which is *per se*, i.e. substance, is prior in nature to the relative (for the latter is like an offshoot and accident of being); so that there could not be a common Idea set over all these goods. Further, since 'good' has as many senses as 'being' (for it is predicated both in the category of substance, as of God and of reason, and in quality, i.e. of the virtues, and in quantity, i.e. of that which is moderate, and in relation, i.e. of the useful, and in time, i.e. of the right opportunity, and in place, i.e. of the right locality and the like), clearly it cannot be something universally present in all cases and single; for then it could not have been predicated in all the categories, but in one only. Further, since of the things answering to one Idea there is one science, there would have been one science of all the goods; but as it is there are many sciences even of the things that fall under one category, e.g. of opportunity, for opportunity in war is studied by strategics and in disease by medicine, and the moderate in food is studied by medicine and in exercise by the science of gymnastics. And one might ask the question, what in the world they *mean* by 'a thing itself', if (as is the case) in 'man himself' and in a particular man the account of man is one and the same. | For in so far as they are men, they will in no respect differ; and if this is so, neither will 'good itself' and particular goods, in so

far as they are good. But again it will not be good any
the more for being eternal, since that which lasts long
is no whiter than that which perishes in a day. The
Pythagoreans seem to give a more plausible account
of the good, when they place the One in the column of
goods; and it is they that Speusippus seems to have
followed.

But let us discuss these matters elsewhere;[1] an objection to what we have said, however, may be discerned
in the fact that the Platonists have not been speaking
about *all* goods, and that the goods that are pursued
and loved for themselves are called good by reference
to a single Form, while those which tend to produce or
to preserve these somehow or to prevent their contraries
are called so by reason of these, and in a different way.
Clearly, then, goods must be spoken of in two ways,
and some must be good in themselves, the others by
reason of these. Let us separate, then, things good in
themselves from things useful, and consider whether
the former are called good by reference to a single
Idea. What sort of goods would one call good in themselves? Is it those that are pursued even when isolated
from others, such as intelligence, sight, and certain
pleasures and honours? Certainly, if we pursue these
also for the sake of something else, yet one would place
them among things good in themselves. Or is nothing
other than the Idea of good good in itself? In that case
the Form will be empty. But if the things we have
named are also things good in themselves, the account
of the good will have to appear as something identical
in them all, as that of whiteness is identical in snow and
in white lead. But of honour, wisdom, and pleasure,
just in respect of their goodness, the accounts are distinct

---

[1] Cf. *Met.* 986ᵃ22–26, 1028ᵇ21–24, 1072ᵇ30–1073ᵃ3, 1091ᵃ29–ᵇ3,
ᵇ13–1092ᵃ17.

and diverse. The good, therefore, is not something common answering to one Idea.

But what then do we mean by the good? It is surely not like the things that only chance to have the same name. Are goods one, then, by being derived from one good or by all contributing to one good, or are they rather one by analogy? Certainly, as sight is in the body, so is reason in the soul, and so on in other cases. But perhaps these subjects had better be dismissed for the present; for perfect precision about them would be more appropriate to another branch of philosophy. And similarly with regard to the Idea; even if there is some one good which is universally predicable of goods, or is capable of separate and independent existence, clearly it could not be achieved or attained by man; but we are now seeking something attainable. Perhaps, however, someone might think it worth while to have knowledge of it with a view to the goods that *are* attainable and achievable; |for, having this as a sort of pattern, we shall know better the goods that are good for us, and if we know them shall attain them. This argument has some plausibility, but seems to clash with the procedure of the sciences; for all of these, though they aim at some good and seek to supply the deficiency of it, leave on one side the knowledge of *the* good. Yet that all the exponents of the arts should be ignorant of, and should not even seek, so great an aid is not probable. It is hard, too, to see how a weaver or a carpenter will be benefited in regard to his own craft by knowing this 'good itself', or how the man who has viewed the Idea itself will be a better doctor or general thereby. For a doctor seems not even to study health in this way, but the health of man, or perhaps rather the health of a particular man; it is individuals that he is healing. But enough of these topics.

The good must be something final and self-sufficient. Definition
of happiness reached by considering the characteristic func-
tion of man

7. Let us again return to the good we are seeking, and
ask what it can be. It seems different in different actions
and arts; it is different in medicine, in strategy, and in the
other arts likewise. What then is the good of each? Surely
that for whose sake everything else is done. In medicine this is health, in strategy victory, in architecture a
house, in any other sphere something else, and in every
action and pursuit the end; for it is for the sake of this
that all men do whatever else they do. Therefore, if
there is an end for all that we do, this will be the good
achievable by action, and if there are more than one,
these will be the goods achievable by action.

So the argument has by a different course reached
the same point; but we must try to state this even more
clearly. Since there are evidently more than one end,
and we choose some of these (e.g. wealth, flutes,[1] and
in general instruments) for the sake of something
else, clearly not all ends are final ends; but the chief
good is evidently something final. Therefore, if there is
only one final end, this will be what we are seeking,
and if there are more than one, the most final of these
will be what we are seeking. Now we call that which
is in itself worthy of pursuit more final than that which
is worthy of pursuit for the sake of something else, and
that which is never desirable for the sake of something
else more final than the things that are desirable both
in themselves and for the sake of that other thing, and
therefore we call final without qualification that which
is always desirable in itself and never for the sake of
something else.

Now such a thing happiness, above all else, is held

[1] Strictly, double-reed instruments.

11

to be; | for this we choose always for itself and never for the sake of something else, but honour, pleasure, reason, and every virtue we choose indeed for themselves (for if nothing resulted from them we should still choose each of them), but we choose them also for the sake of happiness, judging that through them we shall be happy. Happiness, on the other hand, no one chooses for the sake of these, nor, in general, for anything other than itself.

From the point of view of self-sufficiency the same result seems to follow; for the final good is thought to be self-sufficient. Now by self-sufficient we do not mean that which is sufficient for a man by himself, for one who lives a solitary life, but also for parents, children, wife, and in general for his friends and fellow citizens, since man is born for citizenship. But some limit must be set to this; for if we extend our requirement to ancestors and descendants and friends' friends we are in for an infinite series. Let us examine this question, however, on another occasion;[1] the self-sufficient we now define as that which when isolated makes life desirable and lacking in nothing; and such we think happiness to be; and further we think it most desirable of all things, not a thing counted as one good thing among others—if it were so counted it would clearly be made more desirable by the addition of even the least of goods; for that which is added becomes an excess of goods, and of goods the greater is always more desirable. Happiness, then, is something final and self-sufficient, and is the end of action.

Presumably, however, to say that happiness is the chief good seems a platitude, and a clearer account of what it is is still desired. This might perhaps be given, if we could first ascertain the function of man. For just as

[1] i. 10, 11, ix. 10.

12

for a flute-player, a sculptor, or any artist, and, in general, for all things that have a function or activity, the good and the 'well' is thought to reside in the function, so would it seem to be for man, if he has a function. Have the carpenter, then, and the tanner certain functions or activities, and has man none? Is he born without a function? Or as eye, hand, foot, and in general each of the parts evidently has a function, may one lay it down that man similarly has a function apart from all these? What then can this be? Life seems to belong even to plants, but we are seeking what is peculiar to man. Let us exclude, therefore, the life of nutrition and growth. | Next there would be a life of perception, but *it* also seems to be shared even by the horse, the ox, and every animal. There remains, then, an active life of the element that has a rational principle; of this, one part has such a principle in the sense of being obedient to one, the other in the sense of possessing one and exercising thought. And, as 'life of the rational element' also has two meanings, we must state that life in the sense of activity is what we mean; for this seems to be the more proper sense of the term. Now if the function of man is an activity of soul which follows or implies a rational principle, and if we say 'a so-and-so' and 'a good so-and-so' have a function which is the same in kind, e.g. a lyre-player and a good lyre-player, and so without qualification in all cases, eminence in respect of goodness being added to the name of the function (for the function of a lyre-player is to play the lyre, and that of a good lyre-player is to do so well): if this is the case [and we state the function of man to be a certain kind of life, and this to be an activity or actions of the soul implying a rational principle, and the function of a good man to be the good and noble performance of these, and if any action

13

is well performed when it is performed in accordance
with the appropriate excellence: if this is the case],
human good turns out to be activity of soul exhibiting
excellence, and if there are more than one excellence,
in accordance with the best and most complete.

But we must add 'in a complete life'. For one swallow
does not make a summer, nor does one day; and so too
one day, or a short time, does not make a man blessed
and happy.

Let this serve as an outline of the good; for we must
presumably first sketch it roughly, and then later fill in
the details. But it would seem that any one is capable of
carrying on and articulating what has once been well
outlined, and that time is a good discoverer or partner
in such a work; to which facts the advances of the arts
are due; for any one can add what is lacking. And we
must also remember what has been said before,[1] and
not look for precision in all things alike, but in each
class of things such precision as accords with the subject-matter, and so much as is appropriate to the inquiry. For a carpenter and a geometer investigate the
right angle in different ways; the former does so in so
far as the right angle is useful for his work, while the
latter inquires what it is or what sort of thing it is; for
he is a spectator of the truth. We must act in the same
way, then, in all other matters as well, that our main
task may not be subordinated to minor questions. Nor
must we demand the cause in all matters alike; | it is
enough in some cases that the *fact* be well established,
as in the case of the first principles; the fact is a primary thing and first principle. Now of first principles
we see some by induction, some by perception, some
by a certain habituation, and others too in other ways.
But each set of principles we must try to investigate in

[1] 1094ᵇ11–27.

the natural way, and we must take pains to determine
them correctly, since they have a great influence on
what follows. For the beginning is thought to be more
than half of the whole, and many of the questions we
ask are cleared up by it.

Our definition is confirmed by current beliefs about happiness

8. But we must consider happiness in the light not only
of our conclusion and our premises, but also of what is
commonly said about it; for with a true view all the
data harmonize, but with a false one the facts soon
clash. Now goods have been divided into three classes,[1]
and some are described as external, others as relating
to soul or to body; we call those that relate to soul most
properly and truly goods, and psychical actions and
activities we class as relating to soul. Therefore our
account must be sound, at least according to this view,
which is an old one and agreed on by philosophers. It
is correct also in that we identify the end with certain
actions and activities; for thus it falls among goods
of the soul and not among external goods. Another
belief which harmonizes with our account is that the
happy man lives well and fares well; for we have
practically defined happiness as a sort of living and
faring well. The characteristics that are looked for in
happiness seem also, all of them, to belong to what we
have defined happiness as being. For some identify
happiness with virtue, some with practical wisdom,
others with a kind of philosophic wisdom, others with
these, or one of these, accompanied by pleasure or not
without pleasure; while others include also external
prosperity. Now some of these views have been held by
many men and men of old, others by a few eminent
persons; and it is not probable that either of these

[1] Pl. *Euthyd.* 279 ᴀʙ, *Phil.* 48 ᴇ, *Laws*, 743 ᴇ.

should be entirely mistaken, but rather that they should be right in at least some one respect, or even in most respects.

With those who identify happiness with virtue or some one virtue our account is in harmony; for to virtue belongs virtuous activity. But it makes, perhaps, no small difference whether we place the chief good in possession or in use, in state of mind or in activity. For the state of mind may exist without producing any good result, | as in a man who is asleep or in some other way quite inactive, but the activity cannot; for one who has the activity will of necessity be acting, and acting well. And as in the Olympic Games it is not the most beautiful and the strongest that are crowned but those who compete (for it is some of these that are victorious), so those who act win, and rightly win, the noble and good things in life.

Their life is also in itself pleasant. For pleasure is a state of *soul*, and to each man that which he is said to be a lover of is pleasant; e.g. not only is a horse pleasant to the lover of horses, and a spectacle to the lover of sights, but also in the same way just acts are pleasant to the lover of justice and in general virtuous acts to the lover of virtue. Now for most men their pleasures are in conflict with one another because these are not by nature pleasant, but the lovers of what is noble find pleasant the things that are by nature pleasant; and virtuous actions are such, so that these are pleasant for such men as well as in their own nature. Their life, therefore, has no further need of pleasure as a sort of adventitious charm, but has its pleasure in itself. For, besides what we have said, the man who does not rejoice in noble actions is not even good; since no one would call a man just who did not enjoy acting justly, nor any man liberal who did not enjoy liberal actions;

and similarly in all other cases. If this is so, virtuous actions must be in themselves pleasant. But they are also *good* and *noble*, and have each of these attributes in the highest degree, since the good man judges well about these attributes; his judgement is such as we have described.[1] Happiness then is the best, noblest, and most pleasant thing in the world, and these attributes are not severed as in the inscription at Delos—

Most noble is that which is justest, and best is health;
But most pleasant it is to win what we love.

For all these properties belong to the best activities; and these, or one—the best—of these, we identify with happiness.

Yet evidently, as we said,[2] it needs the external goods as well; for it is impossible, or not easy, to do noble acts without the proper equipment. In many actions | we use friends and riches and political power as instruments; and there are some things the lack of which takes the lustre from happiness—good birth, goodly children, beauty; for the man who is very ugly in appearance or ill-born or solitary and childless is not very likely to be happy, and perhaps a man would be still less likely if he had thoroughly bad children or friends or had lost good children or friends by death. As we said,[2] then, happiness seems to need this sort of prosperity in addition; for which reason some identify happiness with good fortune, though others identify it with virtue.

Is happiness acquired by learning or habituation, or sent by God or by chance?

9. For this reason also the question is asked, whether happiness is to be acquired by learning or by habituation or

---

[1] I.e., he judges that virtuous actions are good and noble in the highest degree.   [2] 1098ᵇ26–29.

some other sort of training, or comes in virtue of some divine providence or again by chance. Now if there is *any* gift of the gods to men, it is reasonable that happiness should be god-given, and most surely god-given of all human things inasmuch as it is the best. But this question would perhaps be more appropriate to another inquiry; happiness seems, however, even if it is not god-sent but comes as a result of virtue and some process of learning or training, to be among the most godlike things; for that which is the prize and end of virtue seems to be the best thing in the world, and something godlike and blessed.

It will also on this view be very generally shared; for all who are not maimed as regards their potentiality for virtue may win it by a certain kind of study and care. But if it is better to be happy thus than by chance, it is reasonable that the facts should be so, since everything that depends on the action of nature is by nature as good as it can be, and similarly everything that depends on art or any rational cause, and especially if it depends on the best of all causes. To entrust to chance what is greatest and most noble would be a very defective arrangement.

The answer to the question we are asking is plain also from the definition of happiness; for it has been said[1] to be a virtuous activity of soul, of a certain kind. Of the remaining goods, some must necessarily pre-exist as conditions of happiness, and others are naturally co-operative and useful as instruments. And this will be found to agree with what we said at the outset;[2] for we stated the end of political science to be the best end, and political science spends most of its pains on making the citizens to be of a certain character, viz. good and capable of noble acts.

[1] 1098ᵃ16.   [2] 1094ᵃ27.

It is natural, then, that we call neither ox nor horse nor any other of the animals happy; for none of them is capable of sharing in such activity. | For this reason also a boy is not happy; for he is not yet capable of such acts, owing to his age; and boys who are called happy are being congratulated by reason of the hopes we have for them. For there is required, as we said,[1] not only complete virtue.but also a complete life, since many changes occur in life, and all manner of chances, and the most prosperous may fall into great misfortunes in old age, as is told of Priam in the Trojan Cycle; and one who has experienced such chances and has ended wretchedly no one calls happy.

Should no man be called happy while he lives?

10. Must no one at all, then, be called happy while he lives; must we, as Solon says, see the end? Even if we are to lay down this doctrine, is it also the case that a man *is* happy when he is *dead*? Or is not this quite absurd, especially for us who say that happiness is an activity? But if we do not call the dead man happy, and if Solon does not mean this, but that one can then safely *call* a man blessed, as being at last beyond evils and misfortunes, this also affords matter for discussion; for both evil and good are thought to exist for a dead man, as much as for one who is alive but not aware of them; e.g. honours and dishonours and the good or bad fortunes of children, and in general of descendants. And this also presents a problem; for though a man has lived blessedly until old age and has had a death worthy of his life, many reverses may befall his descendants—some of them may be good and attain the life they deserve, while with others the opposite may be the case; and clearly too the degrees of re-

[1] 1098a18-20.

lationship between them and their ancestors may vary indefinitely. It would be odd, then, if the dead man were to share in these changes and become at one time happy, at another wretched; while it would also be odd if the fortunes of the descendants did not for *some* time have *some* effect on the happiness of their ancestors.

But we must return to our first difficulty;[1] for perhaps by a consideration of it our present problem might be solved. Now if we must see the end and only then call a man blessed, not as being blessed but as having been so before, surely this is a paradox, that when he is happy the attribute that belongs to him is not to be truly predicated of him because we do not wish to call living men happy, |on account of the changes that may befall them, and because we have assumed happiness to be something permanent and by no means easily changed, while a single man may suffer many turns of fortune's wheel. For clearly if we were to follow his fortunes, we should often call the same man happy and again wretched, making the happy man out to be 'a chameleon, and insecurely based'. Or is this following his fortunes quite wrong? Success or failure in life does not depend on these, but human life, as we said,[2] needs these as well, while virtuous activities or their opposites are what determine happiness or the reverse.

The question we have now discussed confirms our definition. For no function of man has so much permanence as virtuous activities (these are thought to be more durable even than knowledge of the sciences), and of these themselves the most valuable are more durable because those who are blessed spend their life most readily and most continuously in these; for this seems to be the reason why we do not forget them. The attribute in question,[3] then, will belong to the happy

[1] Cf. l. 10.   [2] 1099ª31–ᵇ7.   [3] Durability.

man, and he will be happy throughout his life; for always, or by preference to everything else, he will do and contemplate what is excellent, and he will bear the chances of life most nobly and altogether decorously, if he is 'truly good' and 'foursquare beyond reproach'.

Now many events happen by chance, and events differing in importance; small pieces of good fortune or of its opposite clearly do not weigh down the scales of life one way or the other, but a multitude of great events if they turn out well will make life more blessed (for not only are they themselves such as to add beauty to life, but the way a man deals with them may be noble and good), while if they turn out ill they crush and maim blessedness; for they both bring pain with them and hinder many activities. Yet even in these nobility shines through, when a man bears with resignation many great misfortunes, not through insensibility to pain but through nobility and greatness of soul.

If activities are, as we said,[1] what determines the character of life, no blessed man can become miserable; for he will never do the acts that are hateful and mean. For the man who is truly good and wise, |we think, bears all the chances of life becomingly and always makes the best of circumstances, as a good general makes the best military use of the army at his command, and a good shoemaker makes the best shoes out of the hides that are given him; and so with all other craftsmen. And if this is the case, the happy man can never become miserable—though he will not reach *blessedness*, if he meet with fortunes like those of Priam.

Nor, again, is he many-coloured and changeable; for neither will he be moved from his happy state easily

[1] l. 9.

or by any ordinary misadventures, but only by many great ones, nor, if he has had many great misadventures, will he recover his happiness in a short time, but if at all, only in a long and complete one in which he has attained many splendid successes.

Why then should we not say that he is happy who is active in accordance with complete virtue and is sufficiently equipped with external goods, not for some chance period but throughout a complete life? Or must we add 'and who is destined to live thus and die as befits his life'? Certainly the future is obscure to us, while happiness, we claim, is an end and something in every way final. If so, we shall call blessed those among living men in whom these conditions are, and are to be, fulfilled—but blessed *men*. So much for these questions.

Do the fortunes of the living affect the dead?

11.[1] That the fortunes of descendants and of all a man's friends should not affect his happiness at all seems a very unfriendly doctrine, and one opposed to the opinions men hold; but since the events that happen are numerous and admit of all sorts of difference, and some come more near to us and others less so, it seems a long—nay, an infinite—task to discuss each in detail; a general outline will perhaps suffice. If, then, as some of a man's own misadventures have a certain weight and influence on life while others are, as it were, lighter, so too there are differences among the misadventures of our friends taken as a whole, and it makes a difference whether the various sufferings befall the living or the dead (much more even than whether lawless and terrible deeds are presupposed in a tragedy or done on the stage), this difference also must be taken into account; or rather, perhaps, the fact that doubt is felt whether

---

[1] Aristotle now returns to the question stated in 1100ª18–30.

the dead share in any good or evil. | For it seems, from these considerations, that even if anything whether good or evil penetrates to them, it must be something weak and negligible, either in itself or for them, or if not, at least it must be such in degree and kind as not to make happy those who are not happy nor to take away their blessedness from those who are. The good or bad fortunes of friends, then, seem to have some effects on the dead, but effects of such a kind and degree as neither to make the happy unhappy nor to produce any other change of the kind.

Virtue is praiseworthy, but happiness is above praise

12. These questions having been definitely answered, let us consider whether happiness is among the things that are praised or rather among the things that are prized; for clearly it is not to be placed among *potentialities*. Everything that is praised seems to be praised because it is of a certain kind and is related somehow to something else; for we praise the just or brave man, and in general both the good man and virtue itself, because of the actions and functions involved, and we praise the strong man, the good runner, and so on, because he is of a certain kind and is related in a certain way to something good and important. This is clear also from the praise given to the gods; it seems absurd that the gods should be measured by our standard, but we do so measure them, since praise involves a reference, as we said, to something else.[1] But if praise is for things such as we have described, clearly what applies to the best things is not praise, but something greater and better, as is indeed obvious; for what we do to the gods and the most godlike of men is to call them blessed and happy. And so too with good *things*; no one praises

---

[1] i.e. other than what is praised.

23

happiness as he does justice, but rather calls it blessed, as being something more divine and better.

Eudoxus also seems to have been right in his method of advocating the supremacy of pleasure; he thought that the fact that, though a good, it is not praised indicated it to be better than the things that are praised, and that this is what God and the good are; for by reference to these all other things are judged. *Praise* is appropriate to virtue, for as a result of virtue men tend to do noble deeds; but *encomia* are bestowed on acts, whether of the body or of the soul. But perhaps nicety in these matters is more proper to those who have made a study of encomia; to us it is clear from what has been said | that happiness is among the things that are prized and perfect. It seems to be so also from the fact that it is a first principle; for it is for the sake of this that we all do everything else, and the first principle and cause of goods is, we claim, something prized and divine.

KINDS OF VIRTUE

Division of the faculties, and resultant division of virtue into intellectual and moral

13. Since happiness is an activity of soul in accordance with perfect virtue, we must consider the nature of virtue; for perhaps we shall thus see better the nature of happiness. The true student of politics, too, is thought to have studied virtue above all things; for he wishes to make his fellow citizens good and obedient to the laws. As an example of this we have the lawgivers of the Cretans and the Spartans, and any others of the kind that there may have been. And if this inquiry belongs to political science, clearly the pursuit of it will be in accordance with our original plan. But clearly the virtue we must study is human virtue; for the good we were seeking was human good and the happiness human happiness. By human virtue we mean not that of the body but that of the soul; and happiness also we call an activity of soul. But if this is so, clearly the student of politics must know somehow the facts about the soul, as the man who is to heal the eyes must know about the whole body also; and all the more since political science is more prized and better than medical; but even among doctors the best educated spend much labour on acquiring knowledge of the body. The student of politics, then, must study the soul, and must study it with these objetcs in view, and do so just to the extent which is sufficient for the questions we are discussing; for further precision would perhaps involve more labour than our purposes require.

Some things are said about it, adequately enough, even in the discussions outside our school, and we must use these; e.g. that one element in the soul is irrational and one has a rational principle. Whether these are separated as the parts of the body or of anything divisible are, or are distinct by definition but by nature inseparable, like convex and concave in the circumference of a circle, does not affect the present question.

Of the irrational element one division seems to be widely distributed, and vegetative in its nature, I mean that which causes nutrition and growth; for it is this kind of power of the soul that one must assign to all nurslings and to embryos, | and this same power to full-grown creatures; this is more reasonable than to assign some different power to them. Now the excellence of this seems to be common to all species and not specifically human; for this part or faculty seems to function most in sleep, while goodness and badness are least manifest in sleep (whence comes the saying that the

happy are no better off than the wretched for half their
lives; and this happens naturally enough, since sleep
is an inactivity of the soul in that respect in which it is
called good or bad), unless perhaps to a small extent
some of the movements actually penetrate to the soul,
and in this respect the dreams of good men are better
than those of ordinary people. Enough of this subject,
however; let us leave the nutritive faculty alone, since
it has by its nature no share in human excellence.

There seems to be also another irrational element in
the soul—one which in a sense, however, shares in a
rational principle. For we praise the rational principle
of the continent man and of the incontinent, and the
part of their soul that has such a principle, since it
urges them aright and towards the best objects; but
there is found in them also another natural element
beside the rational principle, which fights against and
resists that principle. For exactly as paralysed limbs,
when we intend to move them to the right, turn on the
contrary to the left, so is it with the soul; the impulses
of incontinent people move in contrary directions.
But while in the body we see that which moves astray,
in the soul we do not. No doubt, however, we must
none the less suppose that in the soul too there is something beside the rational principle, resisting and op-
posing it. In what sense it is distinct from the other
elements does not concern us. Now even this seems to
have a share in a rational principle, as we said;[1] at
any rate in the continent man it obeys the rational
principle—and presumably in the temperate and
brave man it is still more obedient; for in him it
speaks, on all matters, with the same voice as the
rational principle.

Therefore the irrational element also appears to be

¹ l. 13.

twofold. For the vegetative element in no way shares
in a rational principle, but the appetitive and in general
the desiring element in a sense shares in it, in so far as
it listens to and obeys it; this is the sense in which we
speak of 'taking account' of one's father or one's friends,
not that in which we speak of 'accounting' for a mathematical property.[1] That the irrational element is in
some sense persuaded by a rational principle is indicated also by the giving of advice and by all reproof
and exhortation. | And if this element also must be said
to have a rational principle, that which has a rational
principle (as well as that which has not) will be twofold, one subdivision having it in the strict sense and
in itself, and the other having a tendency to obey as one
does one's father.

Virtue too is distinguished into kinds in accordance
with this difference; for we say that some of the virtues
are intellectual and others moral, philosophic wisdom
and understanding and practical wisdom being intellectual, liberality and temperance moral. For in
speaking about a man's character we do not say that he
is wise or has understanding, but that he is good-
tempered or temperate; yet we praise the wise man
also with respect to his state of mind; and of states of
mind we call those which merit praise virtues.

---

[1] It is impossible in English to reproduce the play on the meanings
of λόγον ἔχειν, translated above 'have a rational principle' and here
'take account of' and 'account for'. Aristotle's point is that the ἄλογον
(the faculty of desire) can be said to have λόγος only in the sense that it
can obey a λόγος presented to it by reason, not in the sense that it can
originate a λόγος—just as many people can 'take account of' a father's
advice who could not 'account for' a mathematical property.

BOOK II · MORAL VIRTUE

▸▸

MORAL VIRTUE, HOW PRODUCED, IN WHAT
MEDIUM AND IN WHAT MANNER
EXHIBITED

Moral virtue, like the arts, is acquired by repetition of the corresponding acts

1. VIRTUE, then, being of two kinds, intellectual and moral, intellectual virtue in the main owes both its birth and its growth to teaching (for which reason it requires experience and time), while moral virtue comes about as a result of habit, whence also its name (ἠθική) is one that is formed by a slight variation from the word ἔθος (habit). From this it is also plain that none of the moral virtues arises in us by nature; for nothing that exists by nature can form a habit contrary to its nature. For instance the stone which by nature moves downwards cannot be habituated to move upwards, not even if one tries to train it by throwing it up ten thousand times; nor can fire be habituated to move downwards, nor can anything else that by nature behaves in one way be trained to behave in another. Neither by nature, then, nor contrary to nature do the virtues arise in us; rather we are adapted by nature to receive them, and are made perfect by habit.

Again, of all the things that come to us by nature we first acquire the potentiality and later exhibit the activity (this is plain in the case of the senses; for it was not by often seeing or often hearing that we got these senses, but on the contrary we had them before we used them, and did not come to have them by using them); but the virtues we get by first exercising them, as also happens in the case of the arts as well. For the things we have to learn before we can do them, we learn by doing them, e.g. men become builders by building and lyre-players by playing the lyre; so too we become just by doing just acts, | temperate by doing temperate acts, brave by doing brave acts.

This is confirmed by what happens in states; for legislators make the citizens good by forming habits in them, and this is the wish of every legislator, and those who do not effect it miss their mark, and it is in this that a good constitution differs from a bad one.

Again, it is from the same causes and by the same means that every virtue is both produced and destroyed, and similarly every art; for it is from playing the lyre that both good and bad lyre-players are produced. And the corresponding statement is true of builders and of all the rest; men will be good or bad builders as a result of building well or badly. For if this were not so, there would have been no need of a teacher, but all men would have been born good or bad at their craft. This, then, is the case with the virtues also; by doing the acts that we do in our transactions with other men we become just or unjust, and by doing the acts that we do in the presence of danger, and by being habituated to feel fear or confidence, we become brave or cowardly. The same is true of appetites and feelings of anger; some men become temperate and good-tempered, others self-indulgent and irascible, by behaving in one way or the other in the appropriate circumstances. Thus, in one word, states of character arise out of like activities. This is why the activities we exhibit must be of a certain kind; it is because the states of character correspond to the differences between these. It makes no small difference, then, whether we form habits of one kind or of another from our very youth; it makes a very great difference, or rather *all* the difference.

These acts cannot be prescribed exactly, but must avoid excess and defect

2. Since, then, the present inquiry does not aim at theoretical knowledge like the others (for we are inquiring not in order to know what virtue is, but in order to become good, since otherwise our inquiry would have been of no use), we must examine the nature of actions, namely how we ought to do them; for these determine also the nature of the states of character that are produced, as we have said.[1] Now, that we must act according to the right rule is a common principle and must be assumed—it will be discussed later,[2] i.e. both what the right rule is, and how it is related to the other virtues. But this must be agreed upon beforehand, | that the whole account of matters of conduct must be given in outline and not precisely, as we said at the very beginning[3] that the accounts we demand must be in accordance with the subject-matter; matters concerned with conduct and questions of what is good for us have no fixity, any more than matters of health. The general account being of this nature, the account of particular cases is yet more lacking in exactness; for they do not fall under any art or precept, but the agents themselves must in each case consider what is appropriate to the occasion, as happens also in the art of medicine or of navigation.

But though our present account is of this nature we must give what help we can. First, then, let us consider this, that it is the nature of such things to be destroyed by defect and excess, as we see in the case of strength and of health (for to gain light on things imperceptible we must use the evidence of sensible things); exercise either excessive or defective destroys the strength,

[1] a31–b25.　　　[2] vi. 13.　　　[3] 1094b11–27.

and similarly drink or food which is above or below a certain amount destroys the health, while that which is proportionate both produces and increases and preserves it. So too is it, then, in the case of temperance and courage and the other virtues. For the man who flies from and fears everything and does not stand his ground against anything becomes a coward, and the man who fears nothing at all but goes to meet every danger becomes rash; and similarly the man who indulges in every pleasure and abstains from none becomes self-indulgent, while the man who shuns every pleasure, as boors do, becomes in a way insensible; temperance and courage, then, are destroyed by excess and defect, and preserved by the mean.

But not only are the sources and causes of their origination and growth the same as those of their destruction, but also the sphere of their actualization will be the same; for this is also true of the things which are more evident to sense, e.g. of strength; it is produced by taking much food and undergoing much exertion, and it is the strong man that will be most able to do these things. So too is it with the virtues; by abstaining from pleasures we become temperate, and it is when we have become so that we are most able to abstain from them; and similarly too in the case of courage; | for by being habituated to despise things that are fearful and to stand our ground against them we become brave, and it is when we have become so that we shall be most able to stand our ground against them.

Pleasure in doing virtuous acts is a sign that the virtuous disposition has been acquired: a variety of considerations show the essential connexion of moral virtue with pleasure and pain

3. We must take as a sign of states of character the

pleasure or pain that supervenes upon acts; for the
man who abstains from bodily pleasures and delights
in this very fact is temperate, while the man who is
annoyed at it is self-indulgent, and he who stands his
ground against things that are terrible and delights in
this or at least is not pained is brave, while the man
who is pained is a coward. For moral excellence is
concerned with pleasures and pains; it is on account of
the pleasure that we do bad things, and on account of
the pain that we abstain from noble ones. Hence we
ought to have been brought up in a particular way
from our very youth, as Plato says,[1] so as both to
delight in and to be pained by the things that we
ought; this is the right education.

Again, if the virtues are concerned with actions and
passions, and every passion and every action is accompanied by pleasure and pain, for this reason also virtue
will be concerned with pleasures and pains. This is indicated also by the fact that punishment is inflicted by
these means; for it is a kind of cure, and it is the nature
of cures to be effected by contraries.

Again, as we said but lately,[2] every state of soul has
a nature relative to and concerned with the kind of
things by which it tends to be made worse or better;
but it is by reason of pleasures and pains that men become bad, by pursuing and avoiding these—either the
pleasures and pains they ought not or when they ought
not or as they ought not, or by going wrong in one of
the other similar ways that may be distinguished.
Hence men[3] even define the virtues as certain states of
impassivity and rest; not well, however, because they
speak absolutely, and do not say 'as one ought' and 'as
one ought not' and 'when one ought or ought not', and

---

[1] *Laws*, 653 A ff., *Rep.* 401 E–402 A.   [2] [a]27–[b]3.
[3] Probably Speusippus is referred to.

the other things that may be added. We assume, then, that this kind of excellence tends to do what is best with regard to pleasures and pains, and vice does the contrary.

The following facts also may show us that virtue and vice are concerned with these same things. There being three objects of choice and three of avoidance, the noble, the advantageous, the pleasant, and their contraries, the base, the injurious, the painful, about all of these the good man tends to go right and the bad man to go wrong, and especially about pleasure; for this is common to the animals, and also it accompanies all objects of choice; for even the noble and the advantageous appear pleasant.|

Again, it has grown up with us all from our infancy; this is why it is difficult to rub off this passion, engrained as it is in our life. And we measure even our actions, some of us more and others less, by the rule of pleasure and pain. For this reason, then, our whole inquiry must be about these; for to feel delight and pain rightly or wrongly has no small effect on our actions.

Again, it is harder to fight with pleasure than with anger, to use Heraclitus' phrase, but both art and virtue are always concerned with what is harder; for even the good is better when it is harder. Therefore for this reason also the whole concern both of virtue and of political science is with pleasures and pains; for the man who uses these well will be good, he who uses them badly bad.

That virtue, then, is concerned with pleasures and pains, and that by the acts from which it arises it is both increased and, if they are done differently, destroyed, and that the acts from which it arose are those in which it actualizes itself—let this be taken as said.

*The actions that produce moral virtue are not good in the same
sense as those that flow from it: the latter must fulfil certain
conditions not necessary in the case of the arts*

4. The question might be asked, what we mean by say-
ing¹ that we must become just by doing just acts, and
temperate by doing temperate acts; for if men do just
and temperate acts, they are already just and temperate, exactly as, if they do what is in accordance with
the laws of grammar and of music, they are gramma-
rians and musicians.

Or is this not true even of the arts? It is possible to do
something that is in accordance with the laws of grammar, either by chance or under the guidance of another. A man will be a grammarian, then, only when he
has both said something grammatical and said it
grammatically; and this means doing it in accordance
with the grammatical knowledge in himself.

Again, the case of the arts and that of the virtues are
not similar; for the products of the arts have their goodness in themselves, so that it is enough that they should
have a certain character, but if the acts that are in accordance with the virtues have themselves a certain
character it does not follow that they are done justly or
temperately. The agent also must be in a certain condition when he does them; in the first place he must have
knowledge, secondly he must choose the acts, and
choose them for their own sakes, and thirdly his action
must proceed from a firm and unchangeable character.
These are not reckoned in as conditions of the posses-
sion of the arts,|except the bare knowledge; but as a con-
dition of the possession of the virtues knowledge has
little or no weight, while the other conditions count not
for a little but for everything, i.e. the very conditions
which result from often doing just and temperate acts.

¹ 1103ᵃ31–ᵇ25, 1104ᵃ27–ᵇ3.

Actions, then, are called just and temperate when they are such as the just or the temperate man would do; but it is not the man who does these that is just and temperate, but the man who also does them *as* just and temperate men do them. It is well said, then, that it is by doing just acts that the just man is produced, and by doing temperate acts the temperate man; without doing these no one would have even a prospect of becoming good.

But most people do not do these, but take refuge in theory and think they are being philosophers and will become good in this way, behaving somewhat like patients who listen attentively to their doctors, but do none of the things they are ordered to do. As the latter will not be made well in body by such a course of treatment, the former will not be made well in soul by such a course of philosophy.

DEFINITION OF MORAL VIRTUE

The genus of moral virtue: it is a state of character, not a passion, nor a faculty

5. Next we must consider what virtue is. Since things that are found in the soul are of three kinds—passions, faculties, states of character—virtue must be one of these. By passions I mean appetite, anger, fear, confidence, envy, joy, friendly feeling, hatred, longing, emulation, pity, and in general the feelings that are accompanied by pleasure or pain; by faculties the things in virtue of which we are said to be capable of feeling these, e.g. of becoming angry or being pained or feeling pity; by states of character the things in virtue of which we stand well or badly with reference to the passions, e.g. with reference to anger we stand badly if we feel it violently or too weakly, and well if we feel it moderately; and similarly with reference to the other passions.

Now neither the virtues nor the vices are *passions*, because we are not called good or bad on the ground of our passions, but are so called on the ground of our virtues and our vices, and because we are neither praised nor blamed for our passions (for the man who feels fear or anger is not praised, nor is the man who simply feels anger blamed, but the man who feels it in a certain way), | but for our virtues and our vices we *are* praised or blamed.

Again, we feel anger and fear without choice, but the virtues are modes of choice or involve choice. Further, in respect of the passions we are said to be moved, but in respect of the virtues and the vices we are said not to be moved but to be disposed in a particular way.

For these reasons also they are not *faculties*; for we are neither called good or bad, nor praised or blamed, for the simple capacity of feeling the passions; again, we have the faculties by nature, but we are not made good or bad by nature; we have spoken of this before.[1]

If, then, the virtues are neither passions nor faculties, all that remains is that they should be *states of character*.

Thus we have stated what virtue is in respect of its genus.

The differentia of moral virtue: it is a disposition to choose the mean

6. We must, however, not only describe virtue as a state of character, but also say what sort of state it is. We may remark, then, that every virtue or excellence both brings into good condition the thing of which it is the excellence and makes the work of that thing be done well; e.g. the excellence of the eye makes both the eye and

---

[1] 1103ᵃ18–ᵇ2.

its work good; for it is by the excellence of the eye that
we see well. Similarly the excellence of the horse makes
a horse both good in itself and good at running and at
carrying its rider and at awaiting the attack of the
enemy. Therefore, if this is true in every case, the virtue
of man also will be the state of character which makes a
man good and which makes him do his own work well.

How this is to happen we have stated already,[1] but it
will be made plain also by the following consideration
of the specific nature of virtue. In everything that is
continuous and divisible it is possible to take more, less,
or an equal amount, and that either in terms of the
thing itself or relatively to us; and the equal is an intermediate between excess and defect. By the intermediate
in the object I mean that which is equidistant from
each of the extremes, which is one and the same for all
men; by the intermediate relatively to us that which is
neither too much nor too little—and this is not one, nor
the same for all. For instance, if ten is many and two is
few, six is the intermediate, taken in terms of the object;
for it exceeds and is exceeded by an equal amount; this
is intermediate according to arithmetical proportion.
But the intermediate relatively to us is not to be taken
so; if ten pounds are too much for a particular person
to eat and two too little, | it does not follow that the
trainer will order six pounds; for this also is perhaps too
much for the person who is to take it, or too little—too
little for Milo,[2] too much for the beginner in athletic
exercises. The same is true of running and wrestling.
Thus a master of any art avoids excess and defect, but
seeks the intermediate and chooses this—the intermediate not in the object but relatively to us.

If it is thus, then, that every art does its work well—
by looking to the intermediate and judging its works by

----

[1] 1104ª11–27.   [2] A famous athlete.

this standard (so that we often say of good works of art that it is not possible either to take away or to add anything, implying that excess and defect destroy the goodness of works of art, while the mean preserves it; and good artists, as we say, look to this in their work), and if, further, virtue is more exact and better than any art, as nature also is, then virtue must have the quality of aiming at the intermediate. I mean moral virtue; for it is this that is concerned with passions and actions, and in these there is excess, defect, and the intermediate. For instance, both fear and confidence and appetite and anger and pity and in general pleasure and pain may be felt both too much and too little, and in both cases not well; but to feel them at the right times, with reference to the right objects, towards the right people, with the right motive, and in the right way, is what is both intermediate and best, and this is characteristic of virtue. Similarly with regard to actions also there is excess, defect, and the intermediate. Now virtue is concerned with passions and actions, in which excess is a form of failure, and so is defect, while the intermediate is praised and is a form of success; and being praised and being successful are both characteristics of virtue. Therefore virtue is a kind of mean, since, as we have seen, it aims at what is intermediate.

Again, it is possible to fail in many ways (for evil belongs to the class of the unlimited, as the Pythagoreans conjectured, and good to that of the limited), while to succeed is possible only in one way (for which reason also one is easy and the other difficult—to miss the mark easy, to hit it difficult); for these reasons also, then, excess and defect are characteristic of vice, and the mean of virtue;

For men are good in but one way, but bad in many.

Virtue, then, is a state of character concerned with choice, lying in a mean, i.e. the mean relative to us, | this being determined by a rational principle, and by that principle by which the man of practical wisdom would determine it. Now it is a mean between two vices, that which depends on excess and that which depends on defect; and again it is a mean because the vices respectively fall short of or exceed what is right in both passions and actions, while virtue both finds and chooses that which is intermediate. Hence in respect of what it is, i.e. the definition which states its essence, virtue is a mean, with regard to what is best and right an extreme.

But not every action nor every passion admits of a mean; for some have names that already imply badness, e.g. spite, shamelessness, envy, and in the case of actions adultery, theft, murder; for all of these and suchlike things imply by their names that they are themselves bad, and not the excesses or deficiencies of them. It is not possible, then, ever to be right with regard to them; one must always be wrong. Nor does goodness or badness with regard to such things depend on committing adultery with the right woman, at the right time, and in the right way, but simply to do any of them is to go wrong. It would be equally absurd, then, to expect that in unjust, cowardly, and voluptuous action there should be a mean, an excess, and a deficiency; for at that rate there would be a mean of excess and of deficiency, an excess of excess, and a deficiency of deficiency. But as there is no excess and deficiency of temperance and courage because what is intermediate is in a sense an extreme, so too of the actions we have mentioned there is no mean nor any excess and deficiency, but however they are done they are wrong; for in general there is neither a mean of excess and deficiency, nor excess and deficiency of a mean.

The above proposition illustrated by reference to particular virtues

7. We must, however, not only make this general statement, but also apply it to the individual facts. For among statements about conduct those which are general apply more widely, but those which are particular are more true, since conduct has to do with individual cases, and our statements must harmonize with the facts in these cases. We may take these cases from our table. With regard to feelings of fear and confidence courage is the mean; | of the people who exceed, he who exceeds in fearlessness has no name (many of the states have no name), while the man who exceeds in confidence is rash, and he who exceeds in fear and falls short in confidence is a coward. With regard to pleasures and pains—not all of them, and not so much with regard to the pains—the mean is temperance, the excess self-indulgence. Persons deficient with regard to the pleasures are not often found; hence such persons also have received no name. But let us call them 'insensible'.

With regard to giving and taking of money the mean is liberality, the excess and the defect prodigality and meanness. In these actions people exceed and fall short in contrary ways; the prodigal exceeds in spending and falls short in taking, while the mean man exceeds in taking and falls short in spending. (At present we are giving a mere outline or summary, and are satisfied with this; later these states will be more exactly determined.)[1] With regard to money there are also other dispositions—a mean, magnificence (for the

[1] v. 1.

magnificent man differs from the liberal man; the former deals with large sums, the latter with small ones), an excess, tastelessness and vulgarity, and a deficiency, niggardliness; these differ from the states opposed to liberality, and the mode of their difference will be stated later.[1]

With regard to honour and dishonour the mean is proper pride, the excess is known as a sort of 'empty vanity', and the deficiency is undue humility; and as we said[2] liberality was related to magnificence, differing from it by dealing with small sums, so there is a state similarly related to proper pride, being concerned with small honours while that is concerned with great. For it is possible to desire honour as one ought, and more than one ought, and less, and the man who exceeds in his desires is called ambitious, the man who falls short unambitious, while the intermediate person has no name. The dispositions also are nameless, except that that of the ambitious man is called ambition. Hence the people who are at the extremes lay claim to the middle place; and we ourselves sometimes call the intermediate person ambitious and sometimes unambitious, and sometimes praise the ambitious man and sometimes the unambitious. | The reason of our doing this will be stated in what follows;[3] but now let us speak of the remaining states according to the method which has been indicated.

With regard to anger also there is an excess, a deficiency, and a mean. Although they can scarcely be said to have names, yet since we call the intermediate person good-tempered let us call the mean good temper; of the persons at the extremes let the one who exceeds be called irascible, and his vice irascibility, and the

---

[1] 1122^{a}20–29, ^{b}10–18.
[2] ll. 17–19.   [3] ^{b}11–26, 1125^{b}14–18.

man who falls short an unirascible sort of person, and the deficiency unirascibility.

There are also three other means, which have a certain likeness to one another, but differ from one another: for they are all concerned with intercourse in words and actions, but differ in that one is concerned with truth in this sphere, the other two with pleasantness; and of this one kind is exhibited in giving amusement, the other in all the circumstances of life. We must therefore speak of these too, that we may the better see that in all things the mean is praiseworthy, and the extremes neither praiseworthy nor right, but worthy of blame. Now most of these states also have no names, but we must try, as in the other cases, to invent names ourselves so that we may be clear and easy to follow. With regard to truth, then, the intermediate is a truthful sort of person and the mean may be called truthfulness, while the pretence which exaggerates is boastfulness and the person characterized by it a boaster, and that which understates is mock modesty and the person characterized by it mock-modest. With regard to pleasantness in the giving of amusement the intermediate person is ready-witted and the disposition ready wit, the excess is buffoonery and the person characterized by it a buffoon, while the man who falls short is a sort of boor and his state is boorishness. With regard to the remaining kind of pleasantness, that which is exhibited in life in general, the man who is pleasant in the right way is friendly and the mean is friendliness, while the man who exceeds is an obsequious person if he has no end in view, a flatterer if he is aiming at his own advantage, and the man who falls short and is unpleasant in all circumstances is a quarrelsome and surly sort of person.

There are also means in the passions and concerned

with the passions; since shame is not a virtue, and yet praise is extended to the modest man. For even in these matters one man is said to be intermediate, and another to exceed, as for instance the bashful man who is ashamed of everything; while he who falls short or is not ashamed of anything at all is shameless, and the intermediate person is modest. Righteous indignation is a mean between envy and spite, | and these states are concerned with the pain and pleasure that are felt at the fortunes of our neighbours; the man who is characterized by righteous indignation is pained at undeserved good fortune, the envious man, going beyond him, is pained at all good fortune, and the spiteful man falls so far short of being pained that he even rejoices.[1] But these states there will be an opportunity of describing elsewhere;[2] with regard to justice, since it has not one simple meaning, we shall, after describing the other states, distinguish its two kinds and say how each of them is a mean;[3] and similarly we shall treat also of the rational virtues.[4]

CHARACTERISTICS OF THE EXTREME AND
MEAN STATES: PRACTICAL COROLLARIES

The extremes are opposed to each other and to the mean

8. There are three kinds of disposition, then, two of them vices, involving excess and deficiency respectively,

---

[1] Aristotle must mean that while the envious man is pained at the good fortune of others, whether deserved or not, the spiteful man is pleased at the *bad* fortune of others, whether deserved or not. But if he had stated this in full, he would have seen that there is no real opposition.

[2] The reference may be to the whole treatment of the moral virtues in iii. 6–iv. 9, or to the discussion of shame in iv. 9 and an intended corresponding discussion of righteous indignation, or to the discussion of these two states in *Rhet.* ii. 6, 9, 10.

[3] 1129ª26–ᵇ1, 1130ª14–ᵇ5, 1131ᵇ9–15, 1132ª24–30, 1133ᵇ30–1134ª1.

[4] Bk. vi.

and one a virtue, viz. the mean, and all are in a sense opposed to all; for the extreme states are contrary both to the intermediate state and to each other, and the intermediate to the extremes; as the equal is greater relatively to the less, less relatively to the greater, so the middle states are excessive relatively to the deficiencies, deficient relatively to the excesses, both in passions and in actions. For the brave man appears rash relatively to the coward, and cowardly relatively to the rash man; and similarly the temperate man appears self-indulgent relatively to the insensible man, insensible relatively to the self-indulgent, and the liberal man prodigal relatively to the mean man, mean relatively to the prodigal. Hence also the people at the extremes push the intermediate man each over to the other, and the brave man is called rash by the coward, cowardly by the rash man, and correspondingly in the other cases.

These states being thus opposed to one another, the greatest contrariety is that of the extremes to each other, rather than to the intermediate; for these are further from each other than from the intermediate, as the great is further from the small and the small from the great than both are from the equal. Again, to the intermediate some extremes show a certain likeness, as that of rashness to courage and that of prodigality to liberality; but the extremes show the greatest unlikeness to each other; now contraries are defined as the things that are furthest from each other, so that things that are further apart are more contrary.

To the mean in some cases the deficiency, | in some the excess, is more opposed; e.g. it is not rashness, which is an excess, but cowardice, which is a deficiency, that is more opposed to courage, and not insensibility, which is a deficiency, but self-indulgence, which is an excess, that is more opposed to temperance. This happens from two reasons, one being drawn from the thing itself; for because one extreme is nearer and liker to the intermediate, we oppose not this but rather its contrary to the intermediate. E.g., since rashness is thought liker and nearer to courage, and cowardice more unlike, we oppose rather the latter to courage; for things that are further from the intermediate are thought more contrary to it. This, then, is one cause, drawn from the thing itself; another is drawn from ourselves; for the things to which we ourselves more naturally tend seem more contrary to the intermediate. For instance, we ourselves tend more naturally to pleasures, and hence are more easily carried away towards self-indulgence than towards propriety. We describe as contrary to the mean, then, rather the directions in which we more often go to great lengths; and therefore self-indulgence, which is an excess, is the more contrary to temperance.

The mean is hard to attain, and is grasped by perception, not by reasoning

9. That moral virtue is a mean, then, and in what sense it is so, and that it is a mean between two vices, the one involving excess, the other deficiency, and that it is such because its character is to aim at what is intermediate in passions and in actions, has been sufficiently stated. Hence also it is no easy task to be good. For in everything it is no easy task to find the middle, e.g. to find the middle of a circle is not for everyone but for him who knows; so, too, anyone can get angry—that is easy—or give or spend money; but to do this to the right person, to the right extent, at the right time, with the right motive, and in the right way, *that* is not for everyone, nor is it easy; wherefore goodness is both rare and laudable and noble.

Hence he who aims at the intermediate must first depart from what is the more contrary to it, as Calypso advises—

Hold the ship out beyond that surf and spray.[1]

For of the extremes one is more erroneous, one less so; therefore, since to hit the mean is hard in the extreme, we must as a second best, as people say, take the least of the evils; and this will be done best in the way we describe.|

But we must consider the things towards which we ourselves also are easily carried away; for some of us tend to one thing, some to another; and this will be recognizable from the pleasure and the pain we feel. We must drag ourselves away to the contrary extreme; for we shall get into the intermediate state by drawing well away from error, as people do in straightening sticks that are bent.

Now in everything the pleasant or pleasure is most to be guarded against; for we do not judge it impartially. We ought, then, to feel towards pleasure as the elders of the people felt towards Helen, and in all circumstances repeat their saying;[2] for if we dismiss pleasure thus we are less likely to go astray. It is by doing this, then, (to sum the matter up) that we shall best be able to hit the mean.

But this is no doubt difficult, and especially in individual cases; for it is not easy to determine both how and with whom and on what provocation and how long one should be angry; for we too sometimes praise those who fall short and call them good-tempered, but sometimes we praise those who get angry and call them manly.

---

[1] *Od.* xii. 219 f. (Mackail's trans.). But it was Circe who gave the advice (xii. 108), and the actual quotation is from Odysseus' orders to his steersman.   [2] *Il.* iii. 156–60.

The man, however, who deviates little from goodness is not blamed, whether he do so in the direction of the more or of the less, but only the man who deviates more widely; for *he* does not fail to be noticed. But up to what point and to what extent a man must deviate before he becomes blameworthy it is not easy to determine by reasoning, any more than anything else that is perceived by the senses; such things depend on particular facts, and the decision rests with perception. So much, then, is plain, that the intermediate state is in all things to be praised, but that we must incline sometimes towards the excess, sometimes towards the deficiency; for so shall we most easily hit the mean and what is right.

••

INNER SIDE OF MORAL VIRTUE: CONDITIONS
OF RESPONSIBILITY FOR ACTION

Praise and blame attach to voluntary actions, i.e. actions done
(1) not under compulsion, and (2) with knowledge of the
circumstances

1. SINCE virtue is concerned with passions and actions,
and on voluntary passions and actions praise and blame
are bestowed, on those that are involuntary pardon,
and sometimes also pity, to distinguish the voluntary
and the involuntary is presumably necessary for those
who are studying the nature of virtue, and useful also for
legislators with a view to the assigning both of honours
and of punishments.

Those things, then, are thought involuntary, which
take place by force or owing to ignorance; | and that is
compulsory of which the moving principle is outside,
being a principle in which nothing is contributed by
the person who acts—or, rather, is acted upon, e.g.
if he were to be carried somewhere by a wind, or by
men who had him in their power.

But with regard to the things that are done from fear
of greater evils or for some noble object (e.g. if a tyrant
were to order one to do something base, having one's
parents and children in his power, and if one did the
action they were to be saved, but otherwise would be
put to death), it may be debated whether such actions
are involuntary or voluntary. Something of the sort
happens also with regard to the throwing of goods over-
board in a storm; for in the abstract no one throws
goods away voluntarily, but on condition of its securing

the safety of himself and his crew any sensible man does
so. Such actions, then, are mixed, but are more like
voluntary actions; for they are worthy of choice at the
time when they are done, and the end of an action is
relative to the occasion. Both the terms, then, 'voluntary' and 'involuntary', must be used with reference to
the moment of action. Now the man acts voluntarily;
for the principle that moves the instrumental parts of
the body in such actions is in him, and the things of
which the moving principle is in a man himself are in
his power to do or not to do. Such actions, therefore,
are voluntary, but in the abstract perhaps involuntary;
for no one would choose any such act in itself.

For such actions men are sometimes even praised,
when they endure something base or painful in return
for great and noble objects gained; in the opposite case
they are blamed, since to endure the greatest indignities
for no noble end or for a trifling end is the mark of an
inferior person. On some actions praise indeed is not
bestowed, but pardon is, when one does a wrongful
act under pressure which overstrains human nature
and which no one could withstand. But some acts,
perhaps, we cannot be forced to do, but ought rather
to face death after the most fearful sufferings; for the
things that 'forced' Euripides' Alcmaeon to slay his
mother seem absurd. It is difficult sometimes to determine what should be chosen at what cost, and what
should be endured in return for what gain, and yet
more difficult to abide by our decisions; for as a rule
what is expected is painful, and what we are forced to
do is base, whence praise and blame are bestowed on
those who have been forced or have not. |

What sort of acts, then, should be called forced?
We answer that without qualification actions are so
when the cause is in the external circumstances and

the agent contributes nothing. But the things that in themselves are involuntary, but now and in return for these gains are worthy of choice, and whose moving principle is in the agent, are in themselves involuntary, but now and in return for these gains voluntary. They are more like voluntary acts; for actions are in the class of particulars, and the particular acts here are voluntary. What sort of things are to be chosen, and in return for what, it is not easy to state; for there are many differences in the particular cases.

But if someone were to say that pleasant and noble objects have a forcing power, forcing us from without, all acts would be for him forced; for it is for these objects that all men do everything they do. And those who act by force and unwillingly act with pain, but those who do acts for their pleasantness or nobility do them with pleasure; it is absurd to make external circumstances responsible, and not oneself, as being easily caught by such attractions, and to make oneself responsible for noble acts but the pleasant objects responsible for base acts. The forced, then, seems to be that whose moving principle is outside, the person forced contributing nothing.

Everything that is done by reason of ignorance is *not* voluntary; it is only what produces pain and regret that is *in*voluntary. For the man who has done something owing to ignorance, and feels not the least vexation at his action, has not acted voluntarily, since he did not know what he was doing, nor yet involuntarily, since he is not pained. Of people, then, who act by reason of ignorance he who regrets is thought an involuntary agent, and the man who does not regret may, since he is different, be called a not voluntary agent; for, since he differs from the other, it is better that he should have a name of his own.

Acting by reason of ignorance seems also to be different from acting *in* ignorance; for the man who is drunk or in a rage is thought to act as a result not of ignorance but of one of the causes mentioned, yet not knowingly but in ignorance.

Now every wicked man is ignorant of what he ought to do and what he ought to abstain from, and error of this kind makes men unjust and in general bad; but the term 'involuntary' tends to be used not if a man is ignorant of what is to his advantage—for it is not mistaken purpose that makes an action involuntary (*it* makes men *wicked*), nor ignorance of the universal (for *that* men are *blamed*), but ignorance of particulars, i.e. of the circumstances of the action and the objects with which it is concerned. | For it is on these that both pity and pardon depend, since the person who is ignorant of any of these acts involuntarily.

Perhaps it is just as well, therefore, to determine their nature and number. A man may be ignorant, then, of who he is, what he is doing, what or whom he is acting on, and sometimes also what (e.g. what instrument) he is doing it with, and to what end (e.g. he may think his act will conduce to someone's safety), and how he is doing it (e.g. whether gently or violently). Now of all of these no one could be ignorant unless he were mad, and evidently also he could not be ignorant of the agent; for how could he not know himself? But of what he is doing a man might be ignorant, as for instance people say 'it slipped out of their mouths as they were speaking', or 'they did not know it was a secret', as Aeschylus said of the mysteries, or a man might say he 'let it go off when he merely wanted to show its working', as the man did with the catapult. Again, one might think one's son was an enemy, as Merope did, or that a pointed spear had a button on it, or that a stone was

51

pumice-stone; or one might give a man a draught to save him, and really kill him; or one might want to touch a man, as people do in sparring, and really wound him. The ignorance may relate, then, to any of these things, and the man who was ignorant of any of these is thought to have acted involuntarily, and especially if he was ignorant on the most important points; and these are thought to be the circumstances of the action and its end. Further, the doing of an act that is called involuntary in virtue of ignorance of this sort must be painful and involve regret.

Since that which is done by force or by reason of ignorance is involuntary, the voluntary would seem to be that of which the moving principle is in the agent himself, he being aware of the particular circumstances of the action. Presumably acts done by reason of anger or appetite are not rightly called involuntary. For in the first place, on that showing none of the other animals will act voluntarily, nor will children; and secondly, is it meant that we do not do voluntarily *any* of the acts that are due to appetite or anger, or that we do the noble acts voluntarily and the base acts involuntarily? Is not this absurd, when one and the same thing is the cause? But it would surely be odd to describe as involuntary the things one ought to desire; and we ought both to be angry at certain things and to have an appetite for certain things, e.g. for health and for learning. Also what is involuntary is thought to be painful, but what is in accordance with appetite is thought to be pleasant. Again, what is the difference in respect of involuntariness between errors committed upon calculation and those committed in anger? Both are to be avoided, | but the irrational passions are thought not less human than reason is, and therefore also the actions which proceed from anger or appetite are the man's actions. It would be odd, then, to treat them as involuntary.

Moral virtue implies that the action is done (3) by choice: the object of choice is the result of previous deliberation

2. Both the voluntary and the involuntary having been delimited, we must next discuss choice;[1] for it is thought to be most closely bound up with virtue, and to discriminate characters better than actions do.

Choice, then, seems to be voluntary, but not the same thing as the voluntary; the latter extends more widely. For both children and the lower animals share in voluntary action, but not in choice, and acts done on the spur of the moment we describe as voluntary, but not as chosen.

Those who say it is appetite or anger or wish or a kind of opinion do not seem to be right. For choice is not common to irrational creatures as well, but appetite and anger are. Again, the incontinent man acts with appetite, but not with choice; while the continent man on the contrary acts with choice, but not with appetite. Again, appetite is contrary to choice, but not appetite to appetite. Again, appetite relates to the pleasant and the painful, choice neither to the painful nor to the pleasant.

Still less is it anger; for acts due to anger are thought to be less than any others objects of choice.

But neither is it wish, though it seems near to it; for choice cannot relate to impossibles, and if any one said he chose them he would be thought silly; but there may

---

[1] Προαίρεσις is a very difficult word to translate. Sometimes 'intention', 'will', or 'purpose' would bring out the meaning better; but I have for the most part used 'choice'. The etymological meaning is 'preferential choice'.

be a wish even for impossibles, e.g. for immortality. And wish may relate to things that could in no way be brought about by one's own efforts, e.g. that a particular actor or athlete should win in a competition; but no one chooses such things, but only the things that he thinks could be brought about by his own efforts. Again, wish relates rather to the end, choice to the means; for instance, we wish to be healthy, but we choose the acts which will make us healthy, and we wish to be happy and say we do, but we cannot well say we choose to be so; for, in general, choice seems to relate to the things that are in our own power.

For this reason, too, it cannot be opinion; for opinion is thought to relate to all kinds of things, no less to eternal things and impossible things than to things in our own power; and it is distinguished by its falsity or truth, not by its badness or goodness, while choice is distinguished rather by these.

Now with opinion in general perhaps no one even says it is identical. | But it is not identical even with any kind of opinion; for by choosing what is good or bad we are men of a certain character, which we are not by holding certain opinions. And we choose to get or avoid something good or bad, but we have opinions about what a thing is or whom it is good for or how it is good for him; we can hardly be said to opine to get or avoid anything. And choice is praised for being related to the right object or for being *right*, opinion for being true. And we choose what we best know to be good, but we opine what we do not in the least know to be good; and it is not the same people that are thought to make the best choices and to have the best opinions, but some are thought to have fairly good opinions, but by reason of vice to choose what they should not. If opinion precedes choice or accompanies it, that

makes no difference; for it is not this that we are
considering, but whether choice is *identical* with some
kind of opinion.

What, then, or what kind of thing is it, since it
is none of the things we have mentioned? It seems
to be voluntary, but not all that is voluntary to be
an object of choice. Is it, then, what has been deliberated about before? At any rate choice involves
a rational principle and thought. Even the name
seems to suggest that it is what is chosen before other
things.

*The nature of deliberation and its objects: choice is deliberate
  desire of things in our own power*

3. Do we deliberate about everything, and is everything
a possible subject of deliberation, or is deliberation
impossible about some things? We ought presumably
to call not what a fool or a madman would deliberate about, but what a sensible man would deliberate
about, a subject of deliberation. Now about eternal
things no one deliberates, e.g. about the material
universe or the incommensurability of the diagonal
and the side of a square. But no more do we deliberate
about the things that involve movement but always
happen in the same way, whether of necessity or by
nature or from any other cause, e.g. the solstices and the
risings of the stars; nor about things that happen now
in one way, now in another, e.g. droughts and rains;
nor about chance events, like the finding of treasure.
But we do not deliberate even about all human affairs;
for instance, no Spartan deliberates about the best
constitution for the Scythians. For none of these things
can be brought about by our own efforts.

We deliberate about things that are in our power
and can be done; and these are in fact what is left. For

nature, necessity, and chance are thought to be causes, and also reason and everything that depends on man. Now every class of men deliberates about the things that can be done by their own efforts. And in the case of exact and self-contained sciences there is no deliberation, | e.g. about the letters of the alphabet (for we have no doubt how they should be written); but the things that are brought about by our own efforts, but not always in the same way, are the things about which we deliberate, e.g. questions of medical treatment or of money-making. And we do so more in the case of the art of navigation than in that of gymnastics, inasmuch as it has been less exactly worked out, and again about other things in the same ratio, and more also in the case of the arts than in that of the sciences; for we have more doubt about the former. Deliberation is concerned with things that happen in a certain way for the most part, but in which the event is obscure, and with things in which it is indeterminate. We call in others to aid us in deliberation on important questions, distrusting ourselves as not being equal to deciding.

We deliberate not about ends but about means. For a doctor does not deliberate whether he shall heal, nor an orator whether he shall convince, nor a statesman whether he shall produce law and order, nor does any one else deliberate about his end. Having set the end, they consider how and by what means it is to be attained; and if it seems to be produced by several means they consider by which it is most easily and best produced, while if it is achieved by one only they consider how it will, be achieved by this and by what means *this* will be achieved, till they come to the first cause, which in the order of discovery is last. For the person who deliberates seems to inquire and analyse in the way described as though he were analysing a geometrical construction[1] (not all inquiry appears to be deliberation—for instance mathematical inquiries —but all deliberation is inquiry), and what is last in the order of analysis seems to be first in the order of becoming. And if we come on an impossibility, we give up the search, e.g. if we need money and this cannot be got; but if a thing appears possible we try to do it. By 'possible' things I mean things that might be brought about by our own efforts; and these in a sense include things that can be brought about by the efforts of our friends, since the moving principle is in ourselves. The subject of investigation is sometimes the instruments, sometimes the use of them; and similarly in the other cases—sometimes the means, sometimes the mode of using it or the means of bringing it about. It seems, then, as has been said, that man is a moving principle of actions; now deliberation is about the things to be done by the agent himself, and actions are for the sake of things other than themselves. For the end cannot be a subject of deliberation, but only the means; nor indeed can the particular facts be a subject of it, e.g. whether this is bread or has been baked as it should; | for these are matters of perception. If we are to be always deliberating, we shall have to go on to infinity.

The same thing is deliberated upon and is chosen, except that the object of choice is already determinate, since it is that which has been decided upon as a result of deliberation that is the object of choice. For everyone ceases to inquire how he is to act when he has brought the moving principle back to himself and to the ruling

---

[1] Aristotle has in mind the method of discovering the solution of a geometrical problem. The problem being to construct a figure of a certain kind, we suppose it constructed and then analyse it to see if there is some figure by constructing which we can construct the required figure, and so on till we come to a figure which our existing knowledge enables us to construct.

part of himself; for this is what chooses. This is plain
also from the ancient constitutions, which Homer represented; for the kings announced their choices to the
people. The object of choice being one of the things in
our own power which is desired after deliberation,
choice will be deliberate desire of things in our own
power; for when we have reached a judgement as a
result of deliberation, we desire in accordance with
our deliberation.

We may take it, then, that we have described choice
in outline; we have stated the nature of its objects and
the fact that it is concerned with means.

*The object of rational wish is the end, i.e. the good or apparent
good*

4. That *wish* is for the end has already been stated;[1]
some think it is for the good, others for the apparent
good. Now those who say that the good is the object of
wish must admit in consequence that that which the
man who does not choose aright wishes for is not an
object of wish (for if it is to be so, it must also be good;
but it may well have been bad); while those who say
the apparent good is the object of wish must admit that
there is no natural object of wish, but only what seems
good to each man. Now different things appear good to
different people, and, if it so happens, even contrary
things.

If these consequences are unpleasing, are we to say
that absolutely and in truth the good is the object of
wish, but for each person the apparent good; that that
which is in truth an object of wish is an object of wish
to the good man, while any chance thing may be so to
the bad man, as in the case of bodies also the things
that are in truth wholesome are wholesome for bodies

[1] 1111b26.

which are in good condition, while for those that are
diseased other things are wholesome—or bitter or
sweet or hot or heavy, and so on; since the good man
judges each class of things rightly, and in each the
truth appears to him? For each state of character has
its own ideas of the noble and the pleasant, and perhaps the good man differs from others most by seeing
the truth in each class of things, being as it were the
norm and measure of them. In most things the error
seems to be due to pleasure; for this appears a good
when it is not. | We therefore choose the pleasant as
a good and avoid pain as an evil.

We are responsible for bad as well as for good actions

5. The end, then, being what we wish for, the means
what we deliberate about and choose, actions concerning means must be according to choice and voluntary.
Now the exercise of the virtues is concerned with means.
Therefore virtue also is in our own power, and so too
vice. For where it is in our power to act it is also in our
power not to act, and *vice versa*; so that, if to act, where
this is noble, is in our power, not to act, which will be
base, will also be in our power, and if not to act, where
this is noble, is in our power, to act, which will be base,
will also be in our power. Now if it is in our power to do
noble or base acts, and likewise in our power not to do
them, and this was what being good or bad meant,[1]
then it is in our power to be virtuous or vicious.

The saying that 'no one is voluntarily wicked nor
involuntarily happy' seems to be partly false and partly
true; for no one is involuntarily happy, but wickedness
is voluntary. Or else we shall have to dispute what has
just been said, at any rate, and deny that man is a moving principle or begetter of his actions, as of children.

---

[1] 1112ᵃ1 f.

But if these facts are evident and we cannot refer actions to moving principles other than those in ourselves, the acts whose moving principles are in us must themselves also be in our power and voluntary.

Witness seems to be borne to this both by individuals in their private capacity and by legislators themselves; for these punish and take vengeance on those who do wicked acts (unless they have acted under compulsion or as a result of ignorance for which they are not themselves responsible), while they honour those who do noble acts, as though they meant to encourage the latter and deter the former. But no one is encouraged to do the things that are neither in our power nor voluntary; it is assumed that there is no gain in being persuaded not to be hot or in pain or hungry or the like, since we shall experience these feelings none the less. Indeed,[1] we punish a man for his very ignorance, if he is thought responsible for the ignorance, as when penalties are doubled in the case of drunkenness;[2] for the moving principle is in the man himself, since he had the power of not getting drunk and his getting drunk was the cause of his ignorance. And we punish those who are ignorant of anything in the laws that they ought to know and that is not difficult, | and so too in the case of anything else that they are thought to be ignorant of through carelessness; we assume that it is in their power not to be ignorant, since they have the power of taking care.

But perhaps a man is the kind of man not to take care. Still they are themselves by their slack lives responsible for becoming men of that kind, and men are themselves responsible for being unjust or self-indul-

---

[1] This connects with the words of ll. 24 f. 'unless they have acted . . . as a result of ignorance for which they are not themselves responsible'.
[2] As by the law of Pittacus; cf. *Pol.* 1274^b19, *Rhet.* 1402^b9.

gent, in that they cheat or spend their time in drinking-bouts and the like; for it is activities exercised on particular objects that make the corresponding character. This is plain from the case of people training for any contest or action; they practise the activity the whole time. Now not to know that it is from the exercise of activities on particular objects that states of character are produced is the mark of a thoroughly senseless person. Again, it is irrational to suppose that a man who acts unjustly does not wish to be unjust or a man who acts self-indulgently to be self-indulgent. But if *without* being ignorant a man does the things which will make him unjust, he will be unjust voluntarily. Yet it does not follow that if he wishes he will cease to be unjust and will be just. For neither does the man who is ill become well on those terms. We may suppose a case in which he is ill voluntarily, through living incontinently and disobeying his doctors. In that case it was *then* open to him not to be ill, but not now, when he has thrown away his chance, just as when you have let a stone go it is too late to recover it; but yet it was in your power to throw it, since the moving principle was in you. So, too, to the unjust and to the self-indulgent man it was open at the beginning not to become men of this kind, and so they are unjust and self-indulgent voluntarily; but now that they have become so it is not possible for them not to be so.

But not only are the vices of the soul voluntary, but those of the body also for some men, whom we accordingly blame; while no one blames those who are ugly by nature, we blame those who are so owing to want of exercise and care. So it is, too, with respect to weakness and infirmity; no one would reproach a man blind from birth or by disease or from a blow, but rather pity him, while every one would blame a man who was blind from drunkenness or some other form of self-indulgence. Of vices of the body, then, those in our own power are blamed, those not in our power are not. And if this be so, in the other cases also the vices that are blamed must be in our own power.

Now someone may say that all men aim at the apparent good, but have no control over the appearance, but the end appears to each man in a form answering to his character. |We reply that if each man is somehow responsible for his state of character, he will also be himself somehow responsible for the appearance; but if not, no one is responsible for his own evildoing, but everyone does evil acts through ignorance of the end, thinking that by these he will get what is best, and the aiming at the end is not self-chosen but one must be born with an eye, as it were, by which to judge rightly and choose what is truly good, and he is well endowed by nature who is well endowed with this. For it is what is greatest and most noble, and what we cannot get or learn from another, but must have just such as it was when given us at birth, and to be well and nobly endowed with this will be perfect and true excellence of natural endowment. If this is true, then, how will virtue be more voluntary than vice? To both men alike, the good and the bad, the end appears and is fixed by nature or however it may be, and it is by referring everything else to this that men do whatever they do.

Whether, then, it is not by nature that the end appears to each man such as it does appear, but something also depends on him, or the end is natural but because the good man adopts the means voluntarily virtue is voluntary, vice also will be none the less voluntary; for in the case of the bad man there is equally present that which depends on himself in his actions even if not in his end. If, then, as is asserted, the virtues are voluntary (for we are ourselves somehow part-causes of our states of character, and it is by being persons of a certain kind that we set the end to be so and so), the vices also will be voluntary; for the same is true of them.

With regard to the virtues *in general* we have stated their genus in outline, viz. that they are means and that they are states of character, and that they tend, and by their own nature, to the doing of the acts by which they are produced, and that they are in our power and voluntary, and act as the right rule prescribes. But actions and states of character are not voluntary in the same way; for we are masters of our actions from the beginning right to the end, if we know the particular facts, but though we control the beginning of our states of character the gradual progress is not obvious,| any more than it is in illnesses; because it was in our power, however, to act in this way or not in this way, therefore the states are voluntary.

Let us take up the several virtues, however, and say which they are and what sort of things they are concerned with and how they are concerned with them; at the same time it will become plain how many they are. And first let us speak of courage.

COURAGE

Courage concerned with the feelings of fear and confidence—strictly speaking, with the fear of death in battle

6. That it is a mean with regard to feelings of fear and confidence has already been made evident;[1] and plainly the things we fear are fearful things, and these are, to speak without qualification, evils; for which reason people even define fear as expectation of evil.

---

[1] 1107^a33–^b4.

Now we fear all evils, e.g. disgrace, poverty, disease, friendlessness, death, but the brave man is not thought to be concerned with all; for to fear some things is even right and noble, and it is base not to fear them—e.g. disgrace; he who fears this is good and modest, and he who does not is shameless. He is, however, by some people called brave, by a transference of the word to a new meaning; for he has in him something which is like the brave man, since the brave man also is a fearless person. Poverty and disease we perhaps ought not to fear, nor in general the things that do not proceed from vice and are not due to a man himself. But not even the man who is fearless of these is brave. Yet we apply the word to him also in virtue of a similarity; for some who in the dangers of war are cowards are liberal and are confident in face of the loss of money. Nor is a man a coward if he fears insult to his wife and children or envy or anything of the kind; nor brave if he is confident when he is about to be flogged. With what sort of fearful things, then, is the brave man concerned? Surely with the greatest; for no one is more likely than he to stand his ground against what is awe-inspiring. Now death is the most fearful of all things; for it is the end, and nothing is thought to be any longer either good or bad for the dead. But the brave man would not seem to be concerned even with death in *all* circumstances, e.g. at sea or in disease. In what circumstances, then? Surely in the noblest. Now such deaths are those in battle; for these take place in the greatest and noblest danger. And these are correspondingly honoured in city-states and at the courts of monarchs. Properly, then, he will be called brave who is fearless in face of a noble death, and of all emergencies that involve death; and the emergencies of war are in the highest degree of this kind. Yet at sea also, and in disease, the brave man

is fearless,|but not in the same way as the seamen; for
he has given up hope of safety, and is disliking the
thought of death in this shape, while they are hopeful
because of their experience. At the same time, we show
courage in situations where there is the opportunity of
showing prowess or where death is noble; but in these
forms of death neither of these conditions is fulfilled.

The motive of courage is the sense of honour: characteristics of
the opposite vices, cowardice and rashness

7. What is fearful is not the same for all men; but
we say there are things fearful even beyond human
strength. These, then, are fearful to every one—at
least to every sensible man; but the fearful things that
are *not* beyond human strength differ in magnitude and
degree, and so too do the things that inspire confidence.
Now the brave man is as dauntless as man may be.
Therefore, while he will fear even the things that are
not beyond human strength, he will face them as he
ought and as the rule directs, for honour's sake; for this
is the end of virtue. But it is possible to fear these more,
or less, and again to fear things that are not fearful as
if they were. Of the faults that are committed, one consists in fearing what we should not, another in fearing
as we should not, another in fearing when we should
not, and so on; and so too with respect to the things that
inspire confidence. The man, then, who faces and who
fears the right things and from the right motive, in the
right way and at the right time, and who feels confidence under the corresponding conditions, is brave; for
the brave man feels and acts according to the merits of
the case and in whatever way the rule directs. Now the
end of every activity is conformity to the corresponding state of character. This is true, therefore, of the
brave man as well as of others. But courage is noble.

Therefore the end also is noble; for each thing is defined by its end. Therefore it is for a noble end that the brave man endures and acts as courage directs.

Of those who go to excess he who exceeds in fearlessness has no name (we have said previously that many states of character have no names),[1] but he would be a sort of madman or insensitive to pain if he feared nothing, neither earthquakes nor the waves, as they say the Celts do not; while the man who exceeds in confidence about what really is fearful is rash. The rash man, however, is also thought to be boastful and only a pretender to courage; at all events, as the brave man *is* with regard to what is fearful, so the rash man wishes to *appear*; and so he imitates him in situations where he can. Hence also most of them are a mixture of rashness and cowardice; for, while in these situations they display confidence, they do not hold their ground against what is really fearful. The man who exceeds in fear is a coward; for he fears both what he ought not and as he ought not, and all the similar characterizations attach to him. He is lacking also in confidence; | but he is more conspicuous for his excess of fear in painful situations. The coward, then, is a despairing sort of person; for he fears everything. The brave man, on the other hand, has the opposite disposition; for confidence is the mark of a hopeful disposition. The coward, the rash man, and the brave man, then, are concerned with the same objects but are differently disposed towards them; for the first two exceed and fall short, while the third holds the middle, which is the right, position; and rash men are precipitate, and wish for dangers beforehand but draw back when they are in them, while brave men are excited in the moment of action, but collected beforehand.

[1] 1107^b2, cf. 1107^b29, 1108^a5.

As we have said, then, courage is a mean with respect to things that inspire confidence or fear, in the circumstances that have been stated;[1] and it chooses or endures things because it is noble to do so, or because it is base not to do so.[2] But to die to escape from poverty or love or anything painful is not the mark of a brave man, but rather of a coward; for it is softness to fly from what is troublesome, and such a man endures death not because it is noble but to fly from evil.

Five kinds of courage improperly so called

8. Courage, then, is something of this sort, but the name is also applied to five other kinds. (1) First comes the courage of the citizen-soldier; for this is most like true courage. Citizen-soldiers seem to face dangers because of the penalties imposed by the laws and the reproaches they would otherwise incur, and because of the honours they win by such action; and therefore those peoples seem to be bravest among whom cowards are held in dishonour and brave men in honour. This is the kind of courage that Homer depicts, e.g. in Diomede and in Hector:

First will Polydamas be to heap reproach on me then;[3]

and

For Hector one day 'mid the Trojans shall utter his vaunting harangue:
'Afraid was Tydeides, and fled from my face.'[4]

This kind of courage is most like to that which we described earlier,[5] because it is due to virtue; for it is due to shame and to desire of a noble object (i.e. honour) and avoidance of disgrace, which is ignoble. One might

---

[1] Ch. 6.   [2] 1115ᵇ11-24.
[3] *Il.* xxii. 100.   [4] *Il.* viii. 148, 149.   [5] Chs. 6, 7

rank in the same class even those who are compelled by
their rulers; but they are inferior, inasmuch as they do
what they do not from shame but from fear, and to
avoid not what is disgraceful but what is painful; for
their masters compel them, as Hector[1] does:

> But if I shall spy any dastard that cowers far from
>   the fight,
> Vainly will such an one hope to escape from the dogs.

And those who give them their posts, and beat them
if they retreat, do the same, and so do those who draw
them up with trenches|or something of the sort behind
them; all of these apply compulsion. But one ought to
be brave not under compulsion but because it is noble
to be so.

(2) Experience with regard to particular facts is also
thought to be courage; this is indeed the reason why
Socrates thought courage was knowledge. Other people
exhibit this quality in other dangers, and professional
soldiers exhibit it in the dangers of war; for there seem
to be many empty alarms in war, of which these have
had the most comprehensive experience; therefore they
seem brave, because the others do not know the nature
of the facts. Again, their experience makes them most
capable in attack and in defence, since they can use
their arms and have the kind that are likely to be best
both for attack and for defence; therefore they fight like
armed men against unarmed or like trained athletes
against amateurs; for in such contests too it is not the
bravest men that fight best, but those who are strongest
and have their bodies in the best condition. Professional
soldiers turn cowards, however, when the danger puts
too great a strain on them and they are inferior in

[1] Aristotle's quotation is more like *Il.* ii. 391–3, where Agamemnon
speaks, than xv. 348–51, where Hector speaks.

numbers and equipment; for they are the first to fly, while citizen-forces die at their posts, as in fact happened at the temple of Hermes.[1] For to the latter flight is disgraceful and death is preferable to safety on those terms; while the former from the very beginning faced the danger on the assumption that they were stronger, and when they know the facts they fly, fearing death more than disgrace; but the brave man is not that sort of person.

(3) Passion also is sometimes reckoned as courage; those who act from passion, like wild beasts rushing at those who have wounded them, are thought to be brave, because brave men also are passionate; for passion above all things is eager to rush on danger, and hence Homer's 'put strength into his passion'[2] and 'aroused their spirit and passion'[3] and 'hard he breathed panting'[4] and 'his blood boiled'.[5] For all such expressions seem to indicate the stirring and onset o. passion. Now brave men act for honour's sake, but passion aids them; while wild beasts act under the influence of pain; for they attack because they have been wounded or because they are afraid, since if they are in a forest they do not come near one. Thus they are not brave because, driven by pain and passion, they rush on danger without foreseeing any of the perils, since at that rate even asses would be brave when they are hungry; for blows will not drive them from their food;|and lust also makes adulterers do many daring things. Those creatures are not brave, then, which are driven on to danger by pain or passion. The 'courage'

---

[1] The reference is to a battle at Coronea in the Sacred War, c. 353 B.C., in which the Phocians defeated the citizens of Coronea and some Boeotian regulars.

[2] This is a conflation of *Il.* xi. 11 or xiv. 151 and xvi. 529.

[3] Cf. *Il.* v. 470, xv. 232, 594.   [4] Cf. *Od.* xxiv. 318 f.

[5] The phrase does not occur in Homer; it is found in Theocr. xx. 15.

that is due to passion seems to be the most natural, and
to be courage if choice and motive be added.

Men, then, as well as beasts, suffer pain when they
are angry, and are pleased when they exact their revenge; those who fight for these reasons, however, are
pugnacious but not brave; for they do not act for
honour's sake nor as the rule directs, but from strength
of feeling; they have, however, something akin to
courage.

(4) Nor are sanguine people brave; for they are
confident in danger only because they have conquered
often and against many foes. Yet they closely resemble
brave men, because both are confident; but brave men
are confident for the reasons stated earlier,[1] while these
are so because they think they are the strongest and
can suffer nothing. (Drunken men also behave in this
way; they become sanguine.) When their adventures
do not succeed, however, they run away; but it was[1]
the mark of a brave man to face things that are, and
seem, terrible for a man, because it is noble to do so and
disgraceful not to do so. Hence also it is thought the
mark of a braver man to be fearless and undisturbed in
sudden alarms than to be so in those that are foreseen;
for it must have proceeded more from a state of character, because less from preparation; acts that are
foreseen may be chosen by calculation and rule, but
sudden actions must be in accordance with one's state
of character.

(5) People who are ignorant of the danger also
appear brave, and they are not far removed from those
of a sanguine temper, but are inferior inasmuch as they
have no self-reliance while these have. Hence also the
sanguine hold their ground for a time; but those who
have been deceived about the facts fly if they know or

[1] 1115ᵇ11-24.

suspect that these are different from what they supposed, as happened to the Argives when they fell in
with the Spartans and took them for Sicyonians.[1]
9. We have, then, described the character both of
brave men and of those who are thought to be brave.

Relation of courage to pain and pleasure

Though courage is concerned with confidence
and fear, it is not concerned with both alike, but more
with the things that inspire fear; for he who is undisturbed in face of these and bears himself as he should
towards these is more truly brave than the man who
does so towards the things that inspire confidence. It is
for facing what is painful, then, as has been said,[2] that
men are called brave. Hence also courage involves
pain, and is justly praised; for it is harder to face what
is painful than to abstain from what is pleasant. Yet the
end which courage sets before itself would seem to be
pleasant, |but to be concealed by the attending circum-
stances, as happens also in athletic contests; for the
end at which boxers aim is pleasant—the crown and
the honours—but the blows they take are distressing
to flesh and blood, and painful, and so is their whole
exertion; and because the blows and the exertions are
many the end, which is but small, appears to have
nothing pleasant in it. And so, if the case of courage is
similar, death and wounds will be painful to the brave
man and against his will, but he will face them because
it is noble to do so or because it is base not to do so. And
the more he is possessed of virtue in its entirety and the
happier he is, the more he will be pained at the thought
of death; for life is best worth living for such a man, and
he is knowingly losing the greatest goods, and this is

---

[1] At the Long Walls of Corinth, 392 B.C. Cf. Xen. *Hell.* iv. 4. 10.
[2] 1115ᵇ7-13.

painful. But he is none the less brave, and perhaps all
the more so, because he chooses noble deeds of war
at that cost. It is not the case, then, with all the virtues
that the exercise of them is pleasant, except in so far as
it attains its end. But it is quite possible that the best soldiers may be not men of this sort but those who are less
brave but have no other good; for these are ready to
face danger, and they sell their life for trifling gains.

So much, then, for courage; it is not difficult to grasp
its nature in outline, at any rate, from what has been
said.

TEMPERANCE

Temperance is limited to certain pleasures of touch

10. After courage let us speak of temperance; for these
seem to be the virtues of the irrational parts. We have
said[1] that temperance is a mean with regard to pleasures (for it is less, and not in the same way, concerned
with pains); self-indulgence also is manifested in the
same sphere. Now, therefore, let us determine with
what sort of pleasures they are concerned. We may
assume the distinction between bodily pleasures and
those of the soul, such as love of honour and love of
learning; for the lover of each of these delights in that
of which he is a lover, the body being in no way
affected, but rather the mind; but men who are concerned with such pleasures are called neither temperate nor self-indulgent. Nor, again, are those who are
concerned with the other pleasures that are not bodily;
for those who are fond of hearing and telling stories and
who spend their days on anything that turns up are
gossips, but not self-indulgent, nor are those who are
pained at the loss of money or of friends.

[1] 1107^{b}4–6.

Temperance must be concerned with bodily pleasures, but not all even of these; for those who delight in
objects of vision, such as colours and shapes and painting, are called neither temperate nor self-indulgent;
yet it would seem possible to delight even in these either
as one should or to excess or to a deficient degree.

And so too is it with objects of hearing; no one calls
those who delight extravagantly in music or acting
self-indulgent, nor those who do so as they ought
temperate.

Nor do we apply these names to those who delight in
odour, unless it be incidentally; we do not call those
self-indulgent who delight in the odour of apples or
roses or incense, but rather those who delight in the
odour of unguents or of dainty dishes; for self-indulgent
people delight in these because these remind them of
the objects of their appetite. And one may see even
other people, when they are hungry, delighting in the
smell of food; but to delight in this kind of thing is the
mark of the self-indulgent man; for these are objects of
appetite to him.

Nor is there in animals other than man any pleasure
connected with these senses, except incidentally. For
dogs do not delight in the scent of hares, but in the
eating of them, but the scent told them the hares were
there; nor does the lion delight in the lowing of the ox,
but in eating it; but he perceived by the lowing that it
was near, and therefore appears to delight in the lowing; and similarly he does not delight because he sees
'a stag or a wild goat',[1] but because he is going to make
a meal of it. Temperance and self-indulgence, however,
are concerned with the kind of pleasures that the other
animals share in, which therefore appear slavish and
brutish; these are touch and taste. But even of taste

[1] *Il.* iii. 24.

they appear to make little or no use; for the business of
taste is the discriminating of flavours, which is done by
wine-tasters and people who season dishes; but they
hardly take pleasure in making these discriminations,
or at least self-indulgent people do not, but in the actual
enjoyment, which in all cases comes through touch,
both in the case of food and in that of drink and in that
of sexual intercourse. This is why a certain gourmand
prayed that his throat might become longer than a
crane's, implying that it was the contact that he took
pleasure in.|Thus the sense with which self-indulgence
is connected is the most widely shared of the senses; and
self-indulgence would seem to be justly a matter of
reproach, because it attaches to us not as men but as
animals. To delight in such things, then, and to love
them above all others, is brutish. For even of the pleasures of touch the most refined have been eliminated,
e.g. those produced in the gymnasium by rubbing and
by the consequent heat; for the contact characteristic
of the self-indulgent man does not affect the whole body
but only certain parts.

*Characteristics of temperance and its opposites, self-indulgence
and 'insensibility'*

11. Of the appetites some seem to be common, others
to be peculiar to individuals and acquired; e.g. the
appetite for food is natural, since everyone who is
without it craves for food or drink, and sometimes for
both, and for love also (as Homer says)[1] if he is young
and lusty; but not everyone craves for this or that kind
of nourishment or love, nor for the same things. Hence
such craving appears to be our very own. Yet it has of
course something natural about it; for different things
are pleasant to different kinds of people, and some

[1] *Il.* xxiv. 130.

74

things are more pleasant to everyone than chance
objects. Now in the natural appetites few go wrong,
and only in one direction, that of excess; for to eat or
drink whatever offers itself till one is surfeited is to
exceed the natural amount, since natural appetite is
the replenishment of one's deficiency. Hence these
people are called belly-gods, this implying that they
fill their belly beyond what is right. It is people of
entirely slavish character that become like this. But
with regard to the pleasures peculiar to individuals
many people go wrong and in many ways. For while
the people who are 'fond of so-and-so' are so-called
because they delight either in the wrong things, or
more than most people do, or in the wrong way, the
self-indulgent exceed in all three ways; they both delight in some things that they ought not to delight in
(since they are hateful), and if one ought to delight
in some of the things they delight in, they do so more
than one ought and than most men do.

Plainly, then, excess with regard to pleasures is self-
indulgence and is culpable; with regard to pains one
is not, as in the case of courage, called temperate for
facing them or self-indulgent for not doing so, but the
self-indulgent man is so called because he is pained
more than he ought at not getting pleasant things (even
his pain being caused by pleasure), and the temperate
man is so called because he is not pained at the absence
of what is pleasant and at his abstinence from it.|

The self-indulgent man, then, craves for all pleasant
things or those that are most pleasant, and is led by his
appetite to choose these at the cost of everything else;
hence he is pained both when he fails to get them and
when he is merely craving for them (for appetite involves pain); but it seems absurd to be pained for the
sake of pleasure. People who fall short with regard to

pleasures and delight in them less than they should are hardly found; for such insensibility is not human. Even the other animals distinguish different kinds of food and enjoy some and not others; and if there is anyone who finds nothing pleasant and nothing more attractive than anything else, he must be something quite different from a man; this sort of person has not received a name because he hardly occurs. The temperate man occupies a middle position with regard to these objects. For he neither enjoys the things that the self-indulgent man enjoys most—but rather dislikes them—nor in general the things that he should not, nor anything of this sort to excess, nor does he feel pain or craving when they are absent, or does so only to a moderate degree, and not more than he should, nor when he should not, and so on; but the things that, being pleasant, make for health or for good condition, he will desire moderately and as he should, and also other pleasant things if they are not hindrances to these ends, or contrary to what is noble, or beyond his means. For he who neglects these conditions loves such pleasures more than they are worth, but the temperate man is not that sort of person, but the sort of person that the right rule prescribes.

Self-indulgence more voluntary than cowardice: comparison of the self-indulgent man to the spoilt child

12. Self-indulgence is more like a voluntary state than cowardice. For the former is actuated by pleasure, the latter by pain, of which the one is to be chosen and the other to be avoided; and pain upsets and destroys the nature of the person who feels it, while pleasure does nothing of the sort. Therefore self-indulgence is more voluntary. Hence also it is more a matter of reproach; for it is easier to become accustomed to its objects, since

there are many things of this sort in life, and the process
of habituation to them is free from danger, while with
terrible objects the reverse is the case. But cowardice
would seem to be voluntary in a different degree from
its particular manifestations; for it is itself painless,
but in these we are upset by pain, so that we even throw
down our arms and disgrace ourselves in other ways;
hence our acts are even thought to be done under
compulsion. For the self-indulgent man, on the other
hand, the particular acts are voluntary (for he does
them with craving and desire), but the whole state is
less so; for no one craves to be self-indulgent.

The name self-indulgence is applied also to childish
faults;[1] for they bear a certain resemblance to what we
have been considering. | Which is called after which,
makes no difference to our present purpose; plainly,
however, the later is called after the earlier. The transference of the name seems not a bad one; for that which
desires what is base and which develops quickly ought
to be kept in a chastened condition, and these characteristics belong above all to appetite and to the child,
since children in fact live at the beck and call of
appetite, and it is in them that the desire for what is
pleasant is strongest. If, then, it is not going to be
obedient and subject to the ruling principle, it will go
to great lengths; for in an irrational being the desire for
pleasure is insatiable even if it tries every source of
gratification, and the exercise of appetite increases its
innate force, and if appetites are strong and violent they
even expel the power of calculation. Hence they should
be moderate and few, and should in no way oppose the
rational principle—and this is what we call an obedient
and chastened state—and as the child should live

---

[1] ἀκόλαστος, which we have translated 'self-indulgent', meant originally 'unchastened' and was applied to the ways of spoilt children.

according to the direction of his tutor, so the appetitive element should live according to rational principle. Hence the appetitive element in a temperate man should harmonize with the rational principle; for the noble is the mark at which both aim, and the temperate man craves for the things he ought, as he ought, and when he ought; and this is what rational principle directs.

Here we conclude our account of temperance.

BOOK IV · MORAL VIRTUE (cont.)

‣‣‣

VIRTUES CONCERNED WITH MONEY

Liberality

1. LET us speak next of liberality. It seems to be the mean with regard to wealth; for the liberal man is praised not in respect of military matters, nor of those in respect of which the temperate man is praised, nor of judicial decisions, but with regard to the giving and taking of wealth, and especially in respect of giving. Now by 'wealth' we mean all the things whose value is measured by money. Further, prodigality and meanness are excesses and defects with regard to wealth; and meanness we always impute to those who care more than they ought for wealth, but we sometimes apply the word 'prodigality' in a complex sense; for we call those men prodigals who are incontinent and spend money on self-indulgence. Hence also they are thought the poorest characters; for they combine more vices than one. Therefore the application of the word to them is not its proper use; for a 'prodigal' means a man who has a single evil quality, that of wasting his substance; | since a prodigal is one who is being ruined by his own fault,[1] and the wasting of substance is thought to be a sort of ruining of oneself, life being held to depend on possession of substance.

This, then, is the sense in which we take the word 'prodigality'. Now the things that have a use may be used either well or badly; and riches are a useful thing; and everything is used best by the man who has the virtue concerned with it; riches, therefore, will be used best by the man who has the virtue concerned with

---

[1] ἄ-σωτος = one who is not saved, who is ruined.

79

wealth; and this is the liberal man. Now spending and giving seem to be the using of wealth; taking and keeping rather the possession of it. Hence it is more the mark of the liberal man to give to the right people than to take from the right sources and not to take from the wrong. For it is more characteristic of virtue to do good than to have good done to one, and more characteristic to do what is noble than not to do what is base; and it is not hard to see that giving implies doing good and doing what is noble, and taking implies having good done to one or not acting basely. And gratitude is felt towards him who gives, not towards him who does not take, and praise also is bestowed more on him. It is easier, also, not to take than to give; for men are apter to give away their own too little than to take what is another's. Givers, too, are called liberal; but those who do not take are not praised for liberality but rather for justice; while those who take are hardly praised at all. And the liberal are almost the most loved of all virtuous characters, since they are useful; and this depends on their giving.

Now virtuous actions are noble and done for the sake of the noble. Therefore the liberal man, like other virtuous men, will give for the sake of the noble, and rightly; for he will give to the right people, the right amounts, and at the right time, with all the other qualifications that accompany right giving; and that too with pleasure or without pain; for that which is virtuous is pleasant or free from pain—least of all will it be painful. But he who gives to the wrong people or not for the sake of the noble but for some other cause, will be called not liberal but by some other name. Nor is he liberal who gives with pain; for he would prefer the wealth to the noble act, and this is not characteristic of a liberal man. But no more will the liberal man take

from wrong sources; for such taking is not characteristic of the man who sets no store by wealth. Nor will
he be a ready asker; for it is not characteristic of a man
who confers benefits to accept them lightly. But he will
take from the right sources, e.g. from his own posses-
sions, | not as something noble but as a necessity, that
he may have something to give. Nor will he neglect his
own property, since he wishes by means of this to help
others. And he will refrain from giving to anybody and
everybody, that he may have something to give to the
right people, at the right time, and where it is noble to
do so. It is highly characteristic of a liberal man also
to go to excess in giving, so that he leaves too little for
himself; for it is the nature of a liberal man not to look
to himself. The term 'liberality' is used relatively to
a man's substance; for liberality resides not in the
multitude of the gifts but in the state of character of
the giver, and this is relative to the giver's substance.
There is therefore nothing to prevent the man who
gives less from being the more liberal man, if he has less
to give. Those are thought to be more liberal who have
not made their wealth but inherited it; for in the first
place they have no experience of want, and secondly
all men are fonder of their own productions, as are
parents and poets. It is not easy for the liberal man to
be rich, since he is not apt either at taking or at keeping,
but at giving away, and does not value wealth for its
own sake but as a means to giving. Hence comes the
charge that is brought against fortune, that those who
deserve riches most get it least. But it is not unreason-
able that it should turn out so; for he cannot have
wealth, any more than anything else, if he does not take
pains to have it. Yet he will not give to the wrong people
nor at the wrong time, and so on; for he would no
longer be acting in accordance with liberality, and if

he spent on these objects he would have nothing to
spend on the right objects. For, as has been said, he is
liberal who spends according to his substance and on
the right objects; and he who exceeds is prodigal. Hence
we do not call despots prodigal; for it is thought not
easy for them to give and spend beyond the amount of
their possessions. Liberality, then, being a mean with
regard to giving and taking of wealth, the liberal man
will both give and spend the right amounts and on the
right objects, alike in small things and in great, and
that with pleasure; he will also take the right amounts
and from the right sources. For, the virtue being a
mean with regard to both, he will do both as he ought;
since this sort of taking accompanies proper giving, and
that which is not of this sort is contrary to it, and accordingly the giving and taking that accompany each
other are present together in the same man, while the
contrary kinds evidently are not. | But if he happens to
spend in a manner contrary to what is right and noble,
he will be pained, but moderately and as he ought; for
it is the mark of virtue both to be pleased and to be
pained at the right objects and in the right way.
Further, the liberal man is easy to deal with in money
matters; for he can be got the better of, since he sets
no store by money, and is more annoyed if he has not
spent something that he ought than pained if he has
spent something that he ought not, and does not agree
with the saying of Simonides.[1]

The prodigal errs in these respects also; for he is
neither pleased nor pained at the right things or in the
right way; this will be more evident as we go on. We
have said[2] that prodigality and meanness are excesses
and deficiencies, and in two things, in giving and taking; for we include spending under giving. Now prodi-

[1] 'It is better to be rich than clever.'   [2] 1119^b27.

gality exceeds in giving and not taking, and falls short
in taking, while meanness falls short in giving, and
exceeds in taking, but only in small things.

The characteristics of prodigality are not often combined; for it is not easy to give to all if you take from
none; private persons soon 'exhaust their substance
with giving, and it is to these that the name of prodigals
is applied—though a man of this sort would seem to be
in no small degree better than a mean man. For he is
easily cured both by age and by poverty, and thus he
may move towards the middle state. For he has the
characteristics of the liberal man, since he both gives
and refrains from taking, though he does neither of
these in the right manner or well. Therefore if he were
brought to do so by habituation or in some other way,
he would be liberal; for he will then give to the right
people, and will not take from the wrong sources. This
is why he is thought to have not a bad character; it is
not the mark of a wicked or ignoble man to go to excess
in giving and not taking, but only of a foolish one. The
man who is prodigal in this way is thought much better
than the mean man both for the aforesaid reasons and
because he benefits many while the other benefits no
one, not even himself.

But most prodigal people, as has been said,[1] also take
from the wrong sources, and are in this respect mean.
They become apt to take because they wish to spend
and cannot do this easily; for their possessions soon
run short. Thus they are forced to provide means from
some other source. | At the same time, because they care
nothing for honour, they take recklessly and from any
source; for they have an appetite for giving, and they
do not mind how or from what source. Hence also their
giving is not liberal; for it is not noble, nor does it aim

[1] ll. 16-19.

at nobility, nor is it done in the right way; sometimes they make rich those who should be poor, and will give nothing to people of respectable character, and much to flatterers or those who provide them with some other pleasure. Hence also most of them are self-indulgent; for they spend lightly and waste money on their indulgences, and incline towards pleasures because they do not live with a view to what is noble.

The prodigal man, then, turns into what we have described if he is left untutored, but if he is treated with care he will arrive at the intermediate and right state. But meanness is both incurable (for old age and every disability is thought to make men mean) and more innate in men than prodigality; for most men are fonder of getting money than of giving. It also extends widely, and is multiform, since there seem to be many kinds of meanness.

For it consists in two things, deficiency in giving and excess in taking, and is not found complete in all men but is sometimes divided; some men go to excess in taking, others fall short in giving. Those who are called by such names as 'miserly', 'close', 'stingy', all fall short in giving, but do not covet the possessions of others nor wish to get them. In some this is due to a sort of honesty and avoidance of what is disgraceful (for some seem, or at least profess, to hoard their money for this reason, that they may not some day be forced to do something disgraceful; to this class belong the cheeseparer and everyone of the sort; he is so called from his excess of unwillingness to give anything); while others again keep their hands off the property of others from fear, on the ground that it is not easy, if one takes the property of others oneself, to avoid having one's own taken by them; they are therefore content neither to take nor to give.

Others again exceed in respect of taking by taking anything and from any source, e.g. those who ply sordid trades, pimps and all such people, and those who lend small sums and at high rates. | For all of these take more than they ought and from wrong sources. What is common to them is evidently sordid love of gain; they all put up with a bad name for the sake of gain, and little gain at that. For those who make great gains but from wrong sources, and not the right gains, e.g. despots when they sack cities and spoil temples, we do not call mean but rather wicked, impious, and unjust. But the gamester and the footpad [and the highwayman] belong to the class of the mean, since they have a sordid love of gain. For it is for gain that both of them ply their craft and endure the disgrace of it, and the one faces the greatest dangers for the sake of the booty, while the other makes gain from his friends, to whom he ought to be giving. Both, then, since they are willing to make gain from wrong sources, are sordid lovers of gain; therefore all such forms of taking are mean.

And it is natural that meanness is described as the contrary of liberality; for not only is it a greater evil than prodigality, but men err more often in this direction than in the way of prodigality as we have described it.

So much, then, for liberality and the opposed vices.

Magnificence

2. It would seem proper to discuss magnificence next. For this also seems to be a virtue concerned with wealth; but it does not, like liberality, extend to all the actions that are concerned with wealth, but only to those that involve expenditure; and in these it surpasses liberality in scale. For, as the name itself suggests, it is

a fitting expenditure involving largeness of scale. But
the scale is relative; for the expense of equipping a
trireme is not the same as that of heading a sacred em-
bassy. It is what is fitting, then, in relation to the agent,
and to the circumstances and the object. The man who
in small or middling things spends according to the
merits of the case is not called magnificent (e.g. the
man who can say 'Many a gift I gave the wanderer'),[1]
but only the man who does so in great things. For the
magnificent man is liberal, but the liberal man is not
necessarily magnificent. The deficiency of this state of
character is called niggardliness, the excess vulgarity,
lack of taste, and the like, which do not go to excess in
the amount spent on right objects, but by showy expenditure in the wrong circumstances and the wrong
manner; we shall speak of these vices later.[2]

The magnificent man is like an artist; for he can see
what is fitting and spend large sums tastefully. For, as
we said at the beginning,[3] | a state of character is deter-
mined by its activities and by its objects. Now the
expenses of the magnificent man are large and fitting.
Such, therefore, are also his results; for thus there will
be a great expenditure and one that is fitting to its
result. Therefore the result should be worthy of the
expense, and the expense should be worthy of the
result, or should even exceed it. And the magnificent
man will spend such sums for honour's sake; for this is
common to the virtues. And further he will do so gladly
and lavishly; for nice calculation is a niggardly thing.
And he will consider how the result can be made most
beautiful and most becoming rather than for how much
it can be produced and how it can be produced most
cheaply. It is necessary, then, that the magnificent man

---

[1] *Od.* xvii. 420.   [2] 1123ª19–33.
[3] Not in so many words, but cf. 1103ᵇ21–23, 1104ª27–29.

be also liberal. For the liberal man also will spend what he ought and as he ought; and it is in these matters that the greatness implied in the name of the magnificent man—his bigness, as it were—is manifested, since liberality is concerned with these matters; and at an equal expense he will produce a more magnificent work of art. For a possession and a work of art have not the same excellence. The most valuable possession is that which is worth most, e.g. gold, but the most valuable work of art is that which is great and beautiful (for the contemplation of such a work inspires admiration, and so does magnificence); and a work has an excellence— viz. magnificence—which involves magnitude. Magnificence is an attribute of expenditures of the kind which we call honourable, e.g. those connected with the gods —votive offerings, buildings, and sacrifices—and similarly with any form of religious worship, and all those that are proper objects of public-spirited ambition, as when people think they ought to equip a chorus or a trireme, or entertain the city, in a brilliant way. But in all cases, as has been said,¹ we have regard to the agent as well and ask who he is and what means he has; for the expenditure should be worthy of his means, and suit not only the result but also the producer. Hence a poor man cannot be magnificent, since he has not the means with which to spend large sums fittingly; and he who tries is a fool, since he spends beyond what can be expected of him and what is proper, but it is *right* expenditure that is virtuous. But great expenditure is becoming to those who have suitable means to start with, acquired by their own efforts or from ancestors or connexions, and to people of high birth or reputation, and so on; for all these things bring with them greatness and prestige. Primarily, then, the magnificent

¹ ᵃ24-26.

man is of this sort, and magnificence is shown in expenditures of this sort, as has been said;[1] for these are
the greatest and most honourable. Of *private* occasions
of expenditure the most suitable are those that take
place once for all, e.g. a wedding or anything of the
kind, | or anything that interests the whole city or the
people of position in it, and also the receiving of foreign
guests and the sending of them on their way, and gifts
and counter-gifts; for the magnificent man spends not
on himself but on public objects, and gifts bear some
resemblance to votive offerings. A magnificent man
will also furnish his house suitably to his wealth (for
even a house is a sort of public ornament), and will
spend by preference on those works that are lasting (for
these are the most beautiful), and on every class of
things he will spend what is becoming; for the same
things are not suitable for gods and for men, nor in
a temple and in a tomb. And since each expenditure
may be great of its kind, and what is most magnificent
absolutely is great expenditure on a great object, but
what is magnificent *here* is what is great in *these* circumstances, and greatness in the work differs from greatness
in the expense (for the most beautiful ball or bottle is
magnificent as a gift to a child, but the price of it is small
and mean),—therefore it is characteristic of the magnificent man, whatever kind of result he is producing, to
produce it magnificently (for such a result is not easily
surpassed) and to make it worthy of the expenditure.

Such, then, is the magnificent man; the man who
goes to excess and is vulgar exceeds, as has been said,[2]
by spending beyond what is right. For on small objects
of expenditure he spends much and displays a tasteless
showiness; e.g. he gives a club dinner on the scale of
a wedding banquet, and when he provides the chorus

[1] ll. 19-23.   [2] 1122^a31-33.

for a comedy he brings them on to the stage in purple,
as they do at Megara. And all such things he will do
not for honour's sake but to show off his wealth, and
because he thinks he is admired for these things,
and where he ought to spend much he spends little and
where little, much. The niggardly man on the other
hand will fall short in everything, and after spending
the greatest sums will spoil the beauty of the result for
a trifle, and whatever he is doing he will hesitate and
consider how he may spend least, and lament even that,
and think he is doing everything on a bigger scale than
he ought.

These states of character, then, are vices; yet they
do not bring *disgrace* because they are neither harmful
to one's neighbour nor very unseemly.

VIRTUES CONCERNED WITH HONOUR

Pride

3. Pride seems even from its name[1] to be concerned
with great things; what sort of great things, is the first
question we must try to answer. It makes no difference
whether we consider the state of character or the man
characterized by it. | Now the man is thought to be
proud who thinks himself worthy of great things, being
worthy of them; for he who does so beyond his deserts is
a fool, but no virtuous man is foolish or silly. The proud
man, then, is the man we have described. For he who
is worthy of little and thinks himself worthy of little is
temperate, but not proud; for pride implies greatness,
as beauty implies a good-sized body, and little people
may be neat and well-proportioned but cannot be
beautiful. On the other hand, he who thinks himself
worthy of great things, being unworthy of them, is

[1] 'Pride' of course has not the etymological associations of μεγαλο-
ψυχία, but seems in other respects the best translation.

vain; though not every one who thinks himself worthy
of more than he really is worthy of is vain. The man
who thinks himself worthy of less than he is really
worthy of is unduly humble, whether his deserts be
great or moderate, or his deserts be small but his claims
yet smaller. And the man whose deserts are great would
seem *most* unduly humble; for what would he have
done if they had been less? The proud man, then, is
an extreme in respect of the greatness of his claims, but
a mean in respect of the rightness of them; for he claims
what is in accordance with his merits, while the others
go to excess or fall short.

If, then, he deserves and claims great things, and
above all the greatest things, he will be concerned with
one thing in particular. Desert is relative to external
goods; and the greatest of these, we should say, is that
which we render to the gods, and which people of
position most aim at, and which is the prize appointed
for the noblest deeds; and this is honour; that is surely
the greatest of external goods. Honours and dishonours, therefore, are the objects with respect to
which the proud man is as he should be. And even
apart from argument it is with honour that proud men
appear to be concerned; for it is honour that they
chiefly claim, but in accordance with their deserts. The
unduly humble man falls short both in comparison
with his own merits and in comparison with the proud
man's claims. The vain man goes to excess in comparison with his own merits, but does not exceed the
proud man's claims.

Now the proud man, since he deserves most, must
be good in the highest degree; for the better man always
deserves more, and the best man most. Therefore the
truly proud man must be good. And greatness in every
virtue would seem to be characteristic of a proud man.

And it would be most unbecoming for a proud man to
fly from danger, swinging his arms by his sides, or to
wrong another; for to what end should he do disgraceful acts, he to whom nothing is great? If we consider
him point by point we shall see the utter absurdity of
a proud man who is not good. Nor, again, would he
be worthy of honour if he were bad; for honour is the
prize of virtue, and it is to the good that it is rendered. |
Pride, then, seems to be a sort of crown of the virtues;
for it makes them greater, and it is not found without
them. Therefore it is hard to be truly proud; for it is
impossible without nobility and goodness of character.
It is chiefly with honours and dishonours, then, that the
proud man is concerned; and at honours that are great
and conferred by good men he will be moderately
pleased, thinking that he is coming by his own or even
less than his own; for there can be no honour that is
worthy of perfect virtue, yet he will at any rate accept
it since they have nothing greater to bestow on him;
but honour from casual people and on trifling grounds
he will utterly despise, since it is not this that he deserves, and dishonour too, since in his case it cannot be
just. In the first place, then, as has been said,[1] the proud
man is concerned with honours; yet he will also bear
himself with moderation towards wealth and power
and all good or evil fortune, whatever may befall him,
and will be neither over-joyed by good fortune nor
over-pained by evil. For not even towards honour does
he bear himself as if it were a very great thing. Power
and wealth are desirable for the sake of honour (at least
those who have them wish to get honour by means of
them); and for him to whom even honour is a little
thing the others must be so too. Hence proud men are
thought to be disdainful.

1123^b15–22.

91

The goods of fortune also are thought to contribute towards pride. For men who are well-born are thought worthy of honour, and so are those who enjoy power or wealth; for they are in a superior position, and everything that has a superiority in something good is held in greater honour. Hence even such things make men prouder; for they are honoured by some for having them; but in truth the good man alone is to be honoured; he, however, who has both advantages is thought the more worthy of honour. But those who without virtue have such goods are neither justified in making great claims nor entitled to the name of 'proud'; for these things imply perfect virtue. Disdainful and insolent, however, even those who have such goods become. For without virtue it is not easy to bear gracefully the goods of fortune; and, being unable to bear them, and thinking themselves superior to others,| they despise others and themselves do what they please. They imitate the proud man without being like him, and this they do where they can; so they do not act virtuously, but they do despise others. For the proud man despises justly (since he thinks truly), but the many do so at random.

He does not run into trifling dangers, nor is he fond of danger, because he honours few things; but he will face great dangers, and when he is in danger he is unsparing of his life, knowing that there are conditions on which life is not worth having. And he is the sort of man to confer benefits, but he is ashamed of receiving them; for the one is the mark of a superior, the other of an inferior. And he is apt to confer greater benefits in return; for thus the original benefactor besides being paid will incur a debt to him, and will be the gainer by the transaction. They seem also to remember any service they have done, but not those they have

received (for he who receives a service is inferior to him
who has done it, but the proud man wishes to be
superior), and to hear of the former with pleasure, of
the latter with displeasure; this, it seems, is why Thetis
did not mention to Zeus the services she had done him,[1]
and why the Spartans did not recount their services
to the Athenians, but those they had received.[2] It is
a mark of the proud man also to ask for nothing or
scarcely anything, but to give help readily, and to be
dignified towards people who enjoy high position and
good fortune, but unassuming towards those of the
middle class; for it is a difficult and lofty thing to be
superior to the former, but easy to be so to the latter,
and a lofty bearing over the former is no mark of ill-
breeding, but among humble people it is as vulgar as
a display of strength against the weak. Again, it is
characteristic of the proud man not to aim at the things
commonly held in honour, or the things in which
others excel; to be sluggish and to hold back except
where great honour or a great work is at stake, and to
be a man of few deeds, but of great and notable ones.
He must also be open in his hate and in his love (for to
conceal one's feelings, i.e. to care less for truth than
for what people will think, is a coward's part), and must
speak and act openly; for he is free of speech because
he is contemptuous, and he is given to telling the truth,
except when he speaks in irony to the vulgar. He must
be unable to make his life revolve round another, unless
it be a friend; | for this is slavish, and for this reason all
flatterers are servile and people lacking in self-respect
are flatterers. Nor is he given to admiration; for

---

[1] In fact she did, *Il.* i. 503.

[2] The Aldine scholiast quotes Callisthenes as stating that the Spartans
behaved in this way when they were asking for help from the Athenians
on the occasion of an invasion by the Thebans. If the reference is to
369 B.C., it does not agree with Xen. *Hell.* vi. 5. 33 f.

nothing to him is great. Nor is he mindful of wrongs; for it is not the part of a proud man to have a long memory, especially for wrongs, but rather to overlook them. Nor is he a gossip; for he will speak neither about himself nor about another, since he cares not to be praised nor for others to be blamed; nor again is he given to praise; and for the same reason he is not an evil-speaker, even about his enemies, except from haughtiness. With regard to necessary or small matters he is least of all men given to lamentation or the asking of favours; for it is the part of one who takes such matters seriously to behave so with respect to them. He is one who will possess beautiful and profitless things rather than profitable and useful ones; for this is more proper to a character that suffices to itself.

Further, a slow step is thought proper to the proud man, a deep voice, and a level utterance; for the man who takes few things seriously is not likely to be hurried, nor the man who thinks nothing great to be excited, while a shrill voice and a rapid gait are the results of hurry and excitement.

Such, then, is the proud man; the man who falls short of him is unduly humble, and the man who goes beyond him is vain. Now these too are not thought to be bad (for they are not evil-doers), but only mistaken. For the unduly humble man, being worthy of good things, robs himself of what he deserves, and seems to have something bad about him from the fact that he does not think himself worthy of good things, and seems also not to know himself; else he would have desired the things he was worthy of, since these were good. Yet such people are not thought to be fools, but rather unduly retiring. Such an estimate, however, seems actually to make them worse; for each class of people aims at what corresponds to its worth, and these

people stand back even from noble actions and undertakings, deeming themselves unworthy, and from external goods no less. Vain people, on the other hand,
are fools and ignorant of themselves, and that mani-
festly; for, not being worthy of them, they attempt
honourable undertakings, and then are found out; and
they adorn themselves with clothing and outward show
and such things, and wish their strokes of good fortune
to be made public, and speak about them as if they
would be honoured for them. But undue humility is
more opposed to pride than vanity is; for it is both
commoner and worse.

Pride, then, is concerned with honour on the grand
scale, as has been said.[1] |

The virtue intermediate between ambition and unambitiousness

4. There seems to be in the sphere of honour also, as
was said in our first remarks on the subject,[2] a virtue
which would appear to be related to pride as liberality
is to magnificence. For neither of these has anything to
do with the grand scale, but both dispose us as is right
with regard to middling and unimportant objects; as
in getting and giving of wealth there is a mean and an
excess and defect, so too honour may be desired more
than is right, or less, or from the right sources and in the
right way. We blame both the ambitious man as aiming
at honour more than is right and from wrong sources,
and the unambitious man as not willing to be honoured
even for noble reasons. But sometimes we praise the
ambitious man as being manly and a lover of what is
noble, and the unambitious man as being moderate
and self-controlled, as we said in our first treatment of
the subject.[3] Evidently, since 'fond of such and such an
object' has more than one meaning, we do not assign

[1] 1107ᵇ26, 1123ª34–ᵇ22.   [2] Ibid. 24–27.   [3] 1107ᵇ3ª.

95

the term 'ambition' or 'love of honour' always to the
same thing, but when we praise the quality we think
of the man who loves honour more than most people,
and when we blame it we think of him who loves it
more than is right. The mean being without a name,
the extremes seem to dispute for its place as though that
were vacant by default. But where there is excess and
defect, there is also an intermediate; now men desire
honour both more than they should and less; therefore
it is possible also to do so as one should; at all events this
is the state of character that is praised, being an unnamed mean in respect of honour. Relatively to ambition it seems to be unambitiousness, and relatively to
unambitiousness it seems to be ambition, while relatively to both severally it seems in a sense to be both
together. This appears to be true of the other virtues
also. But in this case the extremes seem to be contra-
dictories because the mean has not received a name.

THE VIRTUE CONCERNED WITH ANGER

Good temper

5. Good temper is a mean with respect to anger; the
middle state being unnamed, and the extremes almost
without a name as well, we place good temper in the
middle position, though it inclines towards the deficiency, which is without a name. The excess might be
called a sort of 'irascibility'. For the passion is anger,
while its causes are many and diverse.

The man who is angry at the right things and with
the right people, and, further, as he ought, when he
ought, and as long as he ought, is praised. This will be
the good-tempered man, then, since good temper is
praised. For the good-tempered man tends to be un-
perturbed and not to be led by passion, but to be angry
in the manner, at the things, and for the length of time,

that the rule dictates; | but he is thought to err rather in the direction of deficiency; for the good-tempered man is not revengeful, but rather tends to make allowances.

The deficiency, whether it is a sort of 'unirascibility' or whatever it is, is blamed. For those who are not angry at the things they should be angry at are thought to be fools, and so are those who are not angry in the right way, at the right time, or with the right persons; for such a man is thought not to feel things nor to be pained by them, and, since he does not get angry, he is thought unlikely to defend himself; and to endure being insulted and put up with insult to one's friends is slavish.

The excess can be manifested in all the points that have been named (for one can be angry with the wrong persons, at the wrong things, more than is right, too quickly, or too long); yet *all* are not found in the same person. Indeed they could not; for evil destroys even itself, and if it is complete becomes unbearable. Now *hot-tempered* people get angry quickly and with the wrong persons and at the wrong things and more than is right, but their anger ceases quickly—which is the best point about them. This happens to them because they do not restrain their anger but retaliate openly owing to their quickness of temper, and then their anger ceases. By reason of excess *choleric* people are quick-tempered and ready to be angry with everything and on every occasion; whence their name. *Sulky* people are hard to appease, and retain their anger long; for they repress their passion. But it ceases when they retaliate; for revenge relieves them of their anger, producing in them pleasure instead of pain. If this does not happen they retain their burden; for owing to its not being obvious no one even reasons with them, and to digest one's anger in oneself takes time. Such people are most troublesome to themselves and to their dearest friends. We call *bad-tempered* those who are angry at the wrong things, more than is right, and longer, and cannot be appeased until they inflict vengeance or punishment.

To good temper we oppose the excess rather than the defect; for not only is it commoner (since revenge is the more human), but bad-tempered people are worse to live with.

What we have said in our earlier treatment of the subject[1] is plain also from what we are now saying; viz. that it is not easy to define how, with whom, at what, and how long one should be angry, and at what point right action ceases and wrong begins. For the man who strays a little from the path, either towards the more or towards the less, is not blamed; since sometimes we praise those who exhibit the deficiency, and call them good-tempered, | and sometimes we call angry people manly, as being capable of ruling. How far, therefore, and how a man must stray before he becomes blameworthy, it is not easy to state in words; for the decision depends on the particular facts and on perception. But so much at least is plain, that the middle state is praiseworthy—that in virtue of which we are angry with the right people, at the right things, in the right way, and so on, while the excesses and defects are blameworthy —slightly so if they are present in a low degree, more if in a higher degree, and very much if in a high degree. Evidently, then, we must cling to the middle state.— Enough of the states relative to anger.

VIRTUES OF SOCIAL INTERCOURSE

Friendliness

6. In gatherings of men, in social life and the interchange of words and deeds, some men are thought to

---

¹ 1109ᵇ14–26.

be obsequious, viz. those who to give pleasure praise
everything and never oppose, but think it their duty
'to give no pain to the people they meet'; while those
who, on the contrary, oppose everything and care not
a whit about giving pain are called churlish and contentious. That the states we have named are culpable
is plain enough, and that the middle state is laudable—
that in virtue of which a man will put up with, and will
resent, the right things and in the right way; but no
name has been assigned to it, though it most resembles
friendship. For the man who corresponds to this middle
state is very much what, with affection added, we call
a good friend. But the state in question differs from
friendship in that it implies no passion or affection for
one's associates; since it is not by reason of loving or
hating that such a man takes everything in the right
way, but by being a man of a certain kind. For he will
behave so alike towards those he knows and those he
does not know, towards intimates and those who are
not so, except that in each of these cases he will behave
as is befitting; for it is not proper to have the same care
for intimates and for strangers, nor again is it the same
conditions that make it right to give pain to them. Now
we have said generally that he will associate with
people in the right way; but it is by reference to what
is honourable and expedient that he will aim at not
giving pain or at contributing pleasure. For he seems
to be concerned with the pleasures and pains of social
life; and wherever it is not honourable, or is harmful,
for him to contribute pleasure, he will refuse, and will
choose rather to give pain; also if his acquiescence in
another's action would bring disgrace, and that in a
high degree, or injury, *on that other*, while his opposition
brings a little pain, he will not acquiesce but will
decline. He will associate differently with people in

high station and with ordinary people, with closer and more distant acquaintances, | and so too with regard to all other differences, rendering to each class what is befitting, and while for its own sake he chooses to contribute pleasure, and avoids the giving of pain, he will be guided by the consequences, if these are greater, i.e. honour and expediency. For the sake of a great future pleasure, too, he will inflict small pains.

The man who attains the mean, then, is such as we have described, but has not received a name; of those who contribute pleasure, the man who aims at being pleasant with no ulterior object is obsequious, but the man who does so in order that he may get some advantage in the direction of money or the things that money buys is a flatterer; while the man who quarrels with everything is, as has been said,[1] churlish and contentious. And the extremes seem to be contradictory to each other because the mean is without a name.

Truthfulness

7. The mean opposed to boastfulness is found in almost the same sphere; and this also is without a name. It will be no bad plan to describe these states as well; for we shall both know the facts about character better if we go through them in detail, and we shall be convinced that the virtues are means if we see this to be so in all cases. In the field of social life those who make the giving of pleasure or pain their object in associating with others have been described;[2] let us now describe those who pursue truth or falsehood alike in words and deeds and in the claims they put forward. The boastful man, then, is thought to be apt to claim the things that bring glory, when he has not got them, or to claim more of them than he has, and the mock-modest man on the

[1] 1125ᵇ14–16.   [2] Ch. 6.

other hand to disclaim what he has or belittle it, while
the man who observes the mean is one who calls a thing
by its own name, being truthful both in life and in
word, owning to what he has, neither to more nor to less.
Now each of these courses may be adopted either with
or without an object. But each man speaks and acts and
lives in accordance with his character, if he is *not* acting
for some ulterior object. And falsehood is *in itself*[1] mean
and culpable, and truth noble and worthy of praise.
Thus the truthful man is another case of a man who,
being in the mean, is worthy of praise, and both forms
of untruthful man are culpable, and particularly the
boastful man.

Let us discuss them both, but first of all the truthful
man. We are not speaking of the man who keeps faith
in his agreements, i.e. in the things that pertain to
justice or injustice (for this would belong to another
virtue), | but the man who in the matters in which
nothing of this sort is at stake is true both in word and
in life because his character is such. But such a man
would seem to be as a matter of fact equitable. For the
man who loves truth, and is truthful where nothing is
at stake, will still more be truthful where something is at
stake; he will avoid falsehood as something base, seeing
that he avoided it even for its own sake; and such a man
is worthy of praise. He inclines rather to understate the
truth; for this seems in better taste because exaggera-
tions are wearisome.

He who claims more than he has with no ulterior
object is a contemptible sort of fellow (otherwise he
would not have delighted in falsehood), but seems
futile rather than bad; but if he does it for an object,
he who does it for the sake of reputation or honour is
(for a boaster) not very much to be blamed, but he who

---

[1] i.e. apart from any ulterior object it may serve.

does it for money, or the things that lead to money, is
an uglier character (it is not the capacity that makes
the boaster, but the purpose; for it is in virtue of his
state of character and by being a man of a certain kind
that he is a boaster); as one man is a liar because he
enjoys the lie itself, and another because he desires
reputation or gain. Now those who boast for the sake
of reputation claim such qualities as win praise or
congratulation, but those whose object is gain claim
qualities which are of value to one's neighbours and
one's lack of which is not easily detected, e.g. the
powers of a seer, a sage, or a physician. For this reason
it is such things as these that most people claim and
boast about; for in them the above-mentioned qualities
are found.

Mock-modest people, who understate things, seem
more attractive in character; for they are thought to
speak not for gain but to avoid parade; and here too it
is qualities which bring reputation that they disclaim,
as Socrates used to do. Those who disclaim trifling and
obvious qualities are called humbugs and are more
contemptible; and sometimes this seems to be boastfulness, like the Spartan dress; for both excess and great
deficiency are boastful. But those who use understate-
ment with moderation and understate about matters
that do not very much force themselves on our notice
seem attractive. And it is the boaster that seems to be
opposed to the truthful man; for he is the worse
character.

Ready wit

8. Since life includes rest as well as activity, and in this
is included leisure and amusement, there seems here
also to be a kind of intercourse which is tasteful; | there
is such a thing as saying—and again listening to—what

one should and as one should. The kind of people one
is speaking or listening to will also make a difference.
Evidently here also there is both an excess and a deficiency as compared with the mean. Those who carry
humour to excess are thought to be vulgar buffoons,
striving after humour at all costs, and aiming rather at
raising a laugh than at saying what is becoming and
at avoiding pain to the object of their fun; while those
who can neither make a joke themselves nor put up
with those who do are thought to be boorish and
unpolished. But those who joke in a tasteful way are
called ready-witted, which implies a sort of readiness to
turn this way and that; for such sallies are thought
to be movements of the character, and as bodies are
discriminated by their movements, so too are characters. The ridiculous side of things is not far to seek,
however, and most people delight more than they
should in amusement and in jesting, and so even buffoons are called ready-witted because they are found
attractive; but that they differ from the ready-witted
man, and to no small extent, is clear from what has
been said.

To the middle state belongs also tact; it is the mark
of a tactful man to say and listen to such things as befit
a good and well-bred man; for there are some things
that it befits such a man to say and to hear by way of
jest, and the well-bred man's jesting differs from that
of a vulgar man, and the joking of an educated man
from that of an uneducated. One may see this even
from the old and the new comedies; to the authors of
the former indecency of language was amusing, to
those of the latter innuendo is more so; and these differ
in no small degree in respect of propriety. Now should
we define the man who jokes well by his saying what is
not unbecoming to a well-bred man, or by his not giving

pain, or even giving delight, to the hearer? Or is the latter definition, at any rate, itself indefinite, since different things are hateful or pleasant to different people? The kind of jokes he will listen to will be the same; for the kind he can put up with are also the kind he seems to make. There are, then, jokes he will not make; for the jest is a sort of abuse, and there are things that lawgivers forbid us to abuse; and they should, perhaps, have forbidden us even to make a jest of such. The refined and well-bred man, therefore, will be as we have described, being as it were a law to himself.

Such, then, is the man who observes the mean, whether he be called tactful or ready-witted. The buffoon, on the other hand, is the slave of his sense of humour, and spares neither himself nor others if he can raise a laugh, and says things none of which a man of refinement would say, and to some of which he would not even listen. | The boor, again, is useless for such social intercourse; for he contributes nothing and finds fault with everything. But relaxation and amusement are thought to be a necessary element in life.

The means in life that have been described, then, are three in number, and are all concerned with an interchange of words and deeds of some kind. They differ, however, in that one is concerned with truth, and the other two with pleasantness. Of those concerned with pleasure, one is displayed in jests, the other in the general social intercourse of life.

A QUASI-VIRTUE

Shame

9. Shame should not be described as a virtue; for it is more like a passion than a state of character. It is defined, at any rate, as a kind of fear of dishonour, and

produces an effect similar to that produced by fear of
danger; for people who feel disgraced blush, and those
who fear death turn pale. Both, therefore, seem to be in
a sense bodily conditions, which is thought to be characteristic of passion rather than of a state of character.

The passion is not becoming to every age, but only
to youth. For we think young people should be prone
to shame because they live by passion and therefore
commit many errors, but are restrained by shame;
and we praise young people who are prone to this
passion, but an older person no one would praise for
being prone to the sense of disgrace, since we think
he should not do anything that need cause this sense.
For the sense of disgrace is not even characteristic of
a good man,[1] since it is consequent on bad actions (for
such actions should not be done; and if some actions
are disgraceful in very truth and others only according
to common opinion, this makes no difference; for
neither class of actions should be done, so that no disgrace should be felt); and it is a mark of a bad man even
to be such as to do any disgraceful action. To be so
constituted as to feel disgraced if one does such an
action, and for this reason to think oneself good, is
absurd; for it is for voluntary actions that shame is felt,
and the good man will never voluntarily do bad
actions. But shame may be said to be conditionally
a good thing; *if* a good man does such actions, he will
feel disgraced; but the virtues are not subject to such
a qualification. And if shamelessness—not to be
ashamed of doing base actions—is bad, that does not
make it good to be ashamed of doing such actions.
Continence too is not virtue, but a mixed sort of state;
this will be shown later.[2] Now, however, let us discuss
justice. |

[1] *sc.* still less is it itself a virtue.   [2] vii. 1-10.

‣‣

JUSTICE: ITS SPHERE AND OUTER NATURE: IN WHAT SENSE IT IS A MEAN

The just as the lawful (universal justice) and the just as the fair and equal (particular justice): the former considered

1. WITH regard to justice and injustice we must consider (1) what kind of actions they are concerned with, (2) what sort of mean justice is, and (3) between what extremes the just act is intermediate. Our investigation shall follow the same course as the preceding discussions.

We see that all men mean by justice that kind of state of character which makes people disposed to do what is just and makes them act justly and wish for what is just; and similarly by injustice that state which makes them act unjustly and wish for what is unjust. Let us too, then, lay this down as a general basis. For the same is not true of the sciences and the faculties as of states of character. A faculty or a science which is one and the same is held to relate to contrary objects, but a state of character which is one of two contraries does *not* produce the contrary results; e.g. as a result of health we do not do what is the opposite of healthy, but only what is healthy; for we say a man walks healthily, when he walks as a healthy man would.

Now often one contrary state is recognized from its contrary, and often states are recognized from the subjects that exhibit them; for (A) if good condition is known, bad condition also becomes known, and (B) good condition is known from the things that are in good condition, and they from it. If good condition is firmness of flesh, it is necessary both that bad condition should be flabbiness of flesh and that the wholesome should be that which causes firmness in flesh. And it follows for the most part that if one contrary is ambiguous the other also will be ambiguous; e.g. that if 'just' is so, 'unjust' will be so too.

Now 'justice' and 'injustice' seem to be ambiguous, but because their different meanings approach near to one another the ambiguity escapes notice and is not obvious as it is, comparatively, when the meanings are far apart, e.g. (for here the difference in outward form is great) as the ambiguity in the use of *kleis* for the collar-bone of an animal and for that with which we lock a door. Let us take as a starting-point, then, the various meanings of 'an unjust man'. Both the lawless man and the grasping and unfair man are thought to be unjust, so that evidently both the law-abiding and the fair man will be just. The just, then, is the lawful and the fair, the unjust the unlawful and the unfair. |

Since the unjust man is grasping, he must be concerned with goods—not all goods, but those with which prosperity and adversity have to do, which taken absolutely are always good, but for a particular person are not always good. Now men pray for and pursue these things; but they should not, but should pray that the things that are good absolutely may also be good for them, and should choose the things that *are* good for them. The unjust man does not always choose the greater, but also the less—in the case of things bad absolutely; but because the lesser evil is itself thought to be in a sense good, and graspingness is directed at the good, therefore he is thought to be grasping. And he is unfair; for this contains and is common to both.

Since the lawless man was seen[1] to be unjust and the law-abiding man just, evidently all lawful acts are in a sense just acts; for the acts laid down by the legislative

[1] ᵃ32–ᵇ1.

107

art are lawful, and each of these, we say, is just. Now the laws in their enactments on all subjects aim at the common advantage either of all or of the best or of those who hold power, or something of the sort; so that in one sense we call those acts just that tend to produce and preserve happiness and its components for the political society. And the law bids us do both the acts of a brave man (e.g. not to desert our post nor take to flight nor throw away our arms), and those of a temperate man (e.g. not to commit adultery nor to gratify one's lust), and those of a good-tempered man (e.g. not to strike another nor to speak evil), and similarly with regard to the other virtues and forms of wickedness, commanding some acts and forbidding others; and the rightly-framed law does this rightly, and the hastily conceived one less well.

This form of justice, then, is complete virtue, although not without qualification, but in relation to our neighbour. And therefore justice is often thought to be the greatest of virtues, and 'neither evening nor morning star' is so wonderful; and proverbially 'in justice is every virtue comprehended'. And it is complete virtue in its fullest sense because it is the actual exercise of complete virtue. It is complete because he who possesses it can exercise his virtue not only in himself but towards his neighbour also; for many men can exercise virtue in their own affairs, but not in their relations to their neighbour.|This is why the saying of Bias is thought to be true, that 'rule will show the man'; for a ruler is necessarily in relation to other men, and a member of a society. For this same reason justice, alone of the virtues, is thought to be 'another's good',[1] because it is related to our neighbour; for it does what is advantageous to another, either a ruler or a co-partner. Now

[1] Pl. *Rep.* 343 c.

the worst man is he who exercises his wickedness both towards himself and towards his friends, and the best man is not he who exercises his virtue towards himself but he who exercises it towards another; for this is a difficult task. Justice in this sense, then, is not part of virtue but virtue entire, nor is the contrary injustice a part of vice but vice entire. What the difference is between virtue and justice in this sense is plain from what we have said; they are the same but their essence is not the same; what, as a relation to one's neighbour, is justice is, as a certain kind of state without qualification, virtue.

The just as the fair and equal: divided into distributive and rectificatory justice

2. But at all events what we are investigating is the justice which is a *part* of virtue; for there is a justice of this kind, as we maintain. Similarly it is with injustice in the particular sense that we are concerned.

That there is such a thing is indicated by the fact that while the man who exhibits in action the other forms of wickedness acts wrongly indeed, but not graspingly (e.g. the man who throws away his shield through cowardice or speaks harshly through bad temper or fails to help a friend with money through meanness), when a man acts graspingly he often exhibits none of these vices—no, nor all together, but certainly wickedness of some kind (for we blame him) and injustice. There is, then, another kind of injustice which is a part of injustice in the wide sense, and a use of the word 'unjust' which answers to a part of what is unjust in the wide sense of 'contrary to the law'. Again, if one man commits adultery for the sake of gain and makes money by it, while another does so at the bidding of appetite though he loses money and is penalized for it, the latter would be held to be self-indulgent rather than grasping, but the former is unjust, but not self-indulgent; evidently, therefore, he is unjust by reason of his making gain by his act. Again, all other unjust acts are ascribed invariably to some particular kind of wickedness, e.g. adultery to self-indulgence, the desertion of a comrade in battle to cowardice, physical violence to anger; but if a man makes gain, his action is ascribed to no form of wickedness but injustice. Evidently, therefore, there is apart from injustice in the wide sense another, 'particular', injustice which shares the name and nature of the first, because its definition falls within the same genus; | for the significance of both consists in a relation to one's neighbour, but the one is concerned with honour or money or safety—or that which includes all these, if we had a single name for it—and its motive is the pleasure that arises from gain; while the other is concerned with all the objects with which the good man is concerned.

It is clear, then, that there is more than one kind of justice, and that there is one which is distinct from virtue entire; we must try to grasp its genus and differentia.

The unjust has been divided into the unlawful and the unfair, and the just into the lawful and the fair. To the unlawful answers the aforementioned sense of injustice. But since the unfair and the unlawful are not the same, but are different as a part is from its whole (for all that is unfair is unlawful, but not all that is unlawful is unfair), the unjust and injustice in the sense of the unfair are not the same as but different from the former kind, as part from whole; for injustice in this sense is a part of injustice in the wide sense, and similarly justice in the one sense of justice in the other. Therefore we must speak also about particular justice and particular injustice, and similarly about the just and the unjust. The justice, then, which answers to the

whole of virtue, and the corresponding injustice, one
being the exercise of virtue as a whole, and the other
that of vice as a whole, towards one's neighbour, we
may leave on one side. And how the meanings of 'just'
and 'unjust' which answer to these are to be distinguished is evident; for practically the majority of the
acts commanded by the law are those which are prescribed from the point of view of virtue taken as a
whole; for the law bids us practise every virtue and
forbids us to practise any vice. And the things that tend
to produce virtue taken as a whole are those of the acts
prescribed by the law which have been prescribed with
a view to education for the common good. But with
regard to the education of the individual as such, which
makes him without qualification a good *man*, we must
determine later[1] whether this is the function of the
political art or of another; for perhaps it is not the same
to be a good man and a good citizen of any state taken
at random.

Of particular justice and that which is just in the
corresponding sense, (A) one kind is that which is manifested in distributions of honour or money or the other
things that fall to be divided among those who have
a share in the constitution (for in these it is possible for
one man to have a share either unequal or equal to
that of another), and (B) one is that which plays a recti-
fying part in transactions between man and man. |
Of this there are two divisions; of transactions (1) some
are voluntary and (2) others involuntary—voluntary
such transactions as sale, purchase, loan for consumption, pledging, loan for use, depositing, letting (they
are called voluntary because the *origin* of these transactions is voluntary), while of the involuntary (*a*) some

---

[1] 1179ᵇ20–1181ᵇ12. *Pol.* 1276ᵇ16–1277ᵇ32, 1278ᵃ40–ᵇ5, 1288ᵃ32–ᵇ2,
1333ᵃ11–16, 1337ᵃ11–14.

are clandestine, such as theft, adultery, poisoning, procuring, enticement of slaves, assassination, false witness, and (*b*) others are violent, such as assault, imprisonment, murder, robbery with violence, mutilation, abuse, insult.

Distributive justice, in accordance with geometrical proportion

3. (A) We have shown that both the unjust man and the unjust act are unfair or unequal; now it is clear that there is also an intermediate between the two unequals involved in either case. And this is the equal; for in any kind of action in which there is a more and a less there is also what is equal. If, then, the unjust is unequal, the just is equal, as all men suppose it to be, even apart from argument. And since the equal is intermediate, the just will be an intermediate. Now equality implies at least two things. The just, then, must be both intermediate and equal and relative (i.e. for certain persons). And *qua* intermediate it must be between certain things (which are respectively greater and less); *qua* equal, it involves *two* things; *qua* just, it is for certain people. The just, therefore, involves at least four terms; for the persons for whom it is in fact just are two, and the things in which it is manifested, the objects distributed, are two. And the same equality will exist between the persons and between the things concerned; for as the latter—the things concerned—are related, so are the former; if they are not equal, they will not have what is equal, but this is the origin of quarrels and complaints—when either equals have and are awarded unequal shares, or unequals equal shares. Further, this is plain from the fact that awards should be 'according to merit'; for all men agree that what is just in distribution must be according to merit in some sense, though they do not all specify the same sort of merit, but democrats identify it with the status of freeman, supporters of oligarchy with wealth (or with noble birth), and supporters of aristocracy with excellence.

The just, then, is a species of the proportionate (proportion being not a property only of the kind of number which consists of abstract units, but of number in general). For proportion is equality of ratios, and involves four terms at least (that discrete proportion involves four terms is plain, but so does continuous proportion, for it uses one term as two and mentions it twice; | e.g. 'as the line A is to the line B, so is the line B to the line C'; the line B, then, has been mentioned twice, so that if the line B be assumed twice, the proportional terms will be four); and the just, too, involves at least four terms, and the ratio between one pair is the same as that between the other pair; for there is a similar distinction between the persons and between the things. As the term A, then, is to B, so will C be to D, and therefore, *alternando*, as A is to C, B will be to D. Therefore also the whole is in the same ratio to the whole;¹ and this coupling the distribution effects, and, if the terms are so combined, effects justly. The conjunction, then, of the term A with C and of B with D is what is just in distribution,² and this species of the just is intermediate, and the unjust is what violates the proportion; for the proportional is intermediate, and the just is proportional. (Mathematicians call this kind of proportion geometrical; for it is in geometrical proportion that it

¹ Person A + thing C to person B + thing D.

² The problem of distributive justice is to divide the distributable honour or reward into parts which are to one another as are the merits of the persons who are to participate. If

A (first person) : B (second person) :: C (first portion) : D (second portion),

then (*alternando*) A : C :: B : D,

and therefore (*componendo*) A + C : B + D :: A : B.

In other words the position established answers to the relative merits of the parties.

follows that the whole is to the whole as either part is to the corresponding part.) This proportion is not continuous; for we cannot get a single term standing for a person and a thing.

This, then, is what the just is—the proportional; the unjust is what violates the proportion. Hence one term becomes too great, the other too small, as indeed happens in practice; for the man who acts unjustly has too much, and the man who is unjustly treated too little, of what is good. In the case of evil the reverse is true; for the lesser evil is reckoned a good in comparison with the greater evil, since the lesser evil is rather to be chosen than the greater, and what is worthy of choice is good, and what is worthier of choice a greater good.

This, then, is one species of the just.

Rectificatory justice, in accordance with arithmetical progression

4. (B) The remaining one is the rectificatory, which arises in connexion with transactions both voluntary and involuntary. This form of the just has a different specific character from the former. For the justice which distributes common possessions is always in accordance with the kind of proportion mentioned above[1] (for in the case also in which the distribution is made from the common funds of a partnership it will be according to the same ratio which the funds put into the business by the partners bear to one another); and the injustice opposed to this kind of justice is that which violates the proportion. But the justice in transactions between man and man is a sort of equality indeed, and the injustice a sort of inequality; | not according to that kind of proportion, however, but according to arithmetical proportion. For it makes no difference

[1] l. 12 f.

114

whether a good man has defrauded a bad man or a bad man a good one, nor whether it is a good or a bad man that has committed adultery; the law looks only to the distinctive character of the injury, and treats the parties as equal, if one is in the wrong and the other is being wronged, and if one inflicted injury and the other has received it. Therefore, this kind of injustice being an inequality, the judge tries to equalize it; for in the case also in which one has received and the other has inflicted a wound, or one has slain and the other been slain, the suffering and the action have been unequally distributed; but the judge tries to equalize things by means of the penalty, taking away from the gain of the assailant. For the term 'gain' is applied generally to such cases—even if it be not a term appropriate to certain cases, e.g. to the person who inflicts a wound—and 'loss' to the sufferer; at all events when the suffering has been estimated, the one is called loss and the other gain. Therefore the equal is intermediate between the greater and the less, but the gain and the loss are respectively greater and less in contrary ways; more of the good and less of the evil are gain, and the contrary is loss; intermediate between them is, as we saw,[1] the equal, which we say is just; therefore corrective justice will be the intermediate between loss and gain. This is why, when people dispute, they take refuge in the judge; and to go to the judge is to go to justice; for the nature of the judge is to be a sort of animate justice; and they seek the judge as an intermediate, and in some states they call judges mediators, on the assumption that if they get what is intermediate they will get what is just. The just, then, is an intermediate, since the judge is so. Now the judge restores equality; it is as though there were a line divided into

[1] l. 14.

unequal parts, and he took away that by which the greater segment exceeds the half, and added it to the smaller segment. And when the whole has been equally divided, then they say they have 'their own'—i.e. when they have got what is equal. The equal is intermediate between the greater and the lesser line according to arithmetical proportion. It is for this reason also that it is called just (*dikaion*), because it is a division into two equal parts (*dikha*), just as if one were to call it *dikaion*; and the judge (*dikastēs*) is one who bisects (*dikhastēs*). For when something is subtracted from one of two equals and added to the other, the other is in excess by these two; since if what was taken from the one had not been added to the other, the latter would have been in excess by one only. | It therefore exceeds the intermediate by one, and the intermediate exceeds by one that from which something was taken. By this, then, we shall recognize both what we must subtract from that which has more, and what we must add to that which has less; we must add to the latter that by which the intermediate exceeds it, and subtract from the greatest that by which it exceeds the intermediate. Let the lines AA′, BB′, CC′ be equal to one another; from the line AA′ let the segment AE have been subtracted, and to the line CC′ let the segment CD[1] have been added, so that the whole line DCC′ exceeds the line EA′ by the segment CD and the segment CF; therefore it exceeds the line BB′ by the segment CD.

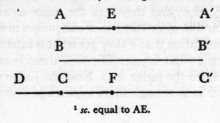

[1] *sc.* equal to AE.

These names, both loss and gain, have come from
voluntary exchange; for to have more than one's own
is called gaining, and to have less than one's original
share is called losing, e.g. in buying and selling and in
all other matters in which the law has left people free
to make their own terms; but when they get neither
more nor less but just what belongs to themselves, they
say that they have their own and that they neither lose
nor gain.

Therefore the just is intermediate between a sort of
gain and a sort of loss, viz. those which are involuntary;[1]
it consists in having an equal amount before and after
the transaction.

*Justice in exchange, reciprocity in accordance with pro-
portion*

5. Some think that *reciprocity* is without qualification
just, as the Pythagoreans said; for they defined justice
without qualification as reciprocity. Now 'reciprocity'
fits neither distributive nor rectificatory justice—yet
people *want* even the justice of Rhadamanthus to mean
this:

Should a man suffer what he did, right justice would
be done

—for in many cases reciprocity and rectificatory justice
are not in accord; e.g. (1) if an official has inflicted
a wound, he should not be wounded in return, and if
someone has wounded an official, he ought not to be
wounded only but punished in addition. Further (2)
there is a great difference between a voluntary and an
involuntary act. But in associations for exchange this
sort of justice does hold men together—reciprocity in
accordance with a proportion and not on the basis of

---

[1] i.e. for the loser.

precisely equal return. For it is by proportionate requital that the city holds together. Men seek to return
either evil for evil—and if they cannot do so, think
their position mere slavery— | or good for good—and if
they cannot do so there is no exchange, but it is by
exchange that they hold together. This is why they give
a prominent place to the temple of the Graces—to
promote the requital of services; for this is characteristic of grace—we should serve in return one who has
shown grace to us, and should another time take the
initiative in showing it.

Now proportionate return is secured by cross-conjunction.[1] Let A be a builder, B a shoemaker, C a house,
D a shoe. The builder, then, must get from the shoemaker the latter's work, and must himself give him in
return his own. If, then, first there is proportionate
equality of goods, and then reciprocal action takes
place, the result we mention will be effected. If not, the
bargain is not equal, and does not hold; for there is
nothing to prevent the work of the one being better
than that of the other; they must therefore be equated.
(And this is true of the other arts also; for they would
have been destroyed if what the patient suffered had
not been just what the agent did, and of the same
amount and kind.[2]) For it is not two doctors that

[1] The working of 'proportionate reciprocity' is not very clearly
described by Aristotle, but seems to be as follows. A and B are workers
in different trades, and will normally be of different degrees of 'worth'.
Their products, therefore, will also have unequal worth, i.e. (though
Aristotle does not expressly reduce the question to one of time) if
$A = nB$, C (what A makes, say, in an hour) will be worth n times as
much as D (what B makes in an hour). A fair exchange will then take
place if A gets nD and B gets 1 C; i.e. if A gives what it takes him an
hour to make, in exchange for what it takes B n hours to make.

[2] This sentence conveys a natural enough thought, and echoes
closely the language of Pl. Gorg. 476 B–D. But it seems to have no
relevance to the context, and probably we have here the unsuccess-
ful attempt of an early editor to find a suitable place for an isolated
note of Aristotle's.

associate for exchange, but a doctor and a farmer, or
in general people who are different and unequal; but
these must be equated. This is why all things that are
exchanged must be somehow comparable. It is for this
end that money has been introduced, and it becomes
in a sense an intermediate; for it measures all things,
and therefore the excess and the defect—how many
shoes are equal to a house or to a given amount of food.
The number of shoes exchanged for a house [or for
a given amount of food] must therefore correspond to
the ratio of builder to shoemaker. For if this be not so,
there will be no exchange and no intercourse. And this
proportion will not be effected unless the goods are
somehow equal. All goods must therefore be measured
by some one thing, as we said before.[1] Now this unit
is in truth demand, which holds all things together (for
if men did not need one another's goods at all, or did
not need them equally, there would be either no exchange or not the same exchange); but money has
become by convention a sort of representative of
demand; and this is why it has the name 'money'
(*nomisma*)—because it exists not by nature but by law
(*nomos*) and it is in our power to change it and make it
useless. There will, then, be reciprocity when the terms
have been equated so that as farmer is to shoemaker,
the amount of the shoemaker's work is to that of the
farmer's work for which it exchanges. | But we must not
bring them into a figure of proportion when they have
already exchanged (otherwise one extreme will have
both excesses), but when they still have their own
goods.[2] Thus they are equals and associates just because

---

[1] l. 19.

[2] Aristotle's meaning, which has caused much difficulty, seems to be
explained by a reference to ix. 1. That chapter concludes with the
observation δεῖ δ' ἴσως οὐ τοσούτου τιμᾶν ὅσου ἔχοντι φαίνεται ἄξιον, ἀλλ'
ὅσου πρὶν ἔχειν ἐτίμα. The reasoning in that chapter shows that

this equality can be effected in their case. Let A be a farmer, C food, B a shoemaker, D his product equated to C. If it had not been possible for reciprocity to be thus effected, there would have been no association of the parties. That demand holds things together as a single unit is shown by the fact that when men do not need one another, i.e. when neither needs the other or one does not need the other, they do not exchange, as we do when someone wants what one has oneself, e.g. when people permit the exportation of corn in exchange for wine. This equation therefore must be established. And for the future exchange—that if we do not need a thing now we shall have it if ever we do need it—money is as it were our surety; for it must be possible for us to get what we want by bringing the money. Now the same thing happens to money itself as to goods—it is not always worth the same; yet it tends to be steadier. This is why all goods must have a price set on them; for then there will always be exchange, and if so, association of man with man. Money, then, acting as a measure, makes goods commensurate and equates them; for neither would there have been association if there were not exchange, nor exchange if there were not equality, nor equality if there were not commensurability. Now in truth it is impossible that things differing so much should become commensurate, but with reference to demand they may

Aristotle's meaning here must be that people must not exchange goods in random amounts and *then* bring themselves into a 'figure of proportion'. For each will then set an unduly high value on the goods he has parted with and an unduly low value on those he has received; and any adjustment that is made will be decided by their respective powers of bluff. One party will have 'both excesses' over the other, since what he gets will exceed the mean and what the other man gets will fall short of it (cf. 1132ᵃ32–ᵇ2). The only fair method is for each to set a value on his own and on the other's goods *before* they exchange, and for them to come to an agreement if they can.

become so sufficiently. There must, then, be a unit, and that fixed by agreement (for which reason it is called money);[1] for it is this that makes all things commensurate, since all things are measured by money. Let A be a house, B ten minae, C a bed. A is half of B, if the house is worth five minae or equal to them; the bed, C, is a tenth of B; it is plain, then, how many beds are equal to a house, viz. five. That exchange took place thus before there was money is plain; for it makes no difference whether it is five beds that exchange for a house, or the money value of five beds.

We have now defined the unjust and the just. These having been marked off from each other, it is plain that just action is intermediate between acting unjustly and being unjustly treated; for the one is to have too much and the other to have too little. Justice is a kind of mean, but not in the same way as the other virtues, but because it relates to an intermediate amount, while injustice relates to the extremes. | And justice is that in virtue of which the just man is said to be a doer, by choice, of that which is just, and one who will distribute either between himself and another or between two others not so as to give more of what is desirable to himself and less to his neighbour (and conversely with what is harmful), but so as to give what is equal in accordance with proportion; and similarly in distributing between two other persons. Injustice on the other hand is similarly related to the unjust, which is excess and defect, contrary to proportion, of the useful or hurtful. For which reason injustice is excess and defect, viz. because it is productive of excess and defect—in one's own case excess of what is in its own nature useful and defect of what is hurtful, while in the case of others it is as a whole like what it is in one's own case, but

_____

[1] Cf. ᵃ30.

proportion may be violated in either direction. In the unjust act to have too little is to be unjustly treated; to have too much is to act unjustly.

Let this be taken as our account of the nature of justice and injustice, and similarly of the just and the unjust in general.

Political justice and analogous kinds of justice

6. Since acting unjustly does not necessarily imply being unjust, we must ask what sort of unjust acts imply that the doer is unjust with respect to each type of injustice, e.g. a thief, an adulterer, or a brigand. Surely the answer does not turn on the difference between these types. For a man might even lie with a woman knowing who she was, but the origin of his act might be not deliberate choice but passion. He acts unjustly, then, but is not unjust; e.g. a man is not a thief, yet he stole, nor an adulterer, yet he committed adultery; and similarly in all other cases.[1]

Now we have previously stated how the reciprocal is related to the just;[2] but we must not forget that what we are looking for is not only what is just without qualification but also political justice. This is found among men who share their life with a view to self-sufficiency, men who are free and either proportionately or arithmetically equal, so that between those who do not fulfil this condition there is no political justice but justice in a special sense and by analogy. For justice exists only between men whose mutual relations are governed by law; and law exists for men between whom there is injustice; for legal justice is the discrimination of the just and the unjust. And between men between whom injustice is done there is also

---

[1] This paragraph has no connexion with what follows; the subject of it is continued in ch. 8.   [2] 1132ᵇ21–1133ᵇ28.

unjust action (though there is not injustice between
all between whom there is unjust action), and this is
assigning too much to oneself of things good in themselves and too little of things evil in themselves. This
is why we do not allow a *man* to rule, but *rational principle*, because a man behaves thus in his own interests
and becomes a tyrant. | The magistrate on the other
hand is the guardian of justice, and, if of justice, then
of equality also. And since he is assumed to have no
more than his share, if he is just (for he does not assign
to himself more of what is good in itself, unless such
a share is proportional to his merits—so that it is for
others that he labours, and it is for this reason that men,
as we stated previously,[1] say that justice is 'another's
good'), therefore a reward must be given him, and this
is honour and privilege; but those for whom such things
are not enough become tyrants.

The justice of a master and that of a father are not
the same as the justice of citizens, though they are like
it; for there can be no injustice in the unqualified sense
towards things that are one's own, but a man's chattel,[2]
and his child until it reaches a certain age and sets up for
itself, are as it were part of himself, and no one chooses
to hurt himself (for which reason there can be no injustice towards oneself). Therefore the justice or injustice of citizens is not manifested in these relations;
for it was as we saw[3] according to law, and between
people naturally subject to law, and these as we saw[4]
are people who have an equal share in ruling and being
ruled. Hence justice can more truly be manifested towards a wife than towards children and chattels, for
the former is household justice; but even this is different
from political justice.

Natural and legal justice

7. Of political justice part is natural, part legal,— natural, that which everywhere has the same force and does not exist by people's thinking this or that; legal, that which is originally indifferent, but when it has been laid down is not indifferent, e.g. that a prisoner's ransom shall be a mina, or that a goat and not two sheep shall be sacrificed, and again all the laws that are passed for particular cases, e.g. that sacrifice shall be made in honour of Brasidas,[1] and the provisions of decrees. Now some think that all justice is of this sort, because that which is by nature is unchangeable and has everywhere the same force (as fire burns both here and in Persia), while they see change in the things recognized as just. This, however, is not true in this unqualified way, but is true in a sense; or rather, with the gods it is perhaps not true at all, while with us there is something that is just even by nature, yet all of it is changeable; but still some is by nature, some not by nature. It is evident which sort of thing, among things capable of being otherwise, is by nature; and which is not but is legal and conventional, assuming that both are equally changeable. And in all other things the same distinction will apply; by nature the right hand is stronger, yet it is possible that all men should come to be ambidextrous. The things which are just by virtue of convention and expediency are like measures; | for wine and corn measures are not everywhere equal, but larger in wholesale and smaller in retail markets. Similarly, the things which are just not by nature but by human enactment are not everywhere the same, since constitutions also are not the same, though there is but one which is everywhere by nature the best.

[1] Thuc. v. 11.

Of things just and lawful each is related as the universal to its particulars; for the things that are done
are many, but of *them* each is one, since it is universal.

There is a difference between the act of injustice and
what is unjust, and between the act of justice and what
is just; for a thing is unjust by nature or by enactment;
and this very thing, when it has been done, is an act of
injustice, but before it is done is not yet that but is unjust. So, too, with an act of justice (though the general
term is rather 'just action', and 'act of justice' is applied
to the correction of the act of injustice).

Each of these must later[1] be examined separately
with regard to the nature and number of its species and
the nature of the things with which it is concerned.

JUSTICE: ITS INNER NATURE AS INVOLVING
CHOICE

The scale of degrees of wrongdoing

8. Acts just and unjust being as we have described
them, a man acts unjustly or justly whenever he does
such acts voluntarily; when involuntarily, he acts
neither unjustly nor justly except in an incidental way;
for he does things which happen to be just or unjust.
Whether an act is or is not one of injustice (or of justice)
is determined by its voluntariness or involuntariness;
for when it is voluntary it is blamed, and at the same
time is then an act of injustice; so that there will be
things that are unjust but not yet acts of injustice, if
voluntariness be not present as well. By the voluntary
I mean, as has been said before,[2] any of the things in a
man's own power which he does with knowledge, i.e.
not in ignorance either of the person acted on or of the

---

[1] Possibly a reference to an intended (or now lost) book of the *Politics*
on laws.   [2] 1109ᵇ35–1111ᵃ24.

instrument used or of the end that will be attained
(e.g. whom he is striking, with what, and to what end),
each such act being done not incidentally nor under
compulsion (e.g. if A takes B's hand and therewith
strikes C, B does not act voluntarily; for the act was
not in his own power). The person struck may be the
striker's father, and the striker may know that it is a
man or one of the persons present, but not know that it
is his father; a similar distinction may be made in the
case of the end, and with regard to the whole action.
Therefore that which is done in ignorance, or though
not done in ignorance is not in the agent's power, or
is done under compulsion, is involuntary (for many
natural processes too, we knowingly perform or
undergo, |none of which is either voluntary or in-
voluntary; e.g. growing old or dying). But in the case
of unjust and just acts alike the injustice or justice may
be only incidental; for a man might return a deposit
unwillingly and from fear, and then he must not be said
either to do what is just or to act justly, except in an
incidental way. Similarly the man who under compulsion and unwillingly fails to return the deposit must
be said to act unjustly, and to do what is unjust, only
incidentally. Of voluntary acts we do some by choice,
others not by choice; by choice those which we do after
deliberation, not by choice those which we do without
previous deliberation. Thus there are three kinds of injury in transactions between man and man; those done
in ignorance are *mistakes* when the person acted on, the
act, the instrument, or the end that will be attained is
other than the agent supposed; the agent thought either
that he was not hitting any one or that he was not hitting with this missile or not hitting this person or to this
end, but a result followed other than that which he
thought likely (e.g. he threw not with intent to wound

but only to prick), or the person hit or the missile was
other than he supposed. Now when (1) the injury takes
place contrary to reasonable expectation, it is a *misadventure*. When (2) it is not contrary to reasonable
expectation, but does not imply vice, it is a *mistake* (for
a man makes a mistake when the fault originates in
him, but is the victim of accident when the origin lies
outside him). When (3) he acts with knowledge but
not after deliberation, it is an *act of injustice*—e.g. the
acts due to anger or to other passions necessary or
natural to man; for when men do such harmful and
mistaken acts they act unjustly, and the acts are acts of
injustice, but this does not imply that the doers are
unjust or wicked; for the injury is not due to vice. But
when (4) a man acts from choice, he is an *unjust man*
and a vicious man.

Hence acts proceeding from anger are rightly judged
not to be done of malice aforethought; for it is not the
man who acts in anger but he who enraged him that
starts the mischief. Again, the matter in dispute is not
whether the thing happened or not, but its justice; for
it is apparent injustice that occasions rage. For they do
not dispute about the occurrence of the act—as in
commercial transactions where one of the two parties
must be vicious[1]—unless they do so owing to forgetful-
ness; but, agreeing about the fact, they dispute on
which side justice lies (whereas a man who has deli-
berately injured another cannot help knowing that
he has done so), so that the one thinks he is being
treated unjustly and the other disagrees. |

But if a man harms another by choice, he acts unjustly; and *these* are the acts of injustice which imply
that the doer is an unjust man, provided that the act

[1] The plaintiff, if he brings a false accusation; the defendant, if he
denies a true one.

violates proportion or equality. Similarly, a man *is just* when he acts justly by choice; but he *acts justly* if he merely acts voluntarily.

Of involuntary acts some are excusable, others not. For the mistakes which men make not only in ignorance but also from ignorance are excusable, while those which men do not from ignorance but (though they do them *in* ignorance) owing to a passion which is neither natural nor such as man is liable to, are not excusable.

Can a man be voluntarily treated unjustly? Is it the distributor or the recipient that is guilty of injustice in distribution? Justice not so easy as it might seem, because it is not a way of acting but an inner disposition

9. Assuming that we have sufficiently defined the suffering and doing of injustice, it may be asked (1) whether the truth is expressed in Euripides' paradoxical words:

'I slew my mother, that's my tale in brief.'
'Were you both willing, or unwilling both?'

Is it truly possible to be willingly treated unjustly, or is all suffering of injustice on the contrary involuntary, as all unjust action is voluntary? And is all suffering of injustice of the latter kind or else all of the former, or is it sometimes voluntary, sometimes involuntary? So, too, with the case of being justly treated; all just action is voluntary, so that it is reasonable that there should be a similar opposition in either case—that both being unjustly and being justly treated should be either alike voluntary or alike involuntary. But it would be thought paradoxical even in the case of being justly treated, if it were always voluntary; for some are unwillingly treated justly. (2) One might raise this question also, whether everyone who has suffered what is unjust is being unjustly treated, or on the other hand it is with

suffering as with acting. In action and in passivity alike
it is possible for justice to be done incidentally, and
similarly (it is plain) injustice; for to do what is unjust
is not the same as to act unjustly, nor to suffer what is
unjust as to be treated unjustly, and similarly in the
case of acting justly and being justly treated; for it is
impossible to be unjustly treated if the other does not
act unjustly, or justly treated unless he acts justly. Now
if to act unjustly is simply to harm someone voluntarily,
and 'voluntarily' means 'knowing the person acted on,
the instrument, and the manner of one's acting', and
the incontinent man voluntarily harms himself, not
only will he voluntarily be unjustly treated but it will
be possible to treat oneself unjustly. (This also is one of
the questions in doubt, whether a man can treat him-
self unjustly.) | Again, a man may voluntarily, owing to
incontinence, be harmed by another who acts voluntarily, so that it would be possible to be voluntarily
treated unjustly. Or is our definition incorrect; must
we to 'harming another, with knowledge both of the
person acted on, of the instrument, and of the manner'
add 'contrary to the wish of the person acted on'? Then
a man may be voluntarily harmed and voluntarily
suffer what is unjust, but no one is voluntarily treated
unjustly; for no one wishes to be unjustly treated, not
even the incontinent man. He acts contrary to his wish;
for no one *wishes* for what he does not think to be good,
but the incontinent man does *do* things that he does not
think he ought to do. Again, one who gives what is his
own, as Homer says Glaucus gave Diomede

> Armour of gold for brazen, the price of a hundred
> beeves for nine,[1]

is not unjustly treated; for though to give is in his power,

[1] *Il.* vi. 236.

to be unjustly treated is not, but there must be someone to treat him unjustly. It is plain, then, that being
unjustly treated is not voluntary.

Of the questions we intended to discuss two still
remain for discussion; (3) whether it is the man who
has assigned to another more than his share that acts
unjustly, or he who has the excessive share, and (4)
whether it is possible to treat oneself unjustly. The
questions are connected; for if the former alternative
is possible and the distributor acts unjustly and not the
man who has the excessive share, then if a man assigns
more to another than to himself, knowingly and voluntarily, he treats himself unjustly; which is what modest
people seem to do, since the virtuous man tends to take
less than his share. Or does this statement too need
qualification? For (a) he perhaps gets more than his
share of some other good, e.g. of honour or of intrinsic
nobility. (b) The question is solved by applying the
distinction we applied to unjust action;[1] for he suffers
nothing contrary to his own wish, so that he is not
unjustly treated so far as this goes, but at most only
suffers harm.

It is plain too that the distributor acts unjustly,
but not always the man who has the excessive share;
for it is not he to whom injustice is done that acts
unjustly, but he to whom it appertains to do the unjust
act voluntarily, i.e. the person in whom lies the origin
of the action, and this lies in the distributor, not in the
receiver. Again, since the word 'do' is ambiguous, and
there is a sense in which lifeless things, or a hand, or a
servant who obeys an order, may be said to slay, he who
gets an excessive share does not act unjustly, though he
'does' what is unjust.

Again, if the distributor gave his judgement in ignor-

[1] ll. 3-5.

ance, he does not act unjustly in respect of legal justice, and his judgement is not unjust in this sense, but in a sense it *is* unjust (for legal justice and primordial justice are different); but if with knowledge he judged unjustly,| he is himself aiming at an excessive share either of gratitude or of revenge. As much, then, as if he were to share in the plunder, the man who has judged unjustly for these reasons has got too much; the fact that what he gets is different from what he distributes makes no difference, for even if he awards land with a view to sharing in the plunder he gets not land but money.

Men think that acting unjustly is in their power, and therefore that being just is easy. But it is not; to lie with one's neighbour's wife, to wound another, to deliver a bribe, is easy and in our power, but to do these things as a result of a certain state of character is neither easy nor in our power. Similarly to know what is just and what is unjust requires, men think, no great wisdom, because it is not hard to understand the matters dealt with by the laws (though these are not the things that are just, except incidentally); but how actions must be done and distributions effected in order to be just, to know *this* is a greater achievement than knowing what is good for the health; though even there, while it is easy to know that honey, wine, hellebore, cautery, and the use of the knife are so, to know how, to whom, and when these should be applied with a view to producing health, is no less an achievement than that of being a physician. Again, for this very reason[1] men think that acting unjustly is characteristic of the just man no less than of the unjust, because he would be not less but even more capable of doing each of these unjust acts;[2] for he could lie with a woman or wound a neighbour;

---

[1] i.e. that stated in ll. 4 f., that acting unjustly is in our own power.

[2] Cf. ll. 6–8.

and the brave man could throw away his shield and
turn to flight in this direction or in that. But to play the
coward or to act unjustly consists not in doing these
things, except incidentally, but in doing them as the
result of a certain state of character, just as to practise
medicine and healing consists not in applying or not
applying the knife, in using or not using medicines,
but in doing so in a certain way.

Just acts occur between people who participate in
things good in themselves and can have too much or too
little of them; for some beings (e.g. presumably the gods)
cannot have too much of them, and to others, those
who are incurably bad, not even the smallest share in
them is beneficial but all such goods are harmful, while
to others they are beneficial up to a point; therefore
justice is essentially something human.

Equity, a corrective of legal justice

10. Our next subject is equity and the equitable, and
their respective relations to justice and the just. For on
examination they appear to be neither absolutely the
same nor generically different; and while we sometimes praise what is equitable and the equitable man
(so that we apply the name by way of praise even to
instances of the other virtues, instead of 'good', |
meaning by 'more equitable' that a thing is better), at
other times, when we reason it out, it seems strange if
the equitable, being something different from the just,
is yet praiseworthy; for either the just or the equitable
is not good, if they are different; or, if both are good,
they are the same.

These, then, are pretty much the considerations that
give rise to the problem about the equitable; they are
all in a sense correct and not opposed to one another;
for the equitable, though it is better than one kind of

justice, yet is just, and it is not as being a different class of thing that it is better than the just. The same thing, then, is just and equitable, and while both are good the equitable is superior. What creates the problem is that the equitable is just, but not the legally just but a correction of legal justice. The reason is that all law is universal but about some things it is not possible to make a universal statement which shall be correct. In those cases, then, in which it is necessary to speak universally, but not possible to do so correctly, the law takes the usual case, though it is not ignorant of the possibility of error. And it is none the less correct; for the error is not in the law nor in the legislator but in the nature of the thing, since the matter of practical affairs is of this kind from the start. When the law speaks universally, then, and a case arises on it which is not covered by the universal statement, then it is right, where the legislator fails us and has erred by over-simplicity, to correct the omission—to say what the legislator himself would have said had be been present, and would have put into his law if he had known. Hence the equitable is just, and better than one kind of justice—not better than absolute justice, but better than the error that arises from the absoluteness of the statement. And this is the nature of the equitable, a correction of law where it is defective owing to its universality. In fact this is the reason why all things are not determined by law, viz. that about some things it is impossible to lay down a law, so that a decree is needed. For when the thing is indefinite the rule also is indefinite, like the leaden rule used in making the Lesbian moulding; the rule adapts itself to the shape of the stone and is not rigid, and so too the decree is adapted to the facts.

It is plain, then, what the equitable is, and that it is just and is better than one kind of justice. It is evident also from this who the equitable man is; the man who chooses and does such acts, and is no stickler for his rights in a bad sense but tends to take less than his share| though he has the law on his side, is equitable, and this state of character is equity, which is a sort of justice and not a different state of character.

Can a man treat himself unjustly?

11. Whether a man can treat himself unjustly or not, is evident from what has been said.[1] For (*a*) one class of just acts are those acts in accordance with any virtue which are prescribed by the law; e.g. the law does not expressly permit suicide, and what it does not expressly permit it forbids. Again, when a man in violation of the law harms another (otherwise than in retaliation) voluntarily, he acts unjustly, and a voluntary agent is one who knows both the person he is affecting by his action and the instrument he is using; and he who through anger voluntarily stabs himself does this contrary to the right rule of life, and this the law does not allow; therefore he is acting unjustly. But towards whom? Surely towards the state, not towards himself. For he suffers voluntarily, but no one is voluntarily treated unjustly. This is also the reason why the state punishes; a certain loss of civil rights attaches to the man who destroys himself, on the ground that he is treating the state unjustly.

Further, (*b*) in that sense of 'acting unjustly' in which the man who 'acts unjustly' is unjust only and not bad all round, it is not possible to treat oneself unjustly (this is different from the former sense; the unjust man in one sense of the term is wicked in a particularized way just as the coward is, not in the sense of being wicked all round, so that his 'unjust act' does not mani-

[1] Cf. 1129ª32-^b1, 1136ª10-1137ª4.

fest wickedness in general). For (i) that would imply the
possibility of the same thing's having been subtracted
from and added to the same thing at the same time; but
this is impossible—the just and the unjust always involve more than one person. Further, (ii) unjust action
is voluntary and done by choice, and *takes the initiative*
(for the man who because he has suffered does the same
in return is not thought to act unjustly); but if a man
harms himself he suffers and does the same things *at the
same time*. Further, (iii) if a man could treat himself
unjustly, he could be voluntarily treated unjustly.
Besides, (iv) no one acts unjustly without committing
particular acts of injustice; but no one can commit
adultery with his own wife or housebreaking on his
own house or theft on his own property.

In general, the question 'Can a man treat himself
unjustly?' is solved also by the distinction we applied
to the question 'Can a man be voluntarily treated
unjustly?'[1]

(It is evident too that both are bad, being unjustly
treated and acting unjustly; for the one means having
less and the other having more than the intermediate
amount, which plays the part here that the healthy does
in the medical art, and that good condition does in the
art of bodily training. But still acting unjustly is the
worse, for it involves vice and is blameworthy—involves vice which is either of the complete and unqualified kind or almost so (we must admit the latter
alternative, because not all voluntary unjust action
implies injustice as a state of character), while being
unjustly treated does not involve vice and injustice in
oneself. In itself, then, being unjustly treated is less bad,|
but there is nothing to prevent its being incidentally a
greater evil. But theory cares nothing for this; it calls

[1] Cf. 1136ᵃ31-ᵇ5.

135

pleurisy a more serious mischief than a stumble; yet the latter may become incidentally the more serious, if the fall due to it leads to your being taken prisoner or put to death by the enemy.)

Metaphorically and in virtue of a certain resemblance there is a justice, not indeed between a man and himself, but between certain parts of him; yet not every kind of justice but that of master and servant or that of husband and wife.¹ For these are the ratios in which the part of the soul that has a rational principle stands to the irrational part; and it is with a view to these parts that people also think a man can be unjust to himself, viz. because these parts are liable to suffer something contrary to their respective desires; there is therefore thought to be a mutual justice between them as between ruler and ruled.

Let this be taken as our account of justice and the other, i.e. the other moral, virtues.

¹ Cf. 1134ᵇ15–17.

BOOK VI · INTELLECTUAL
VIRTUE

▶▶▶▶▶▶▶▶▶▶▶▶▶▶▶▶▶▶▶▶▶▶▶▶▶▶▶▶▶▶▶▶

INTRODUCTION

*Reasons for studying intellectual virtue: intellect divided into
the contemplative and the calculative*

1. Since we have previously said that one ought to
choose that which is intermediate, not the excess nor
the defect,[1] and that the intermediate is determined by
the dictates of the right rule,[2] let us discuss the nature of
these dictates. In all the states of character we have
mentioned,[3] as in all other matters, there is a mark to
which the man who has the rule looks, and heightens
or relaxes his activity accordingly, and there is a standard which determines the mean states which we say
are intermediate between excess and defect, being in
accordance with the right rule. But such a statement,
though true, is by no means clear; for not only here but
in all other pursuits which are objects of knowledge it
is indeed true to say that we must not exert ourselves
nor relax our efforts too much or too little, but to an
intermediate extent and as the right rule dictates; but
if a man had only this knowledge he would be none the
wiser—e.g. we should not know what sort of medicines
to apply to our body if someone were to say 'all those
which the medical art prescribes, and which agree with
the practice of one who possesses the art'. Hence it is
necessary with regard to the states of the soul also, not
only that this true statement should be made, but also
that it should be determined what is the right rule and
what is the standard that fixes it.

[1] 1104ᵃ11–27, 1106ᵃ26–1107ᵃ27.
[2] 1107ᵃ1, cf. 1103ᵇ31, 1114ᵇ29.   [3] In iii. 6–v. 11.

We divided the virtues of the soul and said that some
are virtues of character and others of intellect.[1] |Now we
have discussed in detail the moral virtues;[2] with regard
to the others let us express our view as follows, beginning with some remarks about the soul. We said before[3]
that there are two parts of the soul—that which grasps
a rule or rational principle, and the irrational; let us
now draw a similar distinction within the part which
grasps a rational principle. And let it be assumed that
there are two parts which grasp a rational principle—
one by which we contemplate the kind of things whose
originative causes are invariable, and one by which we
contemplate variable things; for where objects differ in
kind the part of the soul answering to each of the two is
different in kind, since it is in virtue of a certain likeness
and kinship with their objects that they have the knowledge they have. Let one of these parts be called the
scientific and the other the calculative; for to deliberate
and to calculate are the same thing, but no one deliberates about the invariable. Therefore the calculative
is one part of the faculty which grasps a rational
principle. We must, then, learn what is the best state
of each of these two parts; for this is the virtue of each.

The proper object of contemplation is truth; that of calcula-
tion is truth corresponding with right desire

2. The virtue of a thing is relative to its proper work.
Now there are three things in the soul which control
action and truth—sensation, reason, desire.

Of these sensation originates no action; this is plain
from the fact that the lower animals have sensation but
no share in action.

What affirmation and negation are in thinking, pursuit and avoidance are in desire; so that since moral

[1] 1103ᵃ3-7.   [2] In iii. 6–v. 11.   [3] 1102ᵃ26-28.

virtue is a state of character concerned with choice, and choice is deliberate desire, therefore both the reasoning must be true and the desire right, if the choice is to be good, and the latter must pursue just what the former asserts. Now this kind of intellect and of truth is practical; of the intellect which is contemplative, not practical nor productive, the good and the bad state are truth and falsity respectively (for this is the work of everything intellectual); while of the part which is practical and intellectual the good state is truth in agreement with right desire.

The origin of action—its efficient, not its final cause—is choice, and that of choice is desire and reasoning with a view to an end. This is why choice cannot exist either without reason and intellect or without a moral state; for good action and its opposite cannot exist without a combination of intellect and character. Intellect itself, however, moves nothing, but only the intellect which aims at an end and is practical; | for this rules the productive intellect as well, since everyone who makes makes for an end, and that which is made is not an end in the unqualified sense (but only an end in a particular relation, and the end of a particular operation)—only that which is *done* is that; for good action is an end, and desire aims at this. Hence choice is either desiderative reason or ratiocinative desire, and such an origin of action is a man. (It is to be noted that nothing that is past is an object of choice, e.g. no one chooses to have sacked Troy; for no one *deliberates* about the past, but about what is future and capable of being otherwise, while what is past is not capable of not having taken place; hence Agathon is right in saying:

For this alone is lacking even to God,
To make undone things that have once been done.)

The work of both the intellectual parts, then, is truth. Therefore the states that are most strictly those in respect of which each of these parts will reach truth are the virtues of the two parts.

THE CHIEF INTELLECTUAL VIRTUES

Science—demonstrative knowledge of the necessary and eternal

3. Let us begin, then, from the beginning, and discuss these states once more. Let it be assumed that the states by virtue of which the soul possesses truth by way of affirmation or denial are five in number, i.e. art, scientific knowledge, practical wisdom, philosophic wisdom, intuitive reason; we do not include judgement and opinion because in these we may be mistaken.

Now what *scientific knowledge* is, if we are to speak exactly and not follow mere similarities, is plain from what follows. We all suppose that what we know is not even capable of being otherwise; of things capable of being otherwise we do not know, when they have passed outside our observation, whether they exist or not. Therefore the object of scientific knowledge is of necessity. Therefore it is eternal; for things that are of necessity in the unqualified sense are all eternal; and things that are eternal are ungenerated and imperishable. Again, every science is thought to be capable of being taught, and its object of being learnt. And all teaching starts from what is already known, as we maintain in the *Analytics* also; for it proceeds sometimes through induction and sometimes by syllogism. Now induction is the starting-point which knowledge even of the universal presupposes, while syllogism proceeds *from* universals. There are therefore starting-points from which syllogism proceeds, which are not reached by syllogism; it is therefore by induction that they are acquired. Scientific knowledge is, then, a state of capacity to demonstrate, and has the other limiting characteristics which we specify in the *Analytics*; for it is when a man believes in a certain way and the starting-points are known to him that he has scientific knowledge, since if they are not better known to him than the conclusion, he will have his knowledge only incidentally.

Let this, then, be taken as our account of scientific knowledge. |

Art—knowledge of how to make things

4. In the variable are included both things made and things done; making and acting are different (for their nature we treat even the discussions outside our school as reliable); so that the reasoned state of capacity to act is different from the reasoned state of capacity to make. Hence too they are not included one in the other; for neither is acting making nor is making acting. Now since architecture is an art and is essentially a reasoned state of capacity to make, and there is neither any art that is not such a state nor any such state that is not an art, *art* is identical with a state of capacity to make, involving a true course of reasoning. All art is concerned with coming into being, i.e. with contriving and considering how something may come into being which is capable of either being or not being, and whose origin is in the maker and not in the thing made; for art is concerned neither with things that are, or come into being, by necessity, nor with things that do so in accordance with nature (since these have their origin in themselves). Making and acting being different, art must be a matter of making, not of acting. And in a sense chance and art are concerned with the same objects; as Agathon says, 'Art loves chance and chance loves art'. Art, then, as has been

said,[1] is a state concerned with making, involving a true course of reasoning, and lack of art on the contrary is a state concerned with making, involving a false course of reasoning; both are concerned with the variable.

Practical wisdom—knowledge of how to secure the ends of human life

5. Regarding *practical wisdom* we shall get at the truth by considering who are the persons we credit with it. Now it is thought to be a mark of a man of practical wisdom to be able to deliberate well about what is good and expedient for himself, not in some particular respect, e.g. about what sorts of thing conduce to health or to strength, but about what sorts of thing conduce to the good life in general. This is shown by the fact that we credit men with practical wisdom in some particular respect when they have calculated well with a view to some good end which is one of those that are not the object of any art. It follows that in the general sense also the man who is capable of deliberating has practical wisdom. Now no one deliberates about things that are invariable, or about things that it is impossible for him to do. Therefore, since scientific knowledge involves demonstration, but there is no demonstration of things whose first principles are variable (for all such things might actually be otherwise), and since it is impossible to deliberate about things that are of necessity, | practical wisdom cannot be scientific knowledge or art; not science because that which can be done is capable of being otherwise, not art because action and making are different kinds of thing. The remaining alternative, then, is that it is a true and reasoned state of capacity to act with regard to the things that are good or bad for man. For while making

[1] l. 9.

has an end other than itself, action cannot; for good
action itself is its end. It is for this reason that we think
Pericles and men like him have practical wisdom, viz.
because they can see what is good for themselves and
what is good for men in general; we consider that those
can do this who are good at managing households or
states. (This is why we call temperance (*sōphrosunē*) by
this name; we imply that it preserves one's practical
wisdom (*sōzousa tēn phronēsin*). Now what it preserves
is a judgement of the kind we have described. For it is
not any and every judgement that pleasant and painful objects destroy and pervert, e.g. the judgement that
the triangle has or has not its angles equal to two right
angles, but only judgements about what is to be done.
For the originating causes of the things that are done
consist in the end at which they are aimed; but the
man who has been ruined by pleasure or pain forthwith fails to see any such originating cause—to see that
for the sake of this or because of this he ought to choose
and do whatever he chooses and does; for vice is de-
structive of the originating cause of action.)

Practical wisdom, then, must be a reasoned and true
state of capacity to act with regard to human goods.
But further, while there is such a thing as excellence in
art, there is no such thing as excellence in practical
wisdom; and in art he who errs willingly is preferable,
but in practical wisdom, as in the virtues, he is the
reverse. Plainly, then, practical wisdom is a virtue and
not an art. There being two parts of the soul that can
follow a course of reasoning, it must be a virtue of one
of the two, i.e. of that part which forms opinions; for
opinion is about the variable and so is practical wisdom. But yet it is not only a reasoned state; this is shown
by the fact that a state of that sort may be forgotten but
practical wisdom cannot.

Intuitive reason—knowledge of the principles from which science proceeds

6. Scientific knowledge is judgement about things that are universal and necessary; and the conclusions of demonstration, and all scientific knowledge, follow from first principles (for scientific knowledge involves proof). This being so, the first principle from which what is scientifically known follows cannot be an object of scientific knowledge, of art, or of practical wisdom; for that which can be scientifically known can be demonstrated, and art and practical wisdom deal with things that are variable. | Nor are these first principles the objects of philosophic wisdom, for it is a mark of the philosopher to have *demonstration* about some things. If, then, the states of mind by which we have truth and are never deceived about things invariable or even variable are scientific knowledge, practical wisdom, philosophic wisdom, and intuitive reason, and it cannot be any of the three (i.e. practical wisdom, scientific knowledge, or philosophic wisdom), the remaining alternative is that it is *intuitive reason* that grasps the first principles.

Philosophic wisdom—the union of intuitive reason and science

7. *Wisdom*[1] (1) in the arts we ascribe to their most finished exponents, e.g. to Phidias as a sculptor and to Polyclitus as a maker of portrait-statues, and here we mean nothing by wisdom except excellence in art; but (2) we think that some people are wise in general, not in some particular field or in any other limited respect, as Homer says in the *Margites*,

[1] In this chapter Aristotle restricts to a very definite meaning the word σοφία, which in ordinary Greek, as the beginning of the chapter points out, was used both of skill in a particular art or craft, and of wisdom in general.

Him did the gods make neither a digger nor yet
  a ploughman
Nor wise in anything else.

Therefore wisdom must plainly be the most finished
of the forms of knowledge. It follows that the wise
man must not only know what follows from the first
principles, but must also possess truth about the first
principles. Therefore wisdom must be intuitive reason
combined with scientific knowledge—scientific knowledge of the highest objects which has received as it
were its proper completion.

Of the highest objects, we say; for it would be strange
to think that the art of politics, or practical wisdom, is
the best knowledge, since man is not the best thing in
the world. Now if what is healthy or good is different
for men and for fishes, but what is white or straight is
always the same, anyone would say that what is wise is
the same but what is practically wise is different; for
it is to that which considers well the various matters
concerning itself that one ascribes practical wisdom,
and it is to this that one will entrust such matters. This
is why we say that some even of the lower animals have
practical wisdom,[1] viz. those which are found to have
a power of foresight with regard to their own life. It is
evident also that philosophic wisdom and the art of
politics cannot be the same; for if the state of mind
concerned with a man's own interests is to be called
philosophic wisdom, there will be many philosophic
wisdoms; there will not be one concerned with the good
of all animals (any more than there is one art of medicine for all existing things), but a different philosophic
wisdom about the good of each species.

---

[1] We do not say this in English; but we call them 'intelligent' or
'sagacious', which comes to the same thing.

But if the argument be that man is the best of the animals, this makes no difference; for there are other things much more divine in their nature even than man, | e.g., most conspicuously, the bodies of which the heavens are framed. From what has been said it is plain, then, that philosophic wisdom is scientific knowledge, combined with intuitive reason, of the things that are highest by nature. This is why we say Anaxagoras, Thales, and men like them have philosophic but not practical wisdom, when we see them ignorant of what is to their own advantage, and why we say that they know things that are remarkable, admirable, difficult, and divine, but useless; viz. because it is not human goods that they seek.

Practical wisdom on the other hand is concerned with things human and things about which it is possible to deliberate; for we say this is above all the work of the man of practical wisdom, to deliberate well, but no one deliberates about things invariable, or about things which have not an end which is a good that can be brought about by action. The man who is without qualification good at deliberating is the man who is capable of aiming in accordance with calculation at the best for man of things attainable by action. Nor is practical wisdom concerned with universals only—it must also recognize the particulars; for it is practical, and practice is concerned with particulars. This is why some who do not know, and especially those who have experience, are more practical than others who know; for if a man knew that light meats are digestible and wholesome, but did not know which sorts of meat are light, he would not produce health, but the man who knows that chicken is wholesome is more likely to produce health.

Now practical wisdom is concerned with action;

therefore one should have both forms of it, or the latter in preference to the former. But here, too, there must be a controlling kind.

Relations between practical wisdom and political science

8. Political wisdom and practical wisdom are the same state of mind, but their essence is not the same. Of the wisdom concerned with the city, the practical wisdom which plays a controlling part is legislative wisdom, while that which is related to this as particulars to their universal is known by the general name 'political wisdom'; this has to do with action and deliberation, for a decree is a thing to be carried out in the form of an individual act. This is why the exponents of this art are alone said to 'take part in politics'; for these alone 'do things' as manual labourers 'do things'.

Practical wisdom also is identified especially with that form of it which is concerned with a man himself— with the individual; and this is known by the general name 'practical wisdom'; of the other kinds one is called household management, another legislation, the third politics, and of the latter one part is called deliberative and the other judicial. Now knowing what is good for oneself will be one kind of knowledge, but it is very different from the other kinds; | and the man who knows and concerns himself with his own interests is thought to have practical wisdom, while politicians are thought to be busybodies; hence the words of Euripides:

> But how could I be wise, who might at ease,
> Numbered among the army's multitude,
> Have had an equal share? . . .
> For those who aim too high and do too much . . . .

Those who think thus seek their own good, and consider

that one ought to do so. From this opinion, then, has come the view that such men have practical wisdom; yet perhaps one's own good cannot exist without household management, nor without a form of government. Further, how one should order one's own affairs is not clear and needs inquiry.

What has been said is confirmed by the fact that while young men become geometricians and mathematicians and wise in matters like these, it is thought that a young man of practical wisdom cannot be found. The cause is that such wisdom is concerned not only with universals but with particulars, which become familiar from experience, but a young man has no experience, for it is length of time that gives experience; indeed one might ask this question too, why a boy may become a mathematician, but not a philosopher or a physicist. Is it because the objects of mathematics exist by abstraction, while the first principles of these other subjects come from experience, and because young men have no conviction about the latter but merely use the proper language, while the essence of mathematical objects is plain enough to them?

Further, error in deliberation may be either about the universal or about the particular; we may fail to know either that all water that weighs heavy is bad, or that this particular water weighs heavy.

That practical wisdom is not scientific knowledge is evident; for it is, as has been said,[1] concerned with the ultimate particular fact, since the thing to be done is of this nature. It is opposed, then, to intuitive reason; for intuitive reason is of the limiting premises, for which no reason can be given, while practical wisdom is concerned with the ultimate particular, which is the object not of scientific knowledge but of perception—not the

---

[1] 1141ᵇ14–22.

perception of qualities peculiar to one sense but a perception akin to that by which we perceive that the particular figure before us is a triangle; for in that direction as well there will be a limit. But this is rather perception than practical wisdom, though it is another kind of perception than that of the qualities peculiar to each sense.

MINOR INTELLECTUAL VIRTUES
CONCERNED WITH CONDUCT

Goodness in deliberation, how related to practical wisdom

9. There is a difference between inquiry and deliberation; for deliberation is a particular kind of inquiry. We must grasp the nature of excellence in deliberation as well—whether it is a form of scientific knowledge, or opinion, or skill in conjecture, or some other kind of thing. *Scientific knowledge* it is not; for men do not inquire about the things they know about, | but good deliberation is a kind of deliberation, and he who deliberates inquires and calculates. Nor is it *skill in conjecture*; for this both involves no reasoning and is something that is quick in its operation, while men deliberate a long time, and they say that one should carry out quickly the conclusions of one's deliberation, but should deliberate slowly. Again, *readiness of mind* is different from excellence in deliberation; it is a sort of skill in conjecture. Nor again is excellence in deliberation *opinion* of any sort. But since the man who deliberates badly makes a mistake, while he who deliberates well does so correctly, excellence in deliberation is clearly a kind of correctness, but neither of knowledge nor of opinion; for there is no such thing as correctness of knowledge (since there is no such thing as error of knowledge), and correctness of opinion is truth; and

at the same time everything that is an object of opinion
is already determined. But again excellence in deliberation involves reasoning. The remaining alternative, then, is that it is *correctness of thinking*; for this is
not yet assertion, since, while even opinion is not
inquiry but has reached the stage of assertion, the man
who is deliberating, whether he does so well or ill, is
searching for something and calculating.

But excellence in deliberation is a certain correctness
of deliberation; hence we must first inquire what
deliberation is and what it is about. And, there being
more than one kind of correctness, plainly excellence
in deliberation is not any and every kind; for (1) the
incontinent man and the bad man, if he is clever, will
reach as a result of his calculation what he sets before
himself, so that he will have deliberated correctly, but
he will have got for himself a great evil. Now to have
deliberated well is thought to be a good thing; for it is
this kind of correctness of deliberation that is excellence
in deliberation, viz. that which tends to attain what is
good. But (2) it is possible to attain even good by a false
syllogism, and to attain what one ought to do but not
by the right means, the middle term being false; so that
this too is not yet excellence in deliberation—this state
in virtue of which one attains what one ought but not
by the right means. Again (3) it is possible to attain
it by long deliberation while another man attains it
quickly. Therefore in the former case we have not yet
got excellence in deliberation, which is rightness with
regard to the expedient—rightness in respect both of
the end, the manner, and the time. (4) Further, it is
possible to have deliberated well either in the unqualified sense or with reference to a particular end. Excellence in deliberation in the unqualified sense, then, is
that which succeeds with reference to what is the end

in the unqualified sense, and excellence in deliberation
in a particular sense is that which succeeds relatively
to a particular end. If, then, it is characteristic of men
of practical wisdom to have deliberated well, excellence in deliberation will be correctness with regard
to what conduces to the end which practical wisdom
apprehends truly.

*Understanding—the critical quality answering to the impera-
tive quality practical wisdom*

10. Understanding, also, and goodness of understanding, in virtue of which men are said to be men of under-
standing or of good understanding, | are neither entirely
the same as opinion or scientific knowledge (for at that
rate all men would have been men of understanding),
nor are they one of the particular sciences, such as
medicine, the science of things connected with health,
or geometry, the science of spatial magnitudes. For
understanding is neither about things that are always
and are unchangeable, nor about any and every one
of the things that come into being, but about things
which may become subjects of questioning and deliberation. Hence it is about the same objects as practical wisdom; but understanding and practical wisdom
are not the same. For practical wisdom issues commands, since its end is what ought to be done or not
to be done; but understanding only judges. (Understanding is identical with goodness of understanding,
men of understanding with men of good understanding.) Now understanding is neither the having nor the
acquiring of practical wisdom; but as learning is called
understanding when it means the exercise of the faculty
of knowledge,[1] so 'understanding' is applicable to the

---

[1] This is a use of μανθάνειν which is not shared by its normal English
equivalent, 'learn'.

exercise of the faculty of opinion for the purpose of judging of what someone else says about matters with which practical wisdom is concerned—and of judging soundly; for 'well' and 'soundly' are the same thing. And from this has come the use of the name 'understanding' in virtue of which men are said to be 'of good understanding', viz. from the application of the word to the grasping of scientific truth; for we often call such grasping understanding.

Judgement—right discrimination of the equitable: the place of intuition in morals

11. What is called judgement, in virtue of which men are said to 'be sympathetic judges' and to 'have judgement', is the right discrimination of the equitable. This is shown by the fact that we say the equitable man is above all others a man of sympathetic judgement, and identify equity with sympathetic judgement about certain facts. And sympathetic judgement is judgement which discriminates what is equitable and does so correctly; and correct judgement is that which judges what is true.

Now all the states we have considered converge, as might be expected, to the same point; for when we speak of judgement and understanding and practical wisdom and intuitive reason we credit the same people with possessing judgement and having reached years of reason and with having practical wisdom and understanding. For all these faculties deal with ultimates, i.e. with particulars; and being a man of understanding and of good or sympathetic judgement consists in being able to judge about the things with which practical wisdom is concerned; for the equities are common to all good men in relation to other men. Now all things which have to be done are included among particulars or ultimates; for not only must the man of practical wisdom know particular facts, but understanding and judgement are also concerned with things to be done, and these are ultimates. And intuitive reason is concerned with the ultimates in both directions; for both the first terms and the last are objects of intuitive reason and not of argument, | and the intuitive reason which is presupposed by demonstrations grasps the unchangeable and first terms, while the intuitive reason involved in practical reasonings grasps the last and variable fact, i.e. the minor premiss. For these variable facts are the starting-points for the apprehension of the end, since the universals are reached from the particulars; of these therefore we must have perception, and this perception is intuitive reason.

This is why these states are thought to be natural endowments—why, while no one is thought to be a philosopher by nature, people are thought to have by nature judgement, understanding, and intuitive reason. This is shown by the fact that we think our powers correspond to our time of life, and that a particular age brings with it intuitive reason and judgement; this implies that nature is the cause. [Hence intuitive reason is both beginning and end; for demonstrations are from these and about these.[1]] Therefore we ought to attend to the undemonstrated sayings and opinions of experienced and older people or of people of practical wisdom not less than to demonstrations; for because experience has given them an eye they see aright.

We have stated, then, what practical and philosophic wisdom are, and with what each of them is concerned, and we have said that each is the virtue of a different part of the soul.

---

[1] This sentence should probably be read, as Bywater suggests, at the end of the previous paragraph.

RELATION OF PHILOSOPHIC TO PRACTICAL
WISDOM

What is the use of philosophic and of practical wisdom? Philo-
sophic wisdom is the formal cause of happiness; practical
wisdom is what ensures the taking of proper means to the
proper ends desired by moral virtue

12. Difficulties might be raised as to the utility of these
qualities of mind. For (1) philosophic wisdom will
contemplate none of the things that will make a man
happy (for it is not concerned with any coming into
being), and though practical wisdom has *this* merit,
for what purpose do we need it? Practical wisdom is
the quality of mind concerned with things just and
noble and good for man, but these are the things which
it is the mark of a *good* man to do, and we are none the
more able to act for *knowing* them if the virtues are states
of *character*, just as we are none the better able to act
for knowing the things that are healthy and sound, in
the sense not of producing but of issuing from the state
of health; for we are none the more able to act for
having the art of medicine or of gymnastics. But (2) if
we are to say that a man should have practical wisdom
not for the sake of knowing moral truths but for the
sake of becoming good, practical wisdom will be of no
use to those who *are* good; but again it is of no use to
those who have *not* virtue; for it will make no difference
whether they have practical wisdom themselves or
obey others who have it, and it would be enough for us
to do what we do in the case of health; though we wish
to become healthy, yet we do not learn the art of medicine. (3) Besides this, it would be thought strange if
practical wisdom, being inferior to philosophic wisdom, is to be put in authority over it, as seems to be

implied by the fact that the art which produces anything rules and issues commands about that thing.

These, then, are the questions we must discuss; so far
we have only stated the difficulties. |

(1) Now first let us say that in themselves these
states must be worthy of choice because they are the
virtues of the two parts of the soul respectively, even
if neither of them produces anything.

(2) Secondly, they do produce something, not as
the art of medicine produces health, however, but as
health produces health;[1] so does philosophic wisdom
produce happiness; for, being a part of virtue entire,
by being possessed and by actualizing itself it makes
a man happy.

(3) Again, the work of man is achieved only in
accordance with practical wisdom as well as with moral
virtue; for virtue makes us aim at the right mark, and
practical wisdom makes us take the right means. (Of
the fourth part of the soul—the nutritive[2]—there is no
such virtue; for there is nothing which it is in its power
to do or not to do.)

(4) With regard to our being none the more able to
do because of our practical wisdom what is noble and
just, let us begin a little further back, starting with the
following principle. As we say that some people who
do just acts are not necessarily just, i.e. those who do the
acts ordained by the laws either unwillingly or owing
to ignorance or for some other reason and not for the
sake of the acts themselves (though, to be sure, they do
what they should and all the things that the good man
ought), so is it, it seems, that in order to be good one
must be in a certain state when one does the several

---

[1] i.e. as health, as an inner state, produces the activities which we
know as constituting health.

[2] The other three being the scientific (τὸ ἐπιστημονικόν), the calculative (τὸ λογιστικόν), and the desiderative (τὸ ὀρεκτικόν).

acts, i.e. one must do them as a result of choice and for
the sake of the acts themselves. Now virtue makes
the choice right, but the question of the things which
should naturally be done to carry out our choice belongs not to virtue but to another faculty. We must
devote our attention to these matters and give a clearer
statement about them. There is a faculty which is called
cleverness; and this is such as to be able to do the
things that tend towards the mark we have set before
ourselves, and to hit it. Now if the mark be noble, the
cleverness is laudable, but if the mark be bad, the
cleverness is mere smartness; hence we call even men
of practical wisdom clever or smart. Practical wisdom
is not the faculty, but it does not exist without this
faculty. And this eye of the soul acquires its formed
state not without the aid of virtue, as has been said[1]
and is plain; for the syllogisms which deal with acts
to be done are things which involve a starting-point,
viz. 'since the end, i.e. what is best, is of such and such
a nature', whatever it may be (let it for the sake of
argument be what we please); and this is not evident
except to the good man; for wickedness perverts us and
causes us to be deceived about the starting-points of
action. Therefore it is evident that it is impossible to be
practically wise without being good. |

Relation of practical wisdom to natural virtue, moral virtue,
*   and the right rule*

13. We must therefore consider virtue also once more;
for virtue too is similarly related; as practical wisdom
is to cleverness—not the same, but like it—so is natural
virtue to virtue in the strict sense. For all men think
that each type of character belongs to its possessors in
some sense by nature; for from the very moment of

---
[1] ll. 6–26.

birth we are just or fitted for self-control or brave or
have the other moral qualities; but yet we seek something else as that which is good in the strict sense—we
seek for the presence of such qualities in another way.
For both children and brutes have the natural dispositions to these qualities, but without reason these are
evidently hurtful. Only we seem to see this much, that,
while one may be led astray by them, as a strong body
which moves without sight may stumble badly because
of its lack of sight, still, if a man once acquires reason,
that makes a difference in action; and his state, while
still like what it was, will then be virtue in the strict
sense. Therefore, as in the part of us which forms
opinions there are two types, cleverness and practical
wisdom, so too in the moral part there are two types,
natural virtue and virtue in the strict sense, and of
these the latter involves practical wisdom. This is why
some say that all the virtues are forms of practical
wisdom, and why Socrates in one respect was on the
right track while in another he went astray; in thinking
that all the virtues were forms of practical wisdom he
was wrong, but in saying they implied practical wisdom he was right. This is confirmed by the fact that
even now all men, when they define virtue, after
naming the state of character and its objects add 'that
(state) which is in accordance with the right rule'; now
the right rule is that which is in accordance with practical wisdom. All men, then, seem somehow to divine
that this kind of state is virtue, viz. that which is in
accordance with practical wisdom. But we must go
a little further. For it is not merely the state in accordance with the right rule, but the state that implies the
presence of the right rule, that is virtue; and practical
wisdom is a right rule about such matters. Socrates,
then, thought the virtues were rules or rational

principles (for he thought they were, all of them, forms of scientific knowledge), while we think they *involve* a rational principle.

It is clear, then, from what has been said, that it is not possible to be good in the strict sense without practical wisdom, or practically wise without moral virtue. But in this way we may also refute the dialectical argument whereby it might be contended that the virtues exist in separation from each other; the same man, it might be said, is not best equipped by nature for all the virtues, so that he will have already acquired one when he has not yet acquired another. This is possible in respect of the natural virtues, but not in respect of those in respect of which a man is called without qualification good; | for with the presence of the one quality, practical wisdom, will be given all the virtues. And it is plain that, even if it were of no practical value, we should have needed it because it is the virtue of the part of us in question; plain too that the choice will not be right without practical wisdom any more than without virtue; for the one determines the end and the other makes us do the things that lead to the end.

But again it is not *supreme* over philosophic wisdom, i.e. over the superior part of us, any more than the art of medicine is over health; for it does not use it but provides for its coming into being; it issues orders, then, for its sake, but not to it. Further, to maintain its supremacy would be like saying that the art of politics rules the gods because it issues orders about all the affairs of the state.

BOOK VII · CONTINENCE AND INCONTINENCE: PLEASURE

Six varieties of character: method of treatment: current opinions

1. LET us now make a fresh beginning and point out that of moral states to be avoided there are three kinds —vice, incontinence, brutishness. The contraries of two of these are evident—one we call virtue, the other continence; to brutishness it would be most fitting to oppose superhuman virtue, a heroic and divine kind of virtue, as Homer has represented Priam saying of Hector that he was very good,

> For he seemed not, he,
> The child of a mortal man, but as one that of God's seed came.[1]

Therefore if, as they say, men become gods by excess of virtue, of this kind must evidently be the state opposed to the brutish state: for as a brute has no vice or virtue, so neither has a god; his state is higher than virtue, and that of a brute is a different kind of state from vice.

Now, since it is rarely that a godlike man is found— to use the epithet of the Spartans, who when they admire anyone highly call him a 'godlike man'—so too the brutish type is rarely found among men; it is found chiefly among barbarians, but some brutish qualities are also produced by disease or deformity; and we also call by this evil name those who surpass ordinary men in vice. Of this kind of disposition, however, we must later make some mention,[2] while we have discussed

Il. xxiv. 258f.   [1] Ch. 5.

vice before;¹ we must now discuss incontinence and
softness (or effeminacy), and continence and endur-
ance; for we must treat each of the two|neither as
identical with virtue or wickedness, nor as a different genus. We must, as in all other cases, set the apparent facts before us and, after first discussing the
difficulties, go on to prove, if possible, the truth of all
the common opinions about these affections of the
mind, or, failing this, of the greater number and the
most authoritative; for if we both resolve the difficulties and leave the common opinions undisturbed, we
shall have proved the case sufficiently.

Now (1) both continence and endurance are thought
to be included among things good and praiseworthy,
and both incontinence and softness among things bad
and blameworthy; and the same man is thought to be
continent and ready to abide by the result of his cal-
culations, or incontinent and ready to abandon them.
And (2) the incontinent man, knowing that what he
does is bad, does it as a result of passion, while the
continent man, knowing that his appetites are bad,
refuses on account of his rational principle to follow
them. (3) The temperate man all men call continent
and disposed to endurance, while the continent man
some maintain to be always temperate but others do
not; and some call the self-indulgent man incontinent
and the incontinent man self-indulgent indiscrimi-
nately, while others distinguish them. (4) The man of
practical wisdom, they sometimes say, cannot be incontinent, while sometimes they say that some who are
practically wise and clever *are* incontinent. Again, (5)
men are said to be incontinent even with respect to
anger, honour, and gain.—These, then, are the things
that are said.

¹ Bks. II–V.

Contradictions involved in the current opinions

2. Now we may ask (1) what kind of right judgement has the man who behaves incontinently. That he should behave so when he has knowledge, some say is impossible; for it would be strange—so Socrates thought—if when knowledge was in a man something else could master it and drag it about like a slave. For *Socrates* was entirely opposed to the view in question, holding that there is no such thing as incontinence; no one, he said, when he judges acts against what he judges best—people act so only by reason of ignorance. Now this view plainly contradicts the apparent facts, and we must inquire about what happens to such a man; if he acts by reason of ignorance, what is the manner of his ignorance? For that the man who behaves incontinently does not, before he gets into this state, *think* he ought to act so, is evident. But there are *some* who concede certain of Socrates' contentions but not others; that nothing is stronger than knowledge they admit, but not that no one acts contrary to what has seemed to him the better course, and therefore they say that the incontinent man has not knowledge when he is mastered by his pleasures, but opinion. But *if* it is opinion and not knowledge, if it is not a strong conviction that resists but a weak one, |as in men who hesitate, we sympathize with their failure to stand by such convictions against strong appetites; but we do not sympathize with wickedness, nor with any of the other blameworthy states. Is it then *practical wisdom* whose resistance is mastered? That is the strongest of all states. But this is absurd; the same man will be at once practically wise and incontinent, but *no one* would say that it is the part of a practically wise man to do willingly the basest acts. Besides, it has been

shown before that the man of practical wisdom is one
who will *act*[1] (for he is a man concerned with the
individual facts)[2] and who has the other virtues.[3]

(2) Further, if continence involves having strong
and bad appetites, the temperate man will not be
continent nor the continent man temperate; for a temperate man will have neither excessive nor bad appetites. But the continent man *must*; for if the appetites
are good, the state of character that restrains us from
following them is bad, so that not all continence will
be good; while if they are weak and not bad, there is
nothing admirable in resisting them, and if they are
weak and bad, there is nothing great in resisting these
either.

(3) Further, if continence makes a man ready to
stand by any and every opinion, it is bad, i.e. if it makes
him stand even by a false opinion; and if incontinence
makes a man apt to abandon any and every opinion,
there will be a good incontinence, of which Sophocles'
Neoptolemus in the *Philoctetes* will be an instance; for
he is to be praised for not standing by what Odysseus
persuaded him to do, because he is pained at telling
a lie.

(4) Further, the sophistic argument presents a difficulty; the syllogism arising from men's wish to expose
paradoxical results arising from an opponent's view,
in order that they may be admired when they succeed,
is one that puts us in a difficulty (for thought is bound
fast when it will not rest because the conclusion does
not satisfy it, and cannot advance because it cannot
refute the argument). There is an argument from
which it follows that folly coupled with incontinence is
virtue; a man does the opposite of what he thinks right,

---

[1] 1140ᵇ4–6.　　　　　[2] 1141ᵇ16, 1142ᵃ24.
[3] 1144ᵇ30–1145ᵃ2.

owing to incontinence, but thinks what is good to be
evil and something that he should not do, and in consequence he will do what is good and not what is
evil.

(5) Further, he who on conviction does and pursues
and chooses what is pleasant would be thought to be
better than one who does so as a result not of calculation
but of incontinence; for he is easier to cure since he may
be persuaded to change his mind. But to the incon-
tinen tman may be applied the proverb 'When water
chokes, what is one to wash it down with?' If he had
been persuaded of the rightness of what he does, he
would have desisted when he was persuaded to change
his mind; | but now he acts in spite of his being per-
suaded of something quite different.

(6) Further, if incontinence and continence are concerned with any and every kind of object, who is it that
is incontinent in the unqualified sense? No one has all
the forms of incontinence, but we say some people are
incontinent without qualification.

*Solution of the problem, how the incontinent man's knowledge
is impaired*

3. Of some such kind are the difficulties that arise;
some of these points must be refuted and the others
left in possession of the field; for the solution of the
difficulty is the discovery of the truth. (1) We must
consider first, then, whether incontinent people act
knowingly or not, and with what sort of knowledge;
then (2) with what sorts of object the incontinent and
the continent man may be said to be concerned (i.e.
whether with any and every pleasure and pain or with
certain determinate kinds), and whether the continent
man and the man of endurance are the same or different; and similarly with regard to the other matters

germane to this inquiry. The starting-point of our investigation is (a) the question whether the continent man and the incontinent are differentiated by their objects or by their attitude, i.e. whether the incontinent man is incontinent simply by being concerned with such-and-such objects, or, instead, by his attitude, or, instead of that, by both these things; (b) the second question is whether incontinence and continence are concerned with any and every object or not. The man who is incontinent in the unqualified sense neither is concerned with any and every object, but with precisely those with which the self-indulgent man is concerned, nor is he characterized by being simply related to these (for then his state would be the same as self-indulgence), but by being related to them in a certain way. For the one is led on in accordance with his own choice, thinking that he ought always to pursue the present pleasure; while the other does not think so, but yet pursues it.

(1) As for the suggestion that it is true opinion and not knowledge against which we act incontinently, that makes no difference to the argument; for some people when in a state of opinion do not hesitate, but think they know exactly. If, then, the notion is that owing to their weak conviction those who have opinion are more likely to act against their judgement than those who know, we answer that there need be no difference between knowledge and opinion in this respect; for some men are no less convinced of what they think than others of what they know; as is shown by the case of Heraclitus. But (a), since we use the word 'know' in two senses (for both the man who has knowledge but is not using it and he who is using it are said to know), it *will* make a difference whether, when a man does what he should not, he has the knowledge

but is not exercising it, or *is* exercising it; for the latter seems strange, but not the former.

(*b*) Further, since there are two kinds of premisses, | there is nothing to prevent a man's having both premisses and acting against his knowledge, provided that he is using only the universal premiss and not the particular; for it is particular acts that have to be done. And there are also two kinds of universal term; one is predicable of the agent, the other of the object; e.g. 'dry food is good for every man', and 'I am a man', or 'such-and-such food is dry'; but whether 'this food is such-and-such', of this the incontinent man either has not or is not exercising the knowledge.[1] There will, then, be, firstly, an enormous difference between these manners of knowing, so that to know in one way when we act incontinently would not seem anything strange, while to know in the other way would be extraordinary.

And further (*c*) the possession of knowledge in another sense than those just named is something that happens to men; for within the case of having knowledge but not using it we see a difference of state, admitting of the possibility of having knowledge in a sense and yet not having it, as in the instance of a man asleep, mad, or drunk. But now this is just the condition of men under the influence of passions; for outbursts of anger and sexual appetites and some other such passions, it is evident, actually alter our bodily condition, and in some men even produce fits of madness. It is plain, then, that incontinent people must be said to be in a similar condition to men asleep, mad, or drunk.

[1] i.e., if I am to be able to deduce from (*a*) 'dry food is good for all men' that 'this food is good for me', I must have (*b*) the premiss 'I am a man' and (*c*) the premisses (i) '*x* food is dry', (ii) 'this food is *x*'. I cannot fail to know (*b*), and I may know (*c* i); but if I do not know (*c* ii), or know it only 'at the back of my mind', I shall not draw the conclusion.

The fact that men use the language that flows from
knowledge proves nothing; for even men under the
influence of these passions utter scientific proofs and
verses of Empedocles, and those who have just begun
to learn a science can string together its phrases, but do
not yet know it; for it has to become part of themselves,
and that takes time; so that we must suppose that the
use of language by men in an incontinent state means
no more than its utterance by actors on the stage.

(d) Again, we may also view the cause as follows
in the way a student of nature would. The one opinion
is universal, the other is concerned with the particular
facts, and here we come to something within the sphere
of perception; when a single opinion results from the
two, the soul must in one type of case[1] affirm the
conclusion, while in the case of opinions concerned
with production it must immediately act (e.g. if 'everything sweet ought to be tasted', and 'this is sweet', in
the sense of being one of the particular sweet things,
the man who can act and is not restrained must at the
same time actually act accordingly). When, then, the
universal opinion is present in us restraining us from
tasting, and there is also the opinion that 'everything
sweet is pleasant', and that 'this is sweet' (now this is
the opinion that is active),[2] and when appetite happens to be present in us, the one opinion bids us avoid
the object, but appetite leads us towards it (for it can
move each of our bodily parts); so that it turns out
that a man behaves incontinently under the influence
(in a sense) of a rule and an opinion,|and of one not
contrary in itself, but only incidentally—for the appetite is contrary, not the opinion—to the right rule.
It also follows that this is the reason why the lower
animals are not incontinent, viz. because they have no

---

[1] i.e. in scientific reasoning.   [2] i.e. determines action (cf. ᵇ10).

universal judgement but only imagination and memory of particulars.

The explanation of how the ignorance is dissolved and the incontinent man regains his knowledge, is the same as in the case of the man drunk or asleep and is not peculiar to this condition; we must go to the students of natural science for it. Now, the last premiss being an opinion about a perceptible object, and being also what determines our actions, this a man either has not when he is in the state of passion, or has it in the sense in which having knowledge did not mean knowing but only talking, as a drunken man may mutter the verses of Empedocles.[1] And because the last term is not universal nor equally an object of scientific knowledge with the universal term, the position that Socrates sought to establish[2] actually seems to result; for it is not in the presence of what is thought to be knowledge proper that the passion occurs (nor is it this that is 'dragged about' as a result of the passion), but in that of perceptual knowledge.[3]

This must suffice as our answer to the question of whether an incontinent man acts knowingly or not, and with what sort of knowledge it is possible to be incontinent.

Solution of the problem, what is the sphere of incontinence: its proper and its extended sense distinguished

4. (2) We must next discuss whether there is any one who is incontinent without qualification, or all men who are incontinent are so in a particular sense, and if there is, with what sort of objects he is concerned.

[1] Cf. ᵃ10–24.   [2] 1145ᵇ22–24.
[3] Even before the minor premiss of the practical syllogism has been obscured by passion, the incontinent man has not scientific knowledge in the strict sense, since his minor premiss is not universal but has for its subject a sensible particular, e.g. 'this glass of wine'.

That both continent persons and persons of endurance, and incontinent and soft persons, are concerned
with pleasures and pains, is evident.

Now of the things that produce pleasure some are
necessary, while others are worthy of choice in themselves but admit of excess, the bodily causes of pleasure
being necessary (by such I mean both those concerned
with food and those concerned with sexual intercourse,
i.e. the bodily matters with which we defined self-
indulgence and temperance as being concerned), while
the others are not necessary but worthy of choice in
themselves (e.g. victory, honour, wealth, and good and
pleasant things of this sort). This being so, (a) those
who go to excess with reference to the latter, contrary
to the right rule which is in themselves, are not called
incontinent simply, but incontinent with the qualification 'in respect of money, gain, honour, or anger'—
not simply incontinent, on the ground that they are
different from incontinent people and are called incontinent by reason of a resemblance. (Compare the
case of Anthropos,[1] who won a contest at the Olympic
games; | in his case the general definition of man differed
little from the definition peculiar to *him*, but yet it *was*
different.) This is shown by the fact that incontinence
either without qualification or in respect of some particular bodily pleasure is blamed not only as a fault but
as a kind of vice, while none of the people who are incontinent in these other respects is so blamed.

But (b) of the people who are incontinent with
respect to bodily enjoyments, with which we say the
temperate and the self-indulgent man are concerned,
he who pursues the excesses of things pleasant—and
shuns those of things painful, of hunger and thirst and

---

[1] 'Anthropos', the Greek for 'man', was the name of an Olympic
victor in 456 B.C.

heat and cold and all the objects of touch and taste—
not by choice but contrary to his choice and his judgement, is called incontinent, not with the qualification
'in respect of this or that', e.g. of anger, but just simply.
This is confirmed by the fact that men are called 'soft'
with regard to these pleasures, but not with regard to
any of the others. And for this reason we group together
the incontinent and the self-indulgent, the continent
and the temperate man—but not any of these other
types—because they are concerned somehow with the
same pleasures and pains; but though these are concerned with the same objects, they are not similarly
related to them, but some of them make a deliberate
choice while the others do not.[1]

This is why we should describe as self-indulgent
rather the man who without appetite or with but a
slight appetite pursues the excesses of pleasure and
avoids moderate pains, than the man who does so
because of his strong appetites; for what would the
former do, if he had in addition a vigorous appetite,
and a violent pain at the lack of the 'necessary' objects?

Now of appetites and pleasures some belong to the
class of things generically noble and good—for some
pleasant things are by nature worthy of choice, while
others are contrary to these, and others are intermediate, to adopt our previous distinction[2]—e.g. wealth,
gain, victory, honour. And with reference to all objects
whether of this or of the intermediate kind men are not
blamed for being affected by them, for desiring and
loving them, but for doing so in a certain way, i.e. for
going to excess. (This is why all those who contrary
to the rule either are mastered by or pursue one

---

[1] i.e. the temperate and the self-indulgent, not the continent and
the incontinent.

[2] 1147ᵇ23-31, where, however, the 'contraries' are not mentioned.

of the objects which are naturally noble and good,
e.g. those who busy themselves more than they ought
about honour or about children and parents, ⟨are not
wicked⟩; for these too are goods, and those who busy
themselves about them are praised; but yet there is an
excess even in them—if like Niobe one were to fight
even against the gods, or were to be as much devoted
to one's father as Satyrus nicknamed 'the filial',| who
was thought to be very silly on this point.⟩[1] There is
no wickedness, then, with regard to these objects, for
the reason named, viz. because each of them is by
nature a thing worthy of choice for its own sake; yet
excesses in respect of them are bad and to be avoided.
Similarly there is no incontinence with regard to them;
for incontinence is not only to be avoided but is also
a thing worthy of blame; but owing to a similarity in
the state of feeling people apply the name incontinence,
adding in each case what it is in respect of, as we may
describe as a bad doctor or a bad actor one whom we
should not call bad, simply. As, then, in this case we do
not apply the term without qualification because each
of these conditions is not badness but only analogous
to it, so it is clear that in the other case also that alone
must be taken to be incontinence and continence which
is concerned with the same objects as temperance and
self-indulgence, but we apply the term to anger by
virtue of a resemblance; and this is why we say with
a qualification 'incontinent in respect of anger' as we
say 'incontinent in respect of honour, or of gain'.

*Incontinence in its extended sense includes a brutish and a
morbid form.*

5. (1) Some things are pleasant by nature, and of

---

[1] Nothing is really known about the Satyrus referred to, but Professor
Burnet's suggestion that he was a king of Bosporus who deified his
father seems probable.

these (a) some are so without qualification, and (b) others are so with reference to particular classes either of animals or of men; while (2) others are not pleasant by nature, but (a) some of them become so by reason of injuries to the system, and (b) others by reason of acquired habits, and (c) others by reason of originally bad natures. This being so, it is possible with regard to each of the latter kinds to discover similar states of character to those recognized with regard to the former; I mean (A) the brutish states,[1] as in the case of the female who, they say, rips open pregnant women and devours the infants, or of the things in which some of the tribes about the Black Sea that have gone savage are said to delight—in raw meat or in human flesh, or in lending their children to one another to feast upon—or of the story told of Phalaris.[2]

These states are brutish, but (B) others arise as a result of disease[3] (or, in some cases, of madness, as with the man who sacrificed and ate his mother, or with the slave who ate the liver of his fellow), and others are morbid states (C) resulting from custom,[4] e.g. the habit of plucking out the hair or of gnawing the nails, or even coals or earth, and in addition to these paederasty; for these arise in some by nature and in others, as in those who have been the victims of lust from childhood, from habit.

Now those in whom nature is the cause of such a state no one would call incontinent, any more than one would apply the epithet to women, because of the passive part they play in copulation; nor would one apply it to those who are in a morbid condition as a result of habit. To have these various types of habit is beyond the limits of vice, as brutishness is too; | for a man who has them to master or be mastered by them is not simple

---

[1] Answering to (2 c).   [2] Sc. and the bull. But cf. 1149^{a}14.
[3] Answering to (2 a).   [4] Answering to (2 b).

⟨continence or⟩ incontinence but that which is so by analogy, as the man who is in this condition in respect of fits of anger is to be called incontinent in respect of that feeling, but not incontinent simply.

For every excessive state whether of folly, of cowardice, of self-indulgence, or of bad temper, is either brutish or morbid; the man who is by nature apt to fear everything, even the squeak of a mouse, is cowardly with a brutish cowardice, while the man who feared a weasel did so in consequence of disease; and of foolish people those who by nature are thoughtless and live by their senses alone are brutish, like some races of the distant barbarians, while those who are so as a result of disease (e.g. of epilepsy) or of madness are morbid. Of these chacteristics it is possible to have some only at times, and not to be mastered by them, e.g. Phalaris may have restrained a desire to eat the flesh of a child or an appetite for unnatural sexual pleasure; but it is also possible to be mastered, not merely to have the feelings. Thus, as the wickedness which is on the human level is called wickedness simply, while that which is not is called wickedness not simply but with the qualification 'brutish' or 'morbid', in the same way it is plain that some incontinence is brutish and some morbid, while only that which corresponds to *human* self-indulgence is incontinence simply.

That incontinence and continence, then, are concerned only with the same objects as self-indulgence and temperance, and that what is concerned with other objects is a type distinct from incontinence, and called incontinence by a metaphor and not simply, is plain.

Incontinence in respect of anger is less disgraceful than incontinence proper

6. That incontinence in respect of anger is less disgrace-

ful than that in respect of the appetites is what we will
now proceed to see. (1) Anger seems to listen to argument to some extent, but to mishear it, as do hasty
servants who run out before they have heard the whole
of what one says, and then muddle the order, or as dogs
bark if there is but a knock at the door, before looking
to see if it is a friend; so anger by reason of the warmth
and hastiness of its nature, though it hears, does not
hear an order, and springs to take revenge. For argument or imagination informs us that we have been insulted or slighted, and anger, reasoning as it were that
anything like this must be fought against, boils up
straightway; while appetite, if argument or perception
merely says that an object is pleasant, springs to the
enjoyment of it. | Therefore anger obeys the argument
in a sense, but appetite does not. It is therefore more
disgraceful; for the man who is incontinent in respect
of anger is in a sense conquered by argument, while the
other is conquered by appetite and not by argument.

(2) Further, we pardon people more easily for
following natural desires, since we pardon them more
easily for following such appetites as are common to
all men, and in so far as they are common; now anger
and bad temper are more natural than the appetites
for excess, i.e. for unnecessary objects. Take for instance
the man who defended himself on the charge of striking
his father by saying 'Yes, but *he* struck *his* father, and *he*
struck *his*, and' (pointing to his child) 'this boy will
strike *me* when he is a man; it runs in the family'; or the
man who when he was being dragged along by his son
bade him stop at the doorway, since he himself had
dragged his father only as far as that.

(3) Further, those who are more given to plotting
against others are more criminal. Now a passionate man
is not given to plotting, nor is anger itself—it is open;

but the nature of appetite is illustrated by what
the poets call Aphrodite, 'guile-weaving daughter
of Cyprus',[1] and by Homer's words about her 'em-
broidered girdle':

> And the whisper of wooing is there,
> Whose subtlety stealeth the wits of the wise, how
>   prudent soe'er.[2]

Therefore if this form of incontinence is more criminal
and disgraceful than that in respect of anger, it is both
incontinence without qualification and in a sense
vice.

(4) Further, no one commits wanton outrage with
a feeling of pain, but everyone who acts in anger acts
with pain, while the man who commits outrage acts
with pleasure. If, then, those acts at which it is most just
to be angry are more criminal than others, the incontinence which is due to appetite is the more criminal; for
there is no wanton outrage involved in anger.

Plainly, then, the incontinence concerned with appetite is more disgraceful than that concerned with anger,
and continence and incontinence are concerned with
bodily appetites and pleasures; but we must grasp the
differences among the latter themselves. For, as has
been said at the beginning,[3] some are human and
natural both in kind and in magnitude, others are
brutish, and others are due to organic injuries and
diseases. Only with the first of these are temperance
and self-indulgence concerned; this is why we call the
lower animals neither temperate nor self-indulgent,
except by a metaphor, and only if some one race of
animals exceeds another as a whole in wantonness,
destructiveness, and omnivorous greed; these have no
power of choice or calculation, but they *are* departures

---

[1] Author unknown.   [2] *Il.* xiv. 214, 217.   [3] 1148ᵇ15-31.

from the natural norm,[1] as, among men, madmen are. |
Now brutishness is a less evil than vice, though more
alarming; for it is not that the better part has been perverted, as in man,—they *have* no better part. Thus it is
like comparing a lifeless thing with a living in respect
of badness; for the badness of that which has no originative source of movement is always less hurtful, and
reason is an originative source. Thus it is like comparing
injustice in the abstract with an unjust man. Each is in
some sense worse; for a bad man will do ten thousand
times as much evil as a brute.[2]

Softness and endurance: two forms of incontinence—weakness and impetuosity

7. With regard to the pleasures and pains and appetites
and aversions arising through touch and taste, to which
both self-indulgence and temperance were formerly
narrowed down,[3] it is possible to be in such a state as to
be defeated even by those of them which most people
master, or to master even those by which most people
are defeated; among these possibilities, those relating
to pleasures are incontinence and continence, those
relating to pains softness and endurance. The state of

---

[1] And therefore cannot be called self-indulgent properly, but *can* be
so called by a metaphor.

[2] The comparison between the badness of a brute and that of a bad
man is illustrated (1) by a comparison between the badness of a lifeless and that of a living thing; a living thing can do more harm than
a lifeless because it has in ψυχή an ἀρχή κινήσεως which the other has
not; and a man can do more harm than a brute because he has in
νοῦς an ἀρχή κινήσεως which the brute has not; (2) by a comparison
between injustice in the abstract and an unjust man; injustice is in
a sense worse—more terrible—because it is what makes the unjust
man unjust, and in a sense less bad because it cannot operate except
as realized in an unjust man; and a brute is more alarming than a
bad man, but (owing to its lack of νοῦς) does much less harm. The
second illustration is very far-fetched, and corruption may be suspected
in l. 6.   [3] iii. 10.

most people is intermediate, even if they lean more towards the worse states.

Now, since some pleasures are necessary while others are not, and are necessary up to a point while the excesses of them are not, nor the deficiencies, and this is equally true of appetites and pains, the man who pursues the excesses of things pleasant, or pursues to excess necessary objects, and does so by choice, for their own sake and not at all for the sake of any result distinct from them, is self-indulgent; for such a man is of necessity without regrets, and therefore incurable, since a man without regrets cannot be cured.[1] The man who is deficient in his pursuit of them is the opposite of self-indulgent; the man who is intermediate is temperate. Similarly, there is the man who avoids bodily pains not because he is defeated by them but by choice. (Of those who do not *choose* such acts, one kind of man is led to them as a result of the pleasure involved, another because he avoids the pain arising from the appetite, so that these types differ from one another. Now any one would think worse of a man if with no appetite or with weak appetite he were to do something disgraceful, than if he did it under the influence of powerful appetite, and worse of him if he struck a blow not in anger than if he did it in anger; for what would he have done if he *had* been strongly affected? This is why the self-indulgent man is worse than the incontinent.) Of the states named, then,[2] the latter is rather a kind of softness;[3] the former is self-indulgence. While to the incontinent man is opposed the continent, to the soft is opposed the man of endurance; for endurance consists in resisting, while continence consists in conquering, and resisting and

[1] ἀνάγκη ... ἀνίατος ll. 21–22 is a note to defend the use of the word ἀκόλαστος, lit. incorrigible.   [2] In ll. 19–25.

[3] Not softness proper, which is non-deliberate avoidance of pain (ll. 13–15).

conquering are different, as not being beaten is different from winning; this is why continence is also more worthy of choice than endurance. | Now the man who is defective in respect of resistance to the things which most men both resist and resist successfully is soft and effeminate; for effeminacy too is a kind of softness; such a man trails his cloak to avoid the pain of lifting it, and plays the invalid without thinking himself wretched, though the man he imitates is a wretched man.

The case is similar with regard to continence and incontinence. For if a man is defeated by violent and excessive pleasures or pains, there is nothing wonderful in that; indeed we are ready to pardon him if he has resisted, as Theodectes' Philoctetes does when bitten by the snake, or Carcinus' Cercyon in the *Alope*, and as people who try to restrain their laughter burst out in a guffaw, as happened to Xenophantus.[1] But it is surprising if a man is defeated by and cannot resist pleasures or pains which most men can hold out against, when this is not due to heredity or disease, like the softness that is hereditary with the kings of the Scythians, or that which distinguishes the female sex from the male.

The lover of amusement, too, is thought to be self-indulgent, but is really soft. For amusement is a relaxation, since it is a rest from work; and the lover of amusement is one of the people who go to excess in this.

Of incontinence one kind is impetuosity, another weakness. For some men after deliberating fail, owing to their emotion, to stand by the conclusions of their deliberation, others because they have not deliberated are led by their emotion; since some men (just as people who first tickle others are not tickled themselves), if they

---

[1] Apparently a musician at Alexander's court.

have first perceived and seen what is coming and have
first roused themselves and their calculative faculty, are not defeated by their emotion, whether it be
pleasant or painful. It is keen and excitable people
that suffer especially from the impetuous form of incontinence; for the former by reason of their quickness
and the latter by reason of the violence of their passions
do not await the argument, because they are apt to
follow their imagination.

Self-indulgence worse than incontinence

8. The self-indulgent man, as was said,[1] has no regrets; for he stands by his choice; but any incontinent
man is subject to regrets. This is why the position is not
as it was expressed in the formulation of the problem,[2]
but the self-indulgent man is incurable and the incontinent man curable; for wickedness is like a disease
such as dropsy or consumption, while incontinence is
like epilepsy; the former is a permanent, the latter an
intermittent badness. And generally incontinence and
vice are different in kind; vice is unconscious of itself,
incontinence is not | (of incontinent men themselves,
those who become temporarily beside themselves are
better than those who have the rational principle but
do not abide by it, since the latter are defeated by a
weaker passion, and do not act without previous deliberation like the others); for the incontinent man is
like the people who get drunk quickly and on little
wine,[3] i.e. on less than most people.

Evidently, then, incontinence is not vice (though
perhaps it is so in a qualified sense); for incontinence is
contrary to choice while vice is in accordance with

---

[1] ᵃ21.   [2] 1146ᵃ31–ᵇ2.

[3] To get a proper sense for this clause it seems necessary to treat
ll. 1–3 as parenthetical.

choice; not but what they are similar in respect of the
actions they lead to; as in the saying of Demodocus
about the Milesians, 'The Milesians are not without
sense, but they do the things that senseless people do',
so too incontinent people are not criminal, but they will
do criminal acts.

Now, since the incontinent man is apt to pursue, not
on conviction, bodily pleasures that are excessive and
contrary to the right rule, while the self-indulgent man
is convinced because he is the sort of man to pursue
them, it is on the contrary the former that is easily persuaded to change his mind, while the latter is not. For
virtue and vice respectively preserve and destroy the
first principle, and in actions the final cause is the first
principle, as the hypotheses[1] are in mathematics;
neither in that case is it argument that teaches the first
principles, nor is it so here—virtue either natural or
produced by habituation is what teaches right opinion
about the first principle. Such a man as this, then, is
temperate; the contrary type is the self-indulgent.

But there is a sort of man who is carried away as a
result of passion and contrary to the right rule—a man
whom passion masters so that he does not act according
to the right rule, but does not master to the extent of
making him ready to believe that he ought to pursue
such pleasures without reserve; this is the incontinent
man, who is better than the self-indulgent man, and
not bad without qualification; for the best thing in him,
the first principle, is preserved. And contrary to him is
another kind of man, he who abides by his convictions
and is not carried away, at least as a result of passion.
It is evident from these considerations that the latter
is a good state and the former a bad one.

---

[1] i.e. the assumptions of the existence of the primary objects of
mathematics, such as the straight line or the unit.

Relation of continence to obstinacy, incontinence, 'insensibility',
    temperance

9. Is the man continent who abides by any and every
rule and any and every choice, or the man who abides
by the right choice, and is he incontinent who abandons any and every choice and any and every rule, or
he who abandons the rule that is not false and the
choice that is right; this is how we put it before in our
statement of the problem.[1] Or is it incidentally any and
every choice but *per se* the true rule and the right choice
by which the one abides and the other does not? If
anyone chooses or pursues this for the sake of that, |
per se he pursues and chooses the latter, but incidentally
the former. But when we speak without qualification
we mean what is *per se*. Therefore in a sense the one
abides by, and the other abandons, any and every
opinion; but without qualification, the true opinion.

There are some who are apt to abide by their
opinion, who are called strong-headed, viz. those who
are hard to persuade in the first instance and are not
easily persuaded to change; these have some likeness to
the continent man, as the prodigal is in a way like the
liberal man and the rash man like the confident man;
but they are different in many respects. For it is to
passion and appetite that the one will not yield,
since on occasion the continent man *will* yield to
argument; but it is to argument that the others refuse
to yield, for they do form appetites and many of them
are led by their pleasures. Now the people who are
strong-headed are the opinionated, the ignorant, and
the boorish—the opinionated being influenced by
pleasure and pain; for they delight in the victory they
gain if they are not persuaded to change, and are

[1] 1146ᵃ16–31.

pained if their decisions become null and void as decrees sometimes do; so that they resemble the incontinent rather than the continent man.

But there are some who fail to abide by their resolutions, not as a result of incontinence, e.g. Neoptolemus in Sophocles' *Philoctetes*; yet it was for the sake of pleasure that he did not stand fast—but a noble pleasure; for telling the truth was noble to him, but he had been persuaded by Odysseus to tell the lie. For not everyone who does anything for the sake of pleasure is either self-indulgent or bad or incontinent, but he who does it for a disgraceful pleasure.

Since there is also a sort of man who takes *less* delight than he should in bodily things, and does not abide by the rule, he who is intermediate between him and the incontinent man is the continent man; for the incontinent man fails to abide by the rule because he delights too much in them, and this man because he delights in them too little; while the continent man abides by the rule and does not change on either account. Now if continence is good, both the contrary states must be bad, as they actually appear to be; but because the other extreme is seen in few people and seldom, as temperance is thought to be contrary only to self-indulgence, so is continence to incontinence.

Since many names are applied analogically, it is by analogy that we have come to speak of the 'continence' of the temperate man; for both the continent man and the temperate man are such as to do nothing contrary to the rule for the sake of the bodily pleasures, | but the former has and the latter has not bad appetites, and the latter is such as not to feel pleasure contrary to the rule, while the former is such as to feel pleasure but not to be led by it. And the incontinent and the self-indulgent man are also like one another; they are different, but both pursue bodily pleasures—the latter, however, also thinking that he ought to do so, while the former does not think this.

Practical wisdom is not compatible with incontinence, but cleverness is

10. Nor can the same man have practical wisdom and be incontinent; for it has been shown[1] that a man is at the same time practically wise, and good in respect of character. Further, a man has practical wisdom not by knowing only but by being able to act; but the incontinent man is unable to act—there is, however, nothing to prevent a *clever* man from being incontinent; this is why it is sometimes actually thought that some people have practical wisdom but are incontinent, viz. because cleverness and practical wisdom differ in the way we have described in our first discussions,[2] and are near together in respect of their reasoning, but differ in respect of their purpose—nor yet is the incontinent man like the man who knows and is contemplating a truth, but like the man who is asleep or drunk. And he acts willingly (for he acts in a sense with knowledge both of what he does and of the end to which he does it), but is not wicked, since his purpose is good; so that he is half-wicked. And he is not a criminal; for he does not act of malice aforethought; of the two types of incontinent man the one does not abide by the conclusions of his deliberation, while the excitable man does not deliberate at all. And thus the incontinent man is like a city which passes all the right decrees and has good laws, but makes no use of them, as in Anaxandrides' jesting remark,

The city willed it, that cares nought for laws;

[1] 1144ᵃ11–ᵇ32.   [2] 1144ᵃ23–ᵇ4.

but the wicked man is like a city that uses its laws, but
has wicked laws to use.

Now incontinence and continence are concerned
with that which is in excess of the state characteristic
of most men; for the continent man abides by his
resolutions more and the incontinent man less than
most men can.

Of the forms of incontinence, that of excitable people
is more curable than that of those who deliberate but do
not abide by their decisions, and those who are incontinent through habituation are more curable than those
in whom incontinence is innate; for it is easier to change
a habit than to change one's nature; even habit is hard
to change just because it is like nature, as Evenus says:

> I say that habit's but long practice, friend,
> And this becomes men's nature in the end.

We have now stated what continence, incontinence,
endurance, and softness are, and how these states are
related to each other.|

PLEASURE

Three views hostile to pleasure and the arguments for them

11. The study of pleasure and pain belongs to the pro-
vince of the political philosopher; for he is the architect
of the end, with a view to which we call one thing bad
and another good without qualification. Further, it is
one of our necessary tasks to consider them; for not
only did we lay it down that moral virtue and vice are
concerned with pains and pleasures,[1] but most people
say that happiness involves pleasure; this is why the
blessed man is called by a name derived from a word
meaning enjoyment.

1104ᵇ8–1105ᵃ13.

Now (1) some people think that no pleasure is a good, either in itself or incidentally, since the good and pleasure are not the same; (2) others think that some pleasures are good but that most are bad. (3) Again there is a third view, that even if all pleasures are goods, yet the best thing in the world cannot be pleasure. (1) The reasons given for the view that pleasure is not a good at all are (a) that every pleasure is a perceptible process to a natural state, and that no process is of the same kind as its end, e.g. no process of building of the same kind as a house. (b) A temperate man avoids pleasures. (c) A man of practical wisdom pursues what is free from pain, not what is pleasant. (d) The pleasures are a hindrance to thought, and the more so the more one delights in them, e.g. in sexual pleasure; for no one could think of anything while absorbed in this. (e) There is no art of pleasure; but every good is the product of some art. (f) Children and the brutes pursue pleasures. (2) The reasons for the view that not all pleasures are good are that (a) there are pleasures that are actually base and objects of reproach, and (b) there are harmful pleasures; for some pleasant things are unhealthy. (3) The reason for the view that the best thing in the world is not pleasure is that pleasure is not an end but a process.

Discussion of the view that pleasure is not a good

12. These are pretty much the things that are said. That it does not follow from these grounds that pleasure is not a good, or even the chief good, is plain from the following considerations. (A)¹ (a) First, since that which is good may be so in either of two senses (one thing good simply and another good for a particular person), natural constitutions and states of being, and

¹ (A) is the answer to (1 a) and (3).

therefore also the corresponding movements and processes, will be correspondingly divisible. Of those which
are thought to be bad some will be bad if taken without qualification but not bad for a particular person,
but worthy of his choice, and some will not be worthy
of choice even for a particular person, but only at a
particular time and for a short period, though not without qualification; while others are not even pleasures,
but seem to be so, viz. all those which involve pain and
whose end is curative, e.g. the processes that go on in
sick persons.

(b) Further, one kind of good being activity and another being state, the processes that restore us to our
natural state are only incidentally pleasant; for that
matter the activity at work in the appetites for them is
the activity of so much of our state and nature as has
remained unimpaired; for there are actually pleasures
that involve *no* pain or appetite (e.g. those of contempla-
tion), | the nature in such a case not being defective at
all. That the others are incidental is indicated by the fact
that men do not enjoy the same pleasant objects when
their nature is in its settled state as they do when it is
being replenished, but in the former case they enjoy
the things that are pleasant without qualification, in
the latter the contraries of these as well; for then they
enjoy even sharp and bitter things, none of which is
pleasant either by nature or without qualification. The
states they produce, therefore, are not pleasures naturally or without qualification; for as pleasant things
differ, so do the pleasures arising from them.

(c) Again, it is not necessary that there should be
something else better than pleasure, as some say the
end is better than the process; for pleasures are not
processes nor do they all involve process—they are
activities and ends; nor do they arise when we are

acquiring some faculty, but when we are exercising it; and not all pleasures have an end different from themselves, but only the pleasures of persons who are being led to the perfecting of their nature. This is why it is not right to say that pleasure is perceptible process, but it should rather be called activity of the natural state, and instead of 'perceptible' 'unimpeded'. It is thought by *some* people to be process just because they think it is in the strict sense *good*; for they think that activity is process, which it is not.

(B)[1] The view that pleasures are bad because some pleasant things are unhealthy is like saying that healthy things are bad because some healthy things are bad for money-making; both are bad in the respect mentioned, but they are not *bad* for *that* reason—indeed, thinking itself is sometimes injurious to health.

Neither practical wisdom nor any state of being is impeded by the pleasure arising from it; it is foreign pleasures that impede, for the pleasures arising from thinking and learning will make us think and learn all the more.

(C)[2] The fact that no pleasure is the product of any art arises naturally enough; there is no art of any other activity either, but only of the corresponding faculty; though for that matter the arts of the perfumer and the cook *are* thought to be arts of pleasure.

(D)[3] The arguments based on the grounds that the temperate man avoids pleasure and that the man of practical wisdom pursues the painless life, and that children and the brutes pursue pleasure, are all refuted by the same consideration. We have pointed out[4] in what sense pleasures are good without qualification and in what sense some are not good; now both the

---

[1] Answer to (2 *b*) and (1 *d*).   [3] Answer to (1 *e*).
[2] Answer to (1 *b*), (1 *c*), (1*f*).   [4] 1152ᵇ26–1153ª7.

brutes and children pursue pleasures of the latter kind (and the man of practical wisdom pursues tranquil freedom from that kind), viz. those which imply appetite and pain, i.e. the bodily pleasures (for it is these that are of this nature) and the excesses of them, in respect of which the self-indulgent man is self-indulgent. This is why the temperate man avoids these pleasures; for even he *has* pleasures of his own. |

Discussion of the view that pleasure is not the chief good

13. But further (E) it is agreed that pain is bad and to be avoided; for some pain is without qualification bad, and other pain is bad because it is in some respect an impediment to us. Now the contrary of that which is to be avoided, *qua* something to be avoided and bad, is good. Pleasure, then, is necessarily a good. For the answer of Speusippus, that pleasure is contrary both to pain and to good, as the greater is contrary both to the less and to the equal, is not successful; since he would not say that pleasure is essentially just a species of evil.

And (F)[1] if certain pleasures are bad, that does not prevent the chief good from being some pleasure, just as the chief good may be some form of knowledge though certain kinds of knowledge are bad. Perhaps it is even necessary, if each disposition has unimpeded activities, that, whether the activity (if unimpeded) of all our dispositions or that of some one of them is happiness, this should be the thing most worthy of our choice; and this activity is pleasure. Thus the chief good would be some pleasure, though most pleasures might perhaps be bad without qualification. And for this reason all men think that the happy life is pleasant and weave pleasure into their ideal of happiness—and reasonably too; for no activity is perfect when it is impeded, and

---

[1] Answer to (2 *a*).

happiness is a perfect thing; this is why the happy man needs the goods of the body and external goods, i.e. those of fortune, viz. in order that he may not be impeded in these ways. Those who say that the victim on the rack or the man who falls into great misfortunes is happy if he is good are, whether they mean to or not, talking nonsense. Now because we need fortune as well as other things, some people think good fortune the same thing as happiness; but it is not that, for even good fortune itself when in excess is an impediment, and perhaps should then be no longer called good fortune; for its limit is fixed by reference to happiness.

And indeed the fact that all things, both brutes and men, pursue pleasure is an indication of its being somehow the chief good:

No voice is wholly lost that many peoples . . . .

But since no one nature or state either is or is thought the best for all, neither do all pursue the same pleasure; yet all pursue pleasure. And perhaps they actually pursue not the pleasure they think they pursue nor that which they would say they pursue, but the same pleasure; for all things have by nature something divine in them. But the bodily pleasures have appropriated the name both because we oftenest steer our course for them and because all men share in them; thus, because they alone are familiar, men think there are no others. |

It is evident also that if pleasure, i.e. the activity of our faculties, is not a good, it will not be the case that the happy man lives a pleasant life; for to what end should he need pleasure, if it is not good but the happy man may even live a painful life? For pain is neither an evil nor a good, if pleasure is not; why then should he avoid it? Therefore, too, the life of the good man will not be pleasanter than that of anyone else, if his activities are not more pleasant.

Discussion of the view that most pleasures are bad, and of the tendency to identify bodily pleasures with pleasure in general

14. (G)¹ With regard to the bodily pleasures, those who say that *some* pleasures are very much to be chosen, viz. the noble pleasures, but not the bodily pleasures, i.e. those with which the self-indulgent man is concerned, must consider why, then, the contrary pains are bad. For the contrary of bad is good. Are the necessary pleasures good in the sense in which even that which is not bad is good? Or are they good up to a point? Is it that where you have states and processes of which there cannot be too much, there cannot be too much of the corresponding pleasure, and that where there can be too much of the one there can be too much of the other also? Now there can be too much of bodily goods, and the bad man is bad by virtue of pursuing the excess, not by virtue of pursuing the necessary pleasures (for *all* men enjoy in some way or other both dainty foods and wines and sexual intercourse, but not all men do so as they ought). The contrary is the case with pain; for he does not avoid the excess of it, he avoids it altogether; and this is peculiar to him, for the alternative to excess of pleasure is not pain, except to the man who pursues this excess.²

Since we should state not only the truth, but also the cause of error—for this contributes towards producing conviction, since when a reasonable explanation is given of why the false view appears true, this

¹ Answer to (2).
² I have expanded this sentence slightly to bring out the rather obscure connexion of thought. To the voluptuary, and to him alone, pain and violent bodily pleasure appear exhaustive alternatives, and because he always pursues the latter he always shuns the former.

tends to produce belief in the true view—therefore we must state why the bodily pleasures appear the more worthy of choice. (*a*) Firstly, then, it is because they expel pain; owing to the excesses of pain that men experience, they pursue excessive and in general bodily pleasure as being a cure for the pain. Now curative agencies produce intense feeling—which is the reason why they are pursued—because they show up against the contrary pain. (Indeed pleasure is thought not to be good for these two reasons, as has been said,[1] viz. that (α) some of them are activities belonging to a bad nature—either congenital, as in the case of a brute, or due to habit, i.e. those of bad men; while (β) others are meant to cure a defective nature, and it is better to be in a healthy state than to be getting into it, | but these arise during the process of being made perfect and are therefore only incidentally good.) (*b*) Further, they are pursued because of their violence by those who cannot enjoy other pleasures. (At all events they go out of their way to manufacture thirsts somehow for themselves. When these are harmless, the practice is irreproachable; when they are hurtful, it is bad.) For they have nothing else to enjoy and, besides, a neutral state is painful to many people because of their nature. For the animal nature is always in travail, as the students of natural science also testify, saying that sight and hearing are painful; but we have become used to this, as they maintain. Similarly, while, in youth, people are, owing to the growth that is going on, in a situation like that of drunken men, and youth is pleasant,[2] on the other hand people of excitable nature[3]

---

[1] 1152ᵇ26–33.

[2] i.e. the growth or replenishment that is going on produces exhilaration and pleasure.

[3] Lit., melancholic people, those characterized by an excess of black bile.

always need relief; for even their body is ever in tor-
ment owing to its special composition, and they are
always under the influence of violent desire; but pain is
driven out both by the contrary pleasure, and by any
chance pleasure if it be strong; and for these reasons
they become self-indulgent and bad. But the pleasures
that do not involve pains do not admit of excess; and
these are among the things pleasant by nature and not
incidentally. By things pleasant incidentally I mean
those that act as cures (for because as a result people
are cured, through some action of the part that remains healthy, for this reason the process is thought
pleasant); by things naturally pleasant I mean those
that stimulate the action of the healthy nature.

There is no one thing that is always pleasant, because our nature is not simple but there is another
element in us as well, inasmuch as we are perishable
creatures, so that if the one element does something,
this is unnatural to the other nature, and when the
two elements are evenly balanced, what is done seems
neither painful nor pleasant; for if the nature of anything were simple, the same action would always be
most pleasant to it. This is why God always enjoys a
single and simple pleasure; for there is not only an
activity of movement but an activity of immobility,
and pleasure is found more in rest than in movement.
But 'change in all things is sweet', as the poet says,
because of some vice; for as it is the vicious man that
is changeable, so the nature that needs change is
vicious; for it is not simple nor good.

We have now discussed continence and incontinence, and pleasure and pain, both what each is and
in what sense some of them are good and others bad;
it remains to speak of friendship. |

BOOK VIII · FRIENDSHIP

̄̄̄

KINDS OF FRIENDSHIP

Friendship both necessary and noble: main questions about it

1. AFTER what we have said, a discussion of friendship would naturally follow, since it is a virtue or implies virtue, and is besides most necessary with a view to living. For without friends no one would choose to live, though he had all other goods; even rich men and those in possession of office and of dominating power are thought to need friends most of all; for what is the use of such prosperity without the opportunity of beneficence, which is exercised chiefly and in its most laudable form towards friends? Or how can prosperity be guarded and preserved without friends? The greater it is, the more exposed is it to risk. And in poverty and in other misfortunes men think friends are the only refuge. It helps the young, too, to keep from error; it aids older people by ministering to their needs and supplementing the activities that are failing from weakness; those in the prime of life it stimulates to noble actions—'two going together'[1]—for with friends men are more able both to think and to act. Again, parent seems by nature to feel it for offspring and offspring for parent, not only among men but among birds and among most animals; it is felt mutually by members of the same race, and especially by men, whence we praise lovers of their fellow men. We may see even in our travels how near and dear every man is to every other. Friendship seems too to hold states together, and lawgivers to care more for it than for justice; for concord seems to be something like friendship, and this

Il. x. 224.

they aim at most of all, and expel faction as their worst enemy; and when men are friends they have no need of justice, while when they are just they need friendship as well, and the truest form of justice is thought to be a friendly quality.

But it is not only necessary but also noble; for we praise those who love their friends, and it is thought to be a fine thing to have many friends; and again we think it is the same people that are good men and are friends.

Not a few things about friendship are matters of debate. Some define it as a kind of likeness and say like people are friends, whence come the sayings 'like to like',¹ 'Birds of a feather flock together',² and so on; others on the contrary say 'Two of a trade never agree'.| On this very question they inquire for deeper and more physical causes, Euripides saying that 'Parched earth loves the rain, and stately heaven when filled with rain loves to fall to earth', and Heraclitus that 'It is what opposes that helps' and 'From different tones comes the fairest tune' and 'all things are produced through strife'; while Empedocles, as well as others, expresses the opposite view that like aims at like. The physical problems we may leave alone (for they do not belong to the present inquiry); let us examine those which are human and involve character and feeling, e.g. whether friendship can arise between any two people or people cannot be friends if they are wicked, and whether there is one species of friendship or more than one. Those who think there is only one because it admits of degrees have relied on an inadequate indication; for even things different in species admit of degree. We have discussed this matter previously.³

¹ *Od.* xvii. 218.   ² Lit. 'Jackdaw to jackdaw'. The source is unknown.
³ Place unknown.

Three objects of love: implications of friendship

2. The kinds of friendship may perhaps be cleared up if we first come to know the object of love. For not everything seems to be loved but only the lovable, and this is good, pleasant, or useful; but it would seem to be that by which some good or pleasure is produced that is useful, so that it is the good and the pleasant that are lovable as ends. Do men love, then, *the* good, or what is good *for them*? These sometimes clash. So too with regard to the pleasant. Now it is thought that each loves what is good for himself, and that the good is without qualification lovable, and what is good for each man is lovable for him; but each man loves not what is good for him but what seems good. This how-ever will make no difference; we shall just have to say that this is 'that which seems lovable'. Now there are three grounds on which people love: of the love of lifeless objects we do not use the word 'friendship', for it is not mutual love, nor is there a wishing of good to the other (for it would surely be ridiculous to wish wine well; if one wishes anything for it, it is that it may keep, so that one may have it oneself); but to a friend we say we ought to wish what is good for his sake. But to those who thus wish good we ascribe only goodwill, if the wish is not reciprocated; goodwill when it *is* reciprocal being friendship. Or must we add 'when it is recognized'? For many people have goodwill to those whom they have not seen but judge to be good or useful; | and one of these might return this feeling. These people seem to bear goodwill to each other; but how could one call them friends when they do not know their mutual feelings? To be friends, then, they must be mutually recognized as bearing goodwill and wish-ing well to each other for one of the aforesaid reasons.

*Three corresponding kinds of friendship: superiority of friend-
ship whose motive is good*

3. Now these reasons differ from each other in kind;
so, therefore, do the corresponding forms of love and
friendship. There are therefore three kinds of friendship, equal in number to the things that are lovable;
for with respect to each there is a mutual and recognized love, and those who love each other wish well to
each other in that respect in which they love one another. Now those who love each other for their utility
do not love each other for themselves but in virtue
of some good which they get from each other. So too
with those who love for the sake of pleasure; it is not
for their character that men love ready-witted people,
but because they find them pleasant. Therefore those
who love for the sake of utility love for the sake of what
is good *for themselves*, and those who love for the sake
of pleasure do so for the sake of what is pleasant *to
themselves*, and not in so far as the other is the person
loved but in so far as he is useful or pleasant. And thus
these friendships are only incidental; for it is not as
being the man he is that the loved person is loved,
but as providing some good or pleasure. Such friendships, then, are easily dissolved, if the parties do not
remain like themselves; for if the one party is no longer
pleasant or useful the other ceases to love him.

Now the useful is not permanent but is always changing. Thus when the motive of the friendship is done
away, the friendship is dissolved, inasmuch as it existed
only for the ends in question. This kind of friendship
seems to exist chiefly between old people (for at that
age people pursue not the pleasant but the useful) and,
of those who are in their prime or young, between those
who pursue utility. And such people do not live much

with each other either; for sometimes they do not even
find each other pleasant; therefore they do not need
such companionship unless they are useful to each
other; for they are pleasant to each other only in so far
as they rouse in each other hopes of something good
to come. Among such friendships people also class
the friendship of host and guest. On the other hand the
friendship of young people seems to aim at pleasure;
for they live under the guidance of emotion, and pursue
above all what is pleasant to themselves and what is
immediately before them; but with increasing age their
pleasures become different. This is why they quickly
become friends and quickly cease to be so; their friendship changes with the object that is found pleasant,
and such pleasure alters quickly. | Young people are
amorous too; for the greater part of the friendship of
love depends on emotion and aims at pleasure; this is
why they fall in love and quickly fall out of love, changing often within a single day. But these people do wish
to spend their days and lives together; for it is thus that
they attain the purpose of their friendship.

Perfect friendship is the friendship of men who are
good, and alike in virtue; for these wish well alike to
each other *qua* good, and they are good in themselves.
Now those who wish well to their friends for their sake
are most truly friends; for they do this by reason of
their own nature and not incidentally; therefore their
friendship lasts as long as they are good—and goodness is an enduring thing. And each is good without
qualification and to his friend, for the good are both
good without qualification and useful to each other.
So too they are pleasant; for the good are pleasant
both without qualification and to each other, since to
each his own activities and others like them are plea-
surable, and the actions of the good *are* the same or

like. And such a friendship is as, might be expected, permanent, since there meet in it all the qualities that friends should have. For all friendship is for the sake of good or of pleasure— good or pleasure either in the abstract or such as will be enjoyed by him who has the friendly feeling—and is based on a certain resemblance; and to a friendship of good men all the qualities we have named belong in virtue of the nature of the friends themselves; for in the case of this kind of friendship the other qualities also[1] are alike in both friends, and that which is good without qualification is also without qualification pleasant, and these are the most lovable qualities. Love and friendship therefore are found most and in their best form between such men.

But it is natural that such friendships should be infrequent; for such men are rare. Further, such friendship requires time and familiarity; as the proverb says, men cannot know each other till they have 'eaten salt together'; nor can they admit each other to friendship or be friends till each has been found lovable and been trusted by each. Those who quickly show the marks of friendship to each other wish to be friends, but are not friends unless they both are lovable and know the fact; for a wish for friendship may arise quickly, but friendship does not.

Contrast between the best and inferior kinds

4. This kind of friendship, then, is perfect both in respect of duration and in all other respects, and in it each gets from each in all respects the same as, or something like what, he gives; which is what ought to happen between friends. Friendship for the sake of pleasure bears a resemblance to this kind; | for good

---

[1] i.e. absolute pleasantness, relative goodness, and relative pleasantness, as well as absolute goodness.

people too *are* pleasant to each other. So too does friendship for the sake of utility; for the good are also useful to each other. Among men of these inferior sorts too, friendships are most permanent when the friends get the same thing from each other (e.g. pleasure), and not only that but also from the same source, as happens between ready-witted people, not as happens between lover and beloved. For these do not take pleasure in the same things, but the one in seeing the beloved and the other in receiving attentions from his lover; and when the bloom of youth is passing the friendship sometimes passes too (for the one finds no pleasure in the sight of the other, and the other gets no attentions from the first); but many lovers on the other hand are constant, if familiarity has led them to love each other's characters, these being alike. But those who exchange not pleasure but utility in their amour are both less truly friends and less constant. Those who are friends for the sake of utility part when the advantage is at an end; for they were lovers not of each other but of profit.

For the sake of pleasure or utility, then, even bad men may be friends of each other, or good men of bad, or one who is neither good nor bad may be a friend to any sort of person, but for their own sake clearly only good men can be friends; for bad men do not delight in each other unless some advantage come of the relation.

The friendship of the good too, and this alone, is proof against slander; for it is not easy to trust anyone's talk about a man who has long been tested by oneself; and it is among good men that trust and the feeling that 'he would never wrong me' and all the other things that are demanded in true friendship are found. In the other kinds of friendship, however, there is nothing to prevent these evils arising.

For men apply the name of friends even to those whose motive is utility, in which sense states are said to be friendly (for the alliances of states seem to aim at advantage), and to those who love each other for the sake of pleasure, in which sense children are called friends. Therefore we too ought perhaps to call such people friends, and say that there are several kinds of friendship—firstly and in the proper sense that of good men *qua* good, and by analogy the other kinds; for it is in virtue of something good and something akin to what is found in true friendship that they are friends, since even the pleasant is good for the lovers of pleasure. But these two kinds of friendship are not often united, nor do the same people become friends for the sake of utility and of pleasure; for things that are only incidentally connected are not often coupled together.|

Friendship being divided into these kinds, bad men will be friends for the sake of pleasure or of utility, being in this respect like each other, but good men will be friends for their own sake, i.e. in virtue of their goodness. These, then, are friends without qualification; the others are friends incidentally and through a resemblance to these.

The state of friendship distinguished from the activity of friendship and from the feeling of friendliness

5. As in regard to the virtues some men are called good in respect of a state of character, others in respect of an activity, so too in the case of friendship; for those who live together delight in each other and confer benefits on each other, but those who are asleep or locally separated are not performing, but are disposed to perform, the activities of friendship; distance does not break off the friendship absolutely, but only the activity of it. But if the absence is lasting, it seems

actually to make men forget their friendship; hence the saying 'Out of sight, out of mind'.[1] Neither old people nor sour people seem to make friends easily; for there is little that is pleasant in them, and no one can spend his days with one whose company is painful, or not pleasant, since nature seems above all to avoid the painful and to aim at the pleasant. Those, however, who approve of each other but do not live together seem to be well disposed rather than actual friends. For there is nothing so characteristic of friends as living together (since while it is people who are in need that desire benefits, even those who are supremely happy desire to spend their days together; for solitude suits such people least of all); but people cannot live together if they are not pleasant and do not enjoy the same things, as friends who are companions seem to do.

The truest friendship, then, is that of the good, as we have frequently said;[2] for that which is without qualification good or pleasant seems to be lovable and desirable, and for each person that which is good or pleasant to him; and the good man is lovable and desirable to the good man for both these reasons. Now it looks as if love were a feeling, friendship a state of character; for love may be felt just as much towards lifeless things, but mutual love involves choice and choice springs from a state of character; and men wish well to those whom they love, for their sake, not as a result of feeling but as a result of a state of character. And in loving a friend men love what is good for themselves; for the good man in becoming a friend becomes a good to his friend. Each, then, both loves what is good for himself, and makes an equal return in goodwill and in pleasantness; for friendship is said to be

[1] Lit. 'Many a friendship has lack of converse broken'. The source is unknown.   [2] 1156ᵇ7, 23, 33, 1157ᵃ30, ᵇ4.

equality, and both of these are found most in the friendship of the good. |

Various relations between the three kinds

6. Between sour and elderly people friendship arises less readily, inasmuch as they are less good-tempered and enjoy companionship less; for these are thought to be the greatest marks of friendship and most productive of it. This is why, while young men become friends quickly, old men do not; it is because men do not become friends with those in whom they do not delight; and similarly sour people do not quickly make friends either. But such men may bear goodwill to each other; for they wish one another well and aid one another in need; but they are hardly *friends*, because they do not spend their days together or delight in each other, and these are thought the greatest marks of friendship.

One cannot be a friend to many people in the sense of having friendship of the perfect type with them, just as one cannot be in love with many people at once (for love is a sort of excess of feeling, and it is the nature of such only to be felt towards one person); and it is not easy for many people at the same time to please the same person very greatly, or perhaps even to be good in his eyes. One must, too, acquire some experience of the other person and become familiar with him, and that is very hard. But with a view to utility or pleasure it is possible that many people should please one; for many people are useful or pleasant, and these services take little time.

Of these two kinds that which is for the sake of pleasure is the more like friendship, when both parties get the same things from each other and delight in each other or in the same things, as in the friendships of the young; for generosity is more found in such friendships. Friendship based on utility is for the commercially minded. People who are supremely happy, too, have no need of useful friends, but do need pleasant friends; for they wish to live with *someone* and, though they can endure for a short time what is painful, no one could put up with it continuously, nor even with the Good itself if it were painful to him; this is why they look out for friends who are pleasant. Perhaps they should look out for friends who, being pleasant, are also good, and good for them too; for so they will have all the characteristics that friends should have.

People in positions of authority seem to have friends who fall into distinct classes; some people are useful to them and others are pleasant, but the same people are rarely both; for they seek neither those whose pleasantness is accompanied by virtue nor those whose utility is with a view to noble objects, but in their desire for pleasure they seek for ready-witted people, and their other friends they choose as being clever at doing what they are told, and these characteristics are rarely combined. Now we have said that the *good* man *is* at the same time pleasant and useful;[1] but such a man does not become the friend of one who surpasses him in station, unless he is surpassed also in virtue; if this is not so, he does not establish equality, by being proportionally exceeded in both respects. But people who surpass him in both respects are not so easy to find. |

However that may be, the aforesaid friendships involve equality; for the friends get the same things from one another and wish the same things for one another, or exchange one thing for another, e.g. pleasure for utility; we have said,[2] however, that they are both less truly friendships and less permanent. But it is from

---

[1] 1156ᵇ13–15, 1157ª1–3.   [2] 1156ª16–24, 1157ª20–33.

their likeness and their unlikeness to the same thing
that they are thought both to be and not to be friendships. It is by their likeness to the friendship of virtue
that they seem to be friendships (for one of them involves pleasure and the other utility, and these characteristics belong to the friendship of virtue as well);
while it is because the friendship of virtue is proof
against slander and permanent, while these quickly
change (besides differing from the former in many
other respects), that they appear *not* to be friendships;
i.e. it is because of their unlikeness to the friendship of
virtue.

RECIPROCITY OF FRIENDSHIP

In unequal friendships a proportion must be maintained

7. But there is another kind of friendship, viz. that
which involves an inequality between the parties, e.g.
that of father to son and in general of elder to younger,
that of man to wife and in general that of ruler to subject. And these friendships differ also from each other;
for it is not the same that exists between parents and
children and between rulers and subjects, nor is even
that of father to son the same as that of son to father, nor
that of husband to wife the same as that of wife to husband. For the virtue and the function of each of these
is different, and so are the reasons for which they love;
the love and the friendship are therefore different also.
Each party, then, neither gets the same from the other,
nor ought to seek it; but when children render to parents
what they ought to render to those who brought them
into the world, and parents render what they should
to their children, the friendship of such persons will be
abiding and excellent. In all friendships implying inequality the love also should be proportional, i.e. the

better should be more loved than he loves, and so should the more useful, and similarly in each of the other cases; for when the love is in proportion to the merit of the parties, then in a sense arises equality, which is certainly held to be characteristic of friendship.

But equality does not seem to take the same form in acts of justice and in friendship; for in acts of justice what is equal in the primary sense is that which is in proportion to merit, while quantitative equality is secondary, but in friendship quantitative equality is primary and proportion to merit secondary. This becomes clear if there is a great interval in respect of virtue or vice or wealth or anything else between the parties; for then they are no longer friends, and do not even expect to be so. And this is most manifest in the case of the gods; for they surpass us most decisively in all good things. But it is clear also in the case of kings; | for with them, too, men who are much their inferiors do not expect to be friends; nor do men of no account expect to be friends with the best or wisest men. In such cases it is not possible to define exactly up to what point friends can remain friends; for much can be taken away and friendship remain, but when one party is removed to a great distance, as God is, the possibility of friendship ceases. This is in fact the origin of the question whether friends really wish for their friends the greatest goods, e.g. that of being gods; since in that case their friends will no longer be friends to them, and therefore will not be good things for them (for friends *are* good things). The answer is that if we were right in saying that friend wishes good to friend for his sake,[1] his friend must remain the sort of being he is, whatever that may be; therefore it is for him only so long as he remains a man that he will wish the greatest goods. But perhaps not

[1] 1155^b31.

all the greatest goods; for it is for himself most of all that each man wishes what is good.

Loving is more of the essence of friendship than being loved

8. Most people seem, owing to ambition, to wish to be loved rather than to love; which is why most men love flattery; for the flatterer is a friend in an inferior position, or pretends to be such and to love more than he is loved; and being loved seems to be akin to being honoured, and this is what most people aim at. But it seems to be not for its own sake that people choose honour, but incidentally. For most people enjoy being honoured by those in positions of authority because of their hopes (for they think that if they want anything they will get it from them; and therefore they delight in honour as a token of favour to come); while those who desire honour from good men, and men who know, are aiming at confirming their own opinion of themselves; they delight in honour, therefore, because they believe in their own goodness on the strength of the judgement of those who speak about them. In being loved, on the other hand, people delight for its own sake; whence it would seem to be better than being honoured, and friendship to be desirable in itself. But it seems to lie in loving rather than in being loved, as is indicated by the delight mothers take in loving; for some mothers hand over their children to be brought up, and so long as they know their fate they love them and do not seek to be loved in return (if they cannot have both), but seem to be satisfied if they see them prospering; and they themselves love their children even if these owing to their ignorance give them nothing of a mother's due. Now since friendship depends more on loving, and it is those who love their friends that are praised, loving seems to be the characteristic virtue of friends, so that it is only those in whom this is found in due measure that are lasting friends, and only their friendship that endures. |

It is in this way more than any other that even un-equals can be friends; they can be equalized. Now equality and likeness are friendship, and especially the likeness of those who are like in virtue; for being stead-fast in themselves they hold fast to each other, and neither ask nor give base services, but (one may say) even prevent them; for it is characteristic of good men neither to go wrong themselves nor to let their friends do so. But wicked men have no steadfastness (for they do not remain even like to themselves), but become friends for a short time because they delight in each other's wickedness. Friends who are useful or pleasant last longer; i.e. as long as they provide each other with en-joyments or advantages. Friendship for utility's sake seems to be that which most easily exists between con-traries, e.g. between poor and rich, between ignorant and learned; for what a man actually lacks he aims at, and one gives something else in return. But under this head, too, one might bring lover and beloved, beautiful and ugly. This is why lovers sometimes seem ridiculous, when they demand to be loved as they love; if they are equally lovable their claim can perhaps be justified, but when they have nothing lovable about them it is ridiculous. Perhaps, however, contrary does not even aim at contrary by its own nature, but only inciden-tally, the desire being for what is intermediate; for that is what is good, e.g. it is good for the dry not to be-come wet[1] but to come to the intermediate state, and similarly with the hot and in all other cases. These sub-jects we may dismiss; for they are indeed somewhat foreign to our inquiry.

[1] Cf. 1155ᵇ3.

RELATION OF RECIPROCITY IN FRIENDSHIP
TO THAT INVOLVED IN OTHER FORMS OF
COMMUNITY

*Parallelism of friendship and justice: the state comprehends
all lesser communities*

9. Friendship and justice seem, as we have said at the
outset of our discussion,[1] to be concerned with the
same objects and exhibited between the same persons.
For in every community there is thought to be some
form of justice, and friendship too; at least men address
as friends their fellow voyagers and fellow soldiers, and
so too those associated with them in any other kind of
community. And the extent of their association is the
extent of their friendship, as it is the extent to which
justice exists between them. And the proverb 'What
friends have is common property' expresses the truth;
for friendship depends on community. Now brothers
and comrades have all things in common, but the
others to whom we have referred have definite things in
common—some more things, others fewer; for of friendships, too, some are more and others less truly friendships. And the claims of justice differ too; the duties of
parents to children | and those of brothers to each other
are not the same, nor those of comrades and those of
fellow citizens, and so, too, with the other kinds of
friendship. There is a difference, therefore, also between the acts that are unjust towards each of these
classes of associates, and the injustice increases by being exhibited towards those who are friends in a fuller
sense; e.g. it is a more terrible thing to defraud a comrade than a fellow citizen, more terrible not to help a
brother than a stranger, and more terrible to wound a

[1] 1155^a22–28.

father than anyone else. And the demands of justice also seem to increase with the intensity of the friendship, which implies that friendship and justice exist between the same persons and have an equal extension.

Now all forms of community are like parts of the political community; for men journey together with a view to some particular advantage, and to provide something that they need for the purposes of life; and it is for the sake of advantage that the political community too seems both to have come together originally and to endure, for this is what legislators aim at, and they call just that which is to the common advantage. Now the other communities aim at advantage bit by bit, e.g. sailors at what is advantageous on a voyage with a view to making money or something of the kind, fellow soldiers at what is advantageous in war, whether it is wealth or victory or the taking of a city that they seek, and members of tribes and demes act similarly [Some communities seem to arise for the sake of pleasure, viz. religious guilds and social clubs; for these exist respectively for the sake of offering sacrifice and of companionship. But all these seem to fall under the political community; for it aims not at present advantage but at what is advantageous for life as a whole],[1] offering sacrifices and arranging gatherings for the purpose, and assigning honours to the gods, and providing pleasant relaxations for themselves. For the ancient sacrifices and gatherings seem to take place after the harvest as a sort of firstfruits, because it was at these seasons that people had most leisure. All the communities, then, seem to be parts of the political community; and the particular kinds of friendship will correspond to the particular kinds of community.

---

[1] It seems best to treat ll. 19–23 as an insertion from an alternative version.

Classification of constitutions: analogies with family relations

10. There are three kinds of constitution, and an equal number of deviation-forms—perversions, as it were, of them. The constitutions are monarchy, aristocracy, and thirdly that which is based on a property qualification, which it seems appropriate to call timocratic, though most people are wont to call it polity. The best of these is monarchy, the worst timocracy. The deviation from monarchy is tyranny; | for both are forms of one-man rule, but there is the greatest difference between them: the tyrant looks to his own advantage, the king to that of his subjects. For a man is not a king unless he is sufficient to himself and excels his subjects in all good things; and such a man needs nothing further; therefore he will not look to his own interests but to those of his subjects; for a king who is not like that would be a mere titular king. Now tyranny is the very contrary of this; the tyrant pursues his own good. And it is clearer in the case of tyranny that it is the worst deviation-form;[1] but it is the contrary of the best that is worst.[2] Monarchy passes over into tyranny; for tyranny is the evil form of one-man rule and the bad king becomes a tyrant. Aristocracy passes over into oligarchy by the badness of the rulers, who distribute contrary to equity what belongs to the city—all or most of the good things to themselves, and office always to the same people, paying most regard to wealth; thus the rulers are few and are bad men instead of the most worthy. Timocracy passes over into democracy; for these are co-terminous, since it is the ideal even of timocracy to be the rule of the majority, and all who have the property qualification count as equal. Democracy

---

[1] *Sc.* than it is that monarchy is the best genuine form (ª35),
[2] Therefore monarchy must be the best.

is the least bad of the deviations; for in its case the form of constitution is but a slight deviation. These then are the changes to which constitutions are most subject; for these are the smallest and easiest transitions.

One may find resemblances to the constitutions and, as it were, patterns of them even in households. For the association of a father with his sons bears the form of monarchy, since the father cares for his children; and this is why Homer calls Zeus 'father';[1] it is the ideal of monarchy to be paternal rule. But among the Persians the rule of the father is tyrannical; they use their sons as slaves. Tyrannical too is the rule of a master over slaves; for it is the advantage of the master that is brought about in it. Now this seems to be a correct form of government, but the Persian type is perverted; for the modes of rule appropriate to different relations are diverse. The association of man and wife seems to be aristocratic; for the man rules in accordance with his worth, and in those matters in which a man should rule, but the matters that befit a woman he hands over to her. If the man rules in everything the relation passes over into oligarchy; for in doing so he is not acting in accordance with their respective worth, and not ruling in virtue of his superiority. | Sometimes, however, women rule, because they are heiresses; so their rule is not in virtue of excellence but due to wealth and power, as in oligarchies. The association of brothers is like timocracy; for they are equal, except in so far as they differ in age; hence if they differ *much* in age, the friendship is no longer of the fraternal type. Democracy is found chiefly in masterless dwellings (for here everyone is on an equality), and in those in which the ruler is weak and every one has licence to do as he pleases.

---

[1] e.g. *Il.* i. 503.

Corresponding forms of friendship, and of justice

11. Each of the constitutions may be seen to involve friendship just in so far as it involves justice. The friendship between a king and his subjects depends on an excess of benefits conferred; for he confers benefits on his subjects if being a good man he cares for them with a view to their well-being, as a shepherd does for his sheep (whence Homer called Agamemnon 'shepherd of the peoples').[1] Such too is the friendship of a father, though this exceeds the other in the greatness of the benefits conferred; for he is responsible for the existence of his children, which is thought the greatest good, and for their nurture and upbringing. These things are ascribed to ancestors as well. Further, by nature a father tends to rule over his sons, ancestors over descendants, a king over his subjects. These friendships imply superiority of one party over the other, which is why ancestors are honoured. The justice therefore that exists between persons so related is not the same on both sides but is in every case proportioned to merit; for that is true of the friendship as well. The friendship of man and wife, again, is the same that is found in an aristocracy; for it is in accordance with virtue—the better gets more of what is good, and each gets what befits him; and so, too, with the justice in these relations. The friendship of brothers is like that of comrades; for they are equal and of like age, and such persons are for the most part like in their feelings and their character. Like this, too, is the friendship appropriate to timocratic government; for in such a constitution the ideal is for the citizens to be equal and fair; therefore rule is taken in turn, and on equal terms; and the friendship appropriate here will correspond.

[1] e.g. *Il.* ii. 243.

But in the deviation-forms, as justice hardly exists, so too does friendship. It exists least in the worst form: in tyranny there is little or no friendship. For where there is nothing common to ruler and ruled, there is not friendship either, since there is not justice; e.g. between craftsman and tool, soul and body, master and slave; the latter in each case is benefited by that which uses it, but there is no friendship or justice towards lifeless things. But neither is there friendship towards a horse or an ox, nor to a slave *qua* slave. For there is nothing common to the two parties; the slave is a living tool and the tool a lifeless slave. *Qua* slave, then, one cannot be friends with him. But *qua* man one can; for there seems to be some justice between any man and any other who can share in a system of law or be a party to an agreement; therefore there can also be friendship with him in so far as he is a man. Therefore while in tyrannies friendship and justice hardly exist, in democracies they exist more fully; for where the citizens are equal they have much in common.

Various forms of friendship between relations

12. Every form of friendship, then, involves association, as has been said.[1] One might, however, mark off from the rest both the friendship of kindred and that of comrades. Those of fellow citizens, fellow tribesmen, fellow voyagers, and the like are more like mere friendships of association; for they seem to rest on a sort of compact. With them we might class the friendship of host and guest.

The friendship of kinsmen itself, while it seems to be of many kinds, appears to depend in every case on parental friendship; for parents love their children as being a part of themselves, and children their parents

[1] 1159ᵇ29–32.

as having themselves originated from them. Now (1) parents know their offspring better than their children know that they are their children, and (2) the originator feels his offspring to be his own more than the offspring do their begetter; for the product belongs to the producer (e.g. a tooth or hair or anything else to him whose it is), but the producer does not belong to the product, or belongs in a less degree. And (3) the length of time produces the same result; parents love their children as soon as these are born, but children love their parents only after time has elapsed and they have acquired understanding or the power of discrimination by the senses. From these considerations it is also plain why mothers love more than fathers do. Parents, then, love their children as themselves (for their issue are by virtue of their separate existence a sort of other selves), while children love their parents as being born of them, and brothers love each other as being born of the same parents; for their identity with them makes them identical with each other (which is the reason why people talk of 'the same blood', 'the same stock', and so on). They are, therefore, in a sense the same thing, though in separate individuals. Two things that contribute greatly to friendship are a common upbringing and similarity of age; for 'two of an age take to each other', and people brought up together tend to be comrades; whence the friendship of brothers is akin to that of comrades. | And cousins and other kinsmen are bound up together by derivation from brothers, viz. by being derived from the same parents. They come to be closer together or farther apart by virtue of the nearness or distance of the original ancestor.

The friendship of children to parents, and of men to gods, is a relation to them as to something good and superior; for they have conferred the greatest benefits,

since they are the causes of their being and of their
nourishment, and of their education from their birth;
and this kind of friendship possesses pleasantness and
utility also, more than that of strangers, inasmuch as
their life is lived more in common. The friendship of
brothers has the characteristics found in that of comrades (and especially when these are good), and in
general between people who are like each other, inasmuch as they belong more to each other and start with
a love for each other from their very birth, and inasmuch as those born of the same parents and brought up
together and similarly educated are more akin in character; and the test of time has been applied most fully
and convincingly in their case.

Between other kinsmen friendly relations are found
in due proportion. Between man and wife friendship
seems to exist by nature; for man is naturally inclined
to form couples—even more than to form cities, inasmuch as the household is earlier and more necessary
than the city, and reproduction is more common to
man with the animals. With the other animals the
union extends only to this point, but human beings live
together not only for the sake of reproduction but also
for the various purposes of life; for from the start the
functions are divided, and those of man and woman
are different; so they help each other by throwing their
peculiar gifts into the common stock. It is for these
reasons that both utility and pleasure seem to be found
in this kind of friendship. But this friendship may be
based also on virtue, if the parties are good; for each
has its own virtue and they will delight in the fact. And
children seem to be a bond of union (which is the reason why childless people part more easily); for children are a good common to both and what is common
holds them together.

How man and wife and in general friend and friend ought mutually to behave seems to be the same question as how it is just for them to behave; for a man does not seem to have the same duties to a friend, a stranger, a comrade, and a schoolfellow.

CASUISTRY OF FRIENDSHIP

Principles to be observed (a) in friendship between equals

13. There are three kinds of friendship, as we said at the outset of our inquiry,[1] and in respect of each some are friends on an equality and others by virtue of a superiority (for not only can equally good men become friends but a better man can make friends with a worse, | and similarly in friendships of pleasure or utility the friends may be equal or unequal in the benefits they confer). This being so, equals must effect the required equalization on a basis of equality in love and in all other respects, while unequals must render what is in proportion to their superiority or inferiority.

Complaints and reproaches arise either only or chiefly in the friendship of utility, and this is only to be expected. For those who are friends on the ground of virtue are anxious to do well by each other (since that is a mark of virtue and of friendship), and between men who are emulating each other in this there cannot be complaints or quarrels; no one is offended by a man who loves him and does well by him—if he is a person of nice feeling he takes his revenge by doing well by the other. And the man who excels the other in the services he renders will not complain of his friend, since he gets what he aims at; for each man desires what is good. Nor do complaints arise much even in friendships of pleasure; for both get at the same time what they desire,

[1] 1156ª7.

215

if they enjoy spending their time together; and even a man who complained of another for *not* affording him pleasure would seem ridiculous, since it is in his power not to spend his days with him.

But the friendship of utility is full of complaints; for as they use each other for their own interests they always want to get the better of the bargain, and think they have got less than they should, and blame their partners because they do not get all they 'want and deserve'; and those who do well by others cannot help them as much as those whom they benefit want.

Now it seems that, as justice is of two kinds, one unwritten and the other legal, one kind of friendship of utility is moral and the other legal. And so complaints arise most of all when men do not dissolve the relation in the spirit of the same type of friendship in which they contracted it. The *legal* type is that which is on fixed terms; its purely commercial variety is on the basis of immediate payment, while the more liberal variety allows time but stipulates for a definite *quid pro quo*. In this variety the debt is clear and not ambiguous, but in the postponement it contains an element of friendliness; and so some states do not allow suits arising out of such agreements, but think men who have bargained on a basis of credit ought to accept the consequences. The *moral* type is not on fixed terms; it makes a gift, or does whatever it does, as to a friend; but one expects to receive as much or more, as having not given but lent; and if a man is worse off when the relation is dissolved than he was when it was contracted he will complain. This happens because all or most men, while they wish for what is noble, choose what is advantageous; now it is noble to do well by another without a view to repayment, but it is the receiving of benefits that is advantageous. |

Therefore if we can we should return the equivalent of what we have received (for we must not make a man our friend against his will; we must recognize that we were mistaken at the first and took a benefit from a person we should not have taken it from—since it was not from a friend, nor from one who did it just for the sake of acting so—and we must settle up just as if we had been benefited on fixed terms). Indeed, one would agree to repay[1] if one could (if one could not, even the giver would not have expected one to do so); therefore if it is possible we must repay. But at the outset we must consider the man by whom we are being benefited and on what terms he is acting, in order that we may accept the benefit on these terms, or else decline it.

It is disputable whether we ought to measure a service by its utility to the receiver and make the return with a view to that, or by the beneficence of the giver. For those who have received say they have received from their benefactors what meant little to the latter and what they might have got from others—minimizing the service; while the givers, on the contrary, say it was the biggest thing they had, and what could not have been got from others, and that it was given in times of danger or similar need. Now if the friendship is one that aims at *utility*, surely the advantage to the receiver is the measure. For it is he that asks for the service, and the other man helps him on the assumption that he will receive the equivalent; so the assistance has been precisely as great as the advantage to the receiver, and therefore he must return as much as he has received, or even more (for that would be nobler). In friendships based on *virtue*, on the other hand, com-

---

[1] It seems possible to keep the MS. reading, and suppose Aristotle to mean that in such a case, though we made no promise when we got the service, we should be willing, if we were asked, to promise to repay if we could.

plaints do not arise, but the purpose of the doer is a sort of measure; for in purpose lies the essential element of virtue and character.

Principles to be observed (b) in friendship between unequals

14. Differences arise also in friendships based on superiority; for each expects to get more out of them, but when this happens the friendship is dissolved. Not only does the better man think he ought to get more, since more should be assigned to a good man, but the more useful similarly expects this; they say a useless man should not get as much as they should, since it becomes an act of public service and not a friendship if the proceeds of the friendship do not answer to the worth of the benefits conferred. For they think that, as in a commercial partnership those who put more in get more out, so it should be in friendship. But the man who is in a state of need and inferiority makes the opposite claim; such men think it is the part of a good friend to help those who are in need; what, they say, is the use of being the friend of a good man or a powerful man, if one is to get nothing out of it? |

At all events it seems that each party is justified in his claim, and that each should get more out of the friendship than the other—not more of the same thing, however, but the superior more honour and the inferior more gain; for honour is the prize of virtue and of beneficence, while gain is the assistance required by inferiority.

It seems to be so in constitutional arrangements also; the man who contributes nothing good to the common stock is not honoured; for what belongs to the public is given to the man who benefits the public, and honour does belong to the public. It is not possible to get wealth from the common stock and at the same time honour. For no one puts up with the smaller share in *all* things; therefore to the man who loses in wealth they assign honour and to the man who is willing to be paid, wealth, since the proportion to merit equalizes the parties and preserves the friendship, as we have said.[1]

This then is also the way in which we should associate with unequals; the man who is benefited in respect of wealth or virtue must give honour in return, repaying what he can. For friendship asks a man to do what he can, not what is proportional to the merits of the case; since that cannot always be done, e.g. in honours paid to the gods or to parents; for no one could ever return to them the equivalent of what he gets, but the man who serves them to the utmost of his power is thought to be a good man.

This is why it would not seem open to a man to disown his father (though a father may disown his son); being in debt, he should repay, but there is nothing by doing which a son will have done the equivalent of what he has received, so that he is always in debt. But creditors can remit a debt; and a father can therefore do so too. At the same time it is thought that presumably no one would repudiate a son who was not far gone in wickedness; for apart from the natural friendship of father and son it is human nature not to reject a son's assistance. But the son, if he *is* wicked, will naturally avoid aiding his father, or not be zealous about it; for most people wish to get benefits, but avoid doing them, as a thing unprofitable.—So much for these questions.

---

[1] 1162ª34–ᵇ4, cf. 1158ᵇ27, 1159ª35–ᵇ3.

*Principles to be observed (c) where the motives on the two sides
are different*

1. In all friendships between dissimilars it is, as we
have said,[1] proportion that equalizes the parties and
preserves the friendship; e.g. in the political form of
friendship the shoemaker gets a return for his shoes in
proportion to his worth, and the weaver and all other
craftsmen do the same. | Now here a common measure
has been provided in the form of money, and therefore
everything is referred to this and measured by this; but
in the friendship of lovers sometimes the lover complains that his excess of love is not met by love in return
(though perhaps there is nothing lovable about him),
while often the beloved complains that the lover who
formerly promised everything now performs nothing.
Such incidents happen when the lover loves the beloved for the sake of pleasure while the beloved loves
the lover for the sake of utility, and they do not both
possess the qualities expected of them. If these be the
objects of the friendship it is dissolved when they do not
get the things that formed the motives of their love; for
each did not love the other person himself but the
qualities he had, and these were not enduring; that is
why the friendships also are transient. But the love of
characters, as has been said, endures because it is self-
dependent.[2] Differences arise when what they get is
something different and not what they desire; for it is
like getting nothing at all when we do not get what we
aim at; compare the story of the person who made

[1] This has not been said precisely of friendship between dissimilars,
but cf. 1132^{b}31–33, 1158^{b}27, 1159^{a}35–^{b}3, 1162^{a}34–^{b}4, 1163^{b}11.
[2] 1156^{b}9–12.

promises to a lyre-player, promising him the more, the better he sang, but in the morning, when the other demanded the fulfilment of his promises, said that he had given pleasure[1] for pleasure. Now if this had been what each wanted, all would have been well; but if the one wanted enjoyment but the other gain, and the one has what he wants while the other has not, the terms of the association will not have been properly fulfilled; for what each in fact wants is what he attends to, and it is for the sake of that that he will give what he has.

But who is to fix the worth of the service; he who makes the sacrifice or he who has got the advantage? At any rate the other seems to leave it to him. This is what they say Protagoras used to do: whenever he taught anything whatsoever, he bade the learner assess the value of the knowledge, and accepted the amount so fixed. But in such matters some men approve of the saying 'Let a man have his fixed reward'.

Those who get the money first and then do none of the things they said they would, owing to the extravagance of their promises, naturally find themselves the objects of complaint; for they do not fulfil what they agreed to. The sophists are perhaps compelled to do this because no one would give money for the things they *do* know. These people, then, if they do not do what they have been paid for, are naturally made the objects of complaint.

But where there is *no* contract of service, those who give up something for the sake of the other party cannot (as we have said)[2] be complained of (for that is the nature of the friendship of virtue), | and the return to them must be made on the basis of their purpose (for it is purpose that is the characteristic thing in a friend and in virtue). And so too, it seems, should one make

---

[1] i.e. the pleasure of expectation.   [2] 1162ᵇ6–13.

a return to those with whom one has studied philosophy; for their worth cannot be measured against
money, and they can get no honour which will balance
their services, but still it is perhaps enough, as it is with
the gods and with one's parents, to give them what
one can.

If the gift was not of this sort, but was made with
a view to a return, it is no doubt preferable that the
return made should be one that seems fair to both
parties, but if this cannot be achieved, it would seem
not only necessary that the person who gets the first
service should fix the reward, but also just; for if the
other gets in return the equivalent of the advantage
the beneficiary has received, or the price he would
have paid for the pleasure, he will have got what is fair
as from the other.

We see this happening too with things put up for
sale, and in some places there are laws providing that
no actions shall arise out of voluntary contracts, on the
assumption that one should settle with a person to
whom one has given credit, in the spirit in which one
bargained with him. The law holds that it is more just
that the person to whom credit was given should fix the
terms than that the person who gave credit should do
so. For most things are not assessed at the same value
by those who have them and those who want them;
each class values highly what is its own and what it is
offering; yet the return is made on the terms fixed by
the receiver. But no doubt the receiver should assess
a thing not at what it seems worth when he has it, but
at what he assessed it at before he had it.

Conflict of obligations

2. A further problem is set by such questions as
whether one should in all things give the preference to

one's father and obey him, or whether when one is ill one should trust a doctor, and when one has to elect a general should elect a man of military skill; and similarly whether one should render a service by preference to a friend or to a good man, and should show gratitude to a benefactor or oblige a friend, if one cannot do both.

All such questions are hard, are they not, to decide with precision? For they admit of many variations of all sorts in respect both of the magnitude of the service and of its nobility and necessity. But that we should not give the preference in all things to the same person is plain enough; and we must for the most part return benefits rather than oblige friends, as we must pay back a loan to a creditor rather than make one to a friend. But perhaps even this is not always true; e.g. should a man who has been ransomed out of the hands of brigands ransom his ransomer in return, whoever he may be (or pay him if he has not been captured but demands payment), or should he ransom his father? | It would seem that he should ransom his father in preference even to himself. As we have said,¹ then, generally the debt should be paid, but if the gift is exceedingly noble or exceedingly necessary, one should defer to these considerations. For sometimes it is not even fair to return the equivalent of what one has received, when the one man has done a service to one whom he knows to be good, while the other makes a return to one whom he believes to be bad. For that matter, one should sometimes not lend in return to one who has lent to oneself; for the one person lent to a good man, expecting to recover his loan, while the other has no hope of recovering from one who is believed to be bad. Therefore if the facts really are so, the demand is not

¹ 1164ᵇ31–1165ᵃ2.

223

fair; and if they are not, but people think they are, they
would be held to be doing nothing strange in refusing.
As we have often pointed out,[1] then, discussions about
feelings and actions have only as much definiteness as
their subject-matter.

That we should not make the same return to everyone, nor give a father the preference in everything, as
one does not sacrifice everything to Zeus,[2] is plain
enough; but since we ought to render different things
to parents, brothers, comrades, and benefactors, we
ought to render to each class what is appropriate and
becoming. And this is what people seem in fact to do:
to marriages they invite their kinsfolk, for these have
a part in the family and therefore in the doings that
affect the family; and at funerals also they think that
kinsfolk, before all others, should meet, for the same
reason. And it would be thought that in the matter
of food we should help our parents before all others,
since we owe our own nourishment to them, and it is
more honourable to help in this respect the authors of
our being even before ourselves; and honour too one
should give to one's parents as one does to the gods,
but not any and every honour; for that matter one
should not give the same honour to one's father and
to one's mother, nor again should one give them the
honour due to a philosopher or to a general, but the
honour due to a father, or again to a mother. To all
older persons, too, one should give honour appropriate
to their age, by rising to receive them and finding seats
for them and so on; while to comrades and brothers
one should allow freedom of speech and common use
of all things. To kinsmen, too, and fellow tribesmen
and fellow citizens and to every other class one should

[1] 1094ᵇ11–27, 1098ª26–29, 1103ᵇ34–1104ª5.
[2] Cf. 1134ᵇ18–24.

always try to assign what is appropriate, and to compare the claims of each class with respect to nearness of relation and to virtue or usefulness. The comparison is easier when the persons belong to the same class, and more laborious when they are different. Yet we must not on *that* account shrink from the task, but decide the question as best we can.

Occasions of breaking off friendship

3. Another question that arises is whether friendships should or should not be broken off when the other party does not remain the same. | Perhaps we may say that there is nothing strange in breaking off a friendship based on utility or pleasantness, when our friends no longer have these attributes. For it was of these attributes that we were the friends; and when these have failed it is reasonable to love no longer. But one might complain of another if, when he loved us for our usefulness or pleasantness, he pretended to love us for our character. For, as we said at the outset,[1] most differences arise between friends when they are not friends in the spirit in which they think they are. So when a man has deceived himself and has thought he was being loved for his character, when the other person was doing nothing of the kind, he must blame himself; but when he has been deceived by the pretences of the other person, it is just that he should complain against his deceiver; he will complain with more justice than one does against people who counterfeit the currency, inasmuch as the wrongdoing is concerned with something more valuable.

But if one accepts another man as good, and he turns out badly and is seen to do so, must one still love him?

[1] 1162ᵇ23-25.

Surely it is impossible, since not everything can be loved, but only what is good. What is evil neither can nor should be loved; for it is not one's duty to be a lover of evil, or to become like what is bad; and we have said[1] that like is dear to like. Must the friendship, then, be forthwith broken off? Or is this not so in all cases, but only when one's friends are incurable in their wickedness? If they are capable of being reformed one should rather come to the assistance of their character or their property, inasmuch as this is better and more characteristic of friendship. But a man who breaks off such a friendship would seem to be doing nothing strange; for it was not to a man of this sort that he was a friend; when his friend has changed, therefore, and he is unable to save him, he gives him up.

But if one friend remained the same while the other became better and far outstripped him in virtue, should the latter treat the former as a friend? Surely he cannot. When the interval is great this becomes most plain, e.g. in the case of childish friendships; if one friend remained a child in intellect while the other became a fully developed man, how could they be friends when they neither approved of the same things nor delighted in and were pained by the same things? For not even with regard to each other will their tastes agree, and without this (as we saw)[2] they cannot be friends; for they cannot live together. But we have discussed these matters.[3]

Should he, then, behave no otherwise towards him than he would if he had never been his friend? Surely he should keep a remembrance of their former intimacy, and as we think we ought to oblige friends rather than strangers, so to those who have been our

---

[1] 1156ᵇ19–21, 1159ᵇ1.   [2] 1157ᵇ22–24.
[3] Ibid. 17–24, 1158ᵇ33–35.

friends we ought to make some allowance for our
former friendship, when the breach has not been due
to excess of wickedness. |

INTERNAL NATURE OF FRIENDSHIP

Friendship is based on self-love

4. Friendly relations with one's neighbours, and the
marks by which friendships are defined, seem to have
proceeded from a man's relations to himself. For (1) we
define a friend as one who wishes and does what is good,
or seems so, for the sake of his friend, or (2) as one who
wishes his friend to exist and live, for his sake; which
mothers do to their children, and friends do who have
come into conflict. And (3) others define him as one
who lives with and (4) has the same tastes as another,
or (5) one who grieves and rejoices with his friend;
and this too is found in mothers most of all. It is by
some one of these characteristics that friendship too is
defined.

Now each of these is true of the good man's relation
to himself (and of all other men in so far as they think
themselves good; virtue and the good man seem, as has
been said,[1] to be the measure of every class of things).
For[2] his opinions are harmonious, and he desires the
same things with all his soul; and therefore[3] he wishes
for himself what is good and what seems so, and does
it (for it is characteristic of the good man to work out
the good), and does so for his own sake (for he does it
for the sake of the intellectual element in him, which is
thought to be the man himself); and[4] he wishes himself
to live and be preserved, and especially the element
by virtue of which he thinks. For existence is good to

---

[1] 1113ᵃ22–33, cf. 1099ᵃ13.   [2] (4) above.
[3] (1) above.   [4] (2) above.

the virtuous man, and each man wishes himself what
is good, while no one chooses to possess the whole world
if he has first to become someone else (for that matter,
even now God possesses the good) ;[1] he wishes for this
only on condition of being whatever he is; and the
element that thinks would seem to be the individual
man, or to be so more than any other element in him.
And[2] such a man wishes to live with himself; for he does
so with pleasure, since the memories of his past acts are
delightful and his hopes for the future are good, and
therefore pleasant. His mind is well stored too with
subjects of contemplation. And[3] he grieves and rejoices,
more than any other, with himself; for the same thing
is always painful, and the same thing always pleasant,
and not one thing at one time and another at another;
he has, so to speak, nothing to regret.

Therefore, since each of these characteristics belongs
to the good man in relation to himself, and he is related
to his friend as to himself (for his friend is another self),
friendship too is thought to be one of these attributes,
and those who have these attributes to be friends.
Whether there is or is not friendship between a man
and himself is a question we may dismiss for the present;[4] there would seem to be friendship in so far as
he is two or more, to judge from the aforementioned
attributes of friendship, | and from the fact that the ex-
treme of friendship is likened to one's love for oneself.

But the attributes named seem to belong even to the
majority of men, poor creatures though they may be.
Are we to say then that in so far as they are satisfied
with themselves and think they are good, they share

---

[1] *Sc.* but as no one gains by God's now having the good, he would
not gain if a new person which was no longer himself were to possess
it. Cf. 1159ª5–11.   [2] (3) above.   [3] (5) above.
[4] Cf. 1168ª28–1169b2.

in these attributes? Certainly no one who is thoroughly
bad and impious has these attributes, or even seems to
do so. They hardly belong even to inferior people; for
they[1] are at variance with themselves, and have appetites for some things and rational desires for others. This
is true, for instance, of incontinent people; for they
choose, instead of the things they themselves think
good, things that are pleasant but hurtful; while others
again, through cowardice and laziness, shrink from
doing what they think best for themselves. And[2] those
who have done many terrible deeds and are hated for
their wickedness even shrink from life and destroy
themselves. Besides,[3] wicked men seek for people with
whom to spend their days, and shun themselves; for
they remember many a grievous deed, and anticipate
others like them, when they are by themselves, but
when they are with others they forget. And[4] having
nothing lovable in them they have no feeling of love
to themselves. Therefore[5] also such men do not rejoice
or grieve with themselves; for their soul is rent by
faction, and one element in it by reason of its wickedness grieves when it abstains from certain acts, while
the other part is pleased, and one draws them this way
and the other that, as if they were pulling them in
pieces. If a man cannot at the same time be pained and
pleased, at all events after a short time he is pained
because he was pleased, and he could have wished that
these things had not been pleasant to him; for bad men
are full of regrets.

Therefore the bad man does not seem to be amicably
disposed even to himself, because there is nothing
in him to love; so that if to be thus is the height of
wretchedness, we should strain every nerve to avoid

----

[1] (4) above.   [2] (2) above.   [3] (3) above.
[4] (1) above.   [5] (5) above.

wickedness and should endeavour to be good; for so and only so can one be either friendly to oneself or a friend to another.

Relation of friendship to goodwill

5. Goodwill is a friendly sort of relation, but is not *identical* with friendship; for one may have goodwill both towards people whom one does not know, and without their knowing it, but not friendship. This has indeed been said already.[1] But goodwill is not even friendly feeling. For it does not involve intensity or desire, whereas these accompany friendly feeling; and friendly feeling implies intimacy while goodwill may arise of a sudden, as it does towards competitors in a contest; | we come to feel goodwill for them and to share in their wishes, but we would not *do* anything with them; for, as we said, we feel goodwill suddenly and love them only superficially.

Goodwill seems, then, to be a beginning of friendship, as the pleasure of the eye is the beginning of love. For no one loves if he has not first been delighted by the form of the beloved, but he who delights in the form of another does not, for all that, love him, but only does so when he also longs for him when absent and craves for his presence; so too it is not possible for people to be friends if they have not come to feel goodwill for each other, but those who feel goodwill are not for all that friends; for they only *wish* well to those for whom they feel goodwill, and would not do anything with them or take trouble for them. And so one might by an extension of the term 'friendship' say that goodwill is inactive friendship, though when it is prolonged and reaches the point of intimacy it becomes friendship— not the friendship based on utility nor that based on

---

[1] 1155ᵇ32–1156ª5.

pleasure; for goodwill too does not arise on those terms. The man who has received a benefit bestows goodwill in return for what has been done to him, but in doing so is only doing what is just; while he who wishes someone to prosper because he hopes for enrichment through him seems to have goodwill not to him but rather to himself, just as a man is not a friend to another if he cherishes him for the sake of some use to be made of him. In general, goodwill arises on account of some excellence and worth, when one man seems to another beautiful or brave or something of the sort, as we pointed out in the case of competitors in a contest.

Relation of friendship to unanimity

6. Concord also seems to be a friendly relation. For this reason it is not identity of opinion; for that might occur even with people who do not know each other; nor do we say that people who have the same views on any and every subject are in accord, e.g. those who agree about the heavenly bodies (for concord about these is not a friendly relation), but we do say that a city is in accord when men have the same opinion about what is to their interest, and choose the same actions, and do what they have resolved in common. It is about things to be done, therefore, that people are said to be in accord, and, among these, about matters of consequence and in which it is possible for both or all parties to get what they want; e.g. a city is in accord when all its citizens think that the offices in it should be elective, or that they should form an alliance with Sparta, or that Pittacus should be their ruler—at a time when he himself was also willing to rule. But when each of two people wishes himself to have the thing in question, like the captains in the *Phoenissae*, they are in a state of faction; for it is not concord when each of

two parties thinks of the same thing, whatever that
may be, but only when they think of the same thing in
the same hands, e.g. when both the common people
and those of the better class wish the best men to rule;|
for thus and thus alone do all get what they aim at.
Concord seems, then, to be political friendship, as
indeed it is commonly said to be; for it is concerned
with things that are to our interest and have an influence on our life.

Now such concord is found among good men; for
they are in accord both in themselves and with one
another, being, so to say, of one mind (for the wishes of
such men are constant and not at the mercy of oppos-
ing currents like a strait of the sea), and they wish for
what is just and what is advantageous, and these are
the objects of their common endeavour as well. But
bad men cannot be in accord except to a small extent,
any more than they can be friends, since they aim at
getting more than their share of advantages, while in
labour and public service they fall short of their share;
and each man wishing for advantage to himself criti-
cizes his neighbour and stands in his way; for if people
do not watch it carefully the common weal is soon destroyed. The result is that they are in a state of faction,
putting compulsion on each other but unwilling themselves to do what is just.

The pleasure of beneficence

7. Benefactors are thought to love those they have
benefited, more than those who have been well treated
love those that have treated them well, and this is discussed as though it were paradoxical. Most people
think it is because the latter are in the position of
debtors and the former of creditors; and therefore as,
in the case of loans, debtors wish their creditors did not

exist, while creditors actually take care of the safety of
their debtors, so it is thought that benefactors wish the
objects of their action to exist since they will then get
their gratitude, while the beneficiaries take no interest
in making this return. Epicharmus would perhaps de-
clare that they say this because they 'look at things on
their bad side', but it is quite like human nature; for
most people are forgetful, and are more anxious to be
well treated than to treat others well. But the cause
would seem to be more deeply rooted in the nature of
things; the case of those who have lent money is not
even analogous. For they have no friendly feeling to
their debtors, but only a wish that they may be kept
safe with a view to what is to be got from them; while
those who have done a service to others feel friendship
and love for those they have served, even if these are
not of any use to them and never will be. This is what
happens with craftsmen too; every man loves his own
handiwork better than he would be loved by it if it
came alive; | and this happens perhaps most of all with
poets; for they have an excessive love for their own
poems, doting on them as if they were their children.
This is what the position of benefactors is like; for that
which they have treated well is their handiwork, and
therefore they love this more than the handiwork does
its maker. The cause of this is that existence is to all
men a thing to be chosen and loved, and that we exist
by virtue of activity (i.e. by living and acting), and that
the handiwork *is*, in a sense, the producer in activity;
he loves his handiwork, therefore, because he loves
existence. And this is rooted in the nature of things;
for what he is in potentiality, his handiwork manifests
in activity.

At the same time, to the benefactor that is noble
which depends on his action, so that he delights in the

object of his action, whereas to the patient there is nothing noble in the agent, but at most something advantageous, and this is less pleasant and lovable. What *is* pleasant is the activity of the present, the hope of the future, the memory of the past; but most pleasant is that which depends on activity, and similarly this is most lovable. Now for a man who has made something his work remains (for the noble is lasting), but for the person acted on the utility passes away. And the memory of noble things is pleasant, but that of useful things is not likely to be pleasant, or is less so; though the reverse seems true of expectation.

Further, love is like activity, being loved like passivity; and loving and its concomitants are attributes of those who are the more active.[1]

Again, all men love more what they have won by labour; e.g. those who have made their money love it more than those who have inherited it; and to be well treated seems to involve no labour, while to treat others well is a laborious task. These are the reasons, too, why mothers are fonder of their children than fathers; bringing them into the world costs them more pains, and they know better that the children are their own. This last point, too, would seem to apply to benefactors.

The nature of true self-love

8. The question is also debated, whether a man should love himself most, or someone else. People criticize those who love themselves most, and call them self-lovers, using this as an epithet of disgrace, and a bad man seems to do everything for his own sake, and the more so the more wicked he is—and so men reproach him, for instance, with doing nothing of his own accord—

[1] i.e. benefactors.

while the good man acts for honour's sake, and the more so the better he is, and acts for his friend's sake, and sacrifices his own interest.

But the facts clash with these arguments, and this is not surprising. | For men say that one ought to love best one's best friend, and a man's best friend is one who wishes well to the object of his wish for his sake, even if no one is to know of it; and these attributes are found most of all in a man's attitude towards himself, and so are all the other attributes by which a friend is defined; for, as we have said,[1] it is from this relation that all the characteristics of friendship have extended to our neighbours. All the proverbs, too, agree with this, e.g. 'A single soul', and 'What friends have is common property', and 'Friendship is equality', and 'Charity begins at home';[2] for all these marks will be found most in a man's relation to himself; he is his own best friend and therefore ought to love himself best. It is therefore a reasonable question, which of the two views we should follow; for both are plausible.

Perhaps we ought to mark off such arguments from each other and determine how far and in what respects each view is right. Now if we grasp the sense in which each school uses the phrase 'lover of self', the truth may become evident. Those who use the term as one of reproach ascribe self-love to people who assign to themselves the greater share of wealth, honours, and bodily pleasures; for these are what most people desire, and busy themselves about as though they were the best of all things, which is the reason, too, why they become objects of competition. So those who are grasping with regard to these things gratify their appetites and in general their feelings and the irrational element of the soul; and most men are of this nature (which is the

[1] Ch. 4.   [2] Lit. 'the knee is nearer than the shin'.

235

reason why the epithet has come to be used as it is—it takes its meaning from the prevailing type of self-love, which is a bad one); justly, therefore, are men who are lovers of self in this way reproached for being so. That it is those who give themselves the preference in regard to objects of this sort that most people usually call lovers of self is plain; for if a man were always anxious that he himself, above all things, should act justly, temperately, or in accordance with any other of the virtues, and in general were always to try to secure for himself the honourable course, no one would call such a man a lover of self or blame him.

But such a man would seem more than the other a lover of self; at all events he assigns to himself the things that are noblest and best, and gratifies the most authoritative element in himself and in all things obeys this; and just as a city or any other systematic whole is most properly identified with the most authoritative element in it, so is a man; and therefore the man who loves this and gratifies it is most of all a lover of self. Besides, a man is said to have or not to have self-control according as his reason has or has not the control, on the assumption that this is the man himself; and the things men have done on a rational principle | are thought most properly their own acts and voluntary acts. That this is the man himself, then, or is so more than anything else, is plain, and also that the good man loves most this part of him. Whence it follows that he is most truly a lover of self, of another type than that which is a matter of reproach, and as different from that as living according to a rational principle is from living as passion dictates, and desiring what is noble from desiring what seems advantageous. Those, then, who busy themselves in an exceptional degree with noble actions all men approve and praise; and if *all* were to strive towards what is noble and strain every nerve to do the noblest deeds, everything would be as it should be for the common weal, and everyone would secure for himself the goods that are greatest, since virtue is the greatest of goods.

Therefore the good man should be a lover of self (for he will both himself profit by doing noble acts, and will benefit his fellows), but the wicked man should not; for he will hurt both himself and his neighbours, following as he does evil passions. For the wicked man, what he does clashes with what he ought to do, but what the good man ought to do he does; for reason in each of its possessors chooses what is best for itself, and the good man obeys his reason. It is true of the good man too that he does many acts for the sake of his friends and his country, and if necessary dies for them; for he will throw away both wealth and honours and in general the goods that are objects of competition, gaining for himself nobility; since he would prefer a short period of intense pleasure to a long one of mild enjoyment, a twelvemonth of noble life to many years of humdrum existence, and one great and noble action to many trivial ones. Now those who die for others doubtless attain this result; it is therefore a great prize that they choose for themselves. They will throw away wealth too on condition that their friends will gain more; for while a man's friend gains wealth he himself achieves nobility; he is therefore assigning the greater good to himself. The same too is true of honour and office; all these things he will sacrifice to his friend; for this is noble and laudable for himself. Rightly then is he thought to be good, since he chooses nobility before all else. But he may even give up actions to his friend; it may be nobler to become the cause of his friend's acting than to act himself. In all the actions, therefore, that men are praised for, the good man is seen to assign to himself the greater share in what is noble. | In this sense, then, as has been said, a man should be a lover of self; but in the sense in which most men are so, he ought not.

THE NEED OF FRIENDSHIP

Why does the happy man need friends?

9. It is also disputed whether the happy man will need friends or not. It is said that those who are supremely happy and self-sufficient have no need of friends; for they have the things that are good, and therefore being self-sufficient they need nothing further, while a friend, being another self, furnishes what a man cannot provide by his own effort; whence the saying 'When fortune is kind, what need of friends?' But it seems strange, when one assigns all good things to the happy man, not to assign friends, who are thought the greatest of external goods. And if it is more characteristic of a friend to do well by another than to be well done by, and to confer benefits is characteristic of the good man and of virtue, and it is nobler to do well by friends than by strangers, the good man will need people to do well by. This is why the question is asked whether we need friends more in prosperity or in adversity, on the assumption that not only does a man in adversity need people to confer benefits on him, but also those who are prospering need people to do well by. Surely it is strange, too, to make the supremely happy man a solitary; for no one would choose the whole world on condition of being alone, since man is a political creature and one whose nature is to live with others. Therefore even the happy man lives with others; for he has the things that are by nature good. And plainly it is better to spend his days with friends and good men than with strangers or any chance persons. Therefore the happy man needs friends.

What then do holders of the first view mean, and in what respect are they right? Is it that most men identify friends with useful people? Of such friends indeed the supremely happy man will have no need, since he already has the things that are good; nor will he need those whom one makes one's friends because of their pleasantness, or he will need them only to a small extent (for his life, being pleasant, has no need of adventitious pleasure); and because he does not need *such* friends he is thought not to need friends.

But that is surely not true. For we have said at the outset[1] that happiness is an activity; and activity plainly comes into being and is not present at the start like a piece of property. If (1) happiness lies in living and being active, and the good man's activity is virtuous and pleasant in itself, as we have said at the outset,[2] and (2) a thing's being one's own is one of the attributes that make it pleasant, and (3) we can contemplate our neighbours better than ourselves and their actions better than our own, and if the actions of virtuous men who are their friends are pleasant to good men | (since these have both the attributes that are naturally pleasant)[3]—if this be so, the supremely happy man will need friends of this sort, since his purpose is to contemplate worthy actions and actions that are his own, and the actions of a good man who is his friend have both these qualities.

Further, men think that the happy man ought to live pleasantly. Now if he were a solitary, life would be hard for him; for by oneself it is not easy to be

---

[1] 1098ᵃ16, ᵇ31–1099ᵃ7.   [2] 1099ᵃ14, 21.
[3] i.e. the attribute of goodness and that of being their own.

continuously active; but with others and towards others it is easier. With others therefore his activity will be more continuous, and it is in itself pleasant, as it ought to be for the man who is supremely happy; for a good man *qua* good delights in virtuous actions and is vexed at vicious ones, as a musical man enjoys beautiful tunes but is pained at bad ones. A certain training in virtue arises also from the company of the good, as Theognis has said before us.

If we look deeper into the nature of things, a virtuous friend seems to be naturally desirable for a virtuous man. For that which is good by nature, we have said,[1] is for the virtuous man good and pleasant in itself. Now life is defined in the case of animals by the power of perception, in that of man by the power of perception or thought; and a power is defined by reference to the corresponding activity, which is the essential thing; therefore life seems to be essentially the act of perceiving or thinking. And life is among the things that are good and pleasant in themselves, since it is determinate and the determinate is of the nature of the good; and that which is good by nature is also good for the virtuous man (which is the reason why life seems pleasant to all men); but we must not apply this to a wicked and corrupt life or to a life spent in pain; for such a life is indeterminate, as are its attributes. The nature of pain will become plainer in what follows.[2] But if life itself is good and pleasant (which it seems to be, from the very fact that all men desire it, and particularly those who are good and supremely happy; for to such men life is most desirable, and their existence is the most supremely happy); and if he who sees perceives that he sees, and he who hears, that he hears, and he who walks, that he walks, and in the case

---

[1] 1099ᵃ7-11, 1113ᵃ25-33.   [2] x. 1-5.

of all other activities similarly there is something which perceives that we are active, so that if we perceive, we perceive that we perceive, and if we think, that we think; and if to perceive that we perceive or think is to perceive that we exist (for existence was defined as perceiving or thinking); | and if perceiving that one lives is in itself one of the things that are pleasant (for life is by nature good, and to perceive what is good present in oneself is pleasant); and if life is desirable, and particularly so for good men, because to them existence is good and pleasant (for they are pleased at the consciousness of the presence in them of what is in itself good); and if as the virtuous man is to himself, he is to his friend also (for his friend is another self)—if all this be true, as his own being is desirable for each man, so, or almost so, is that of his friend. Now his being was seen to be desirable because he perceived his own goodness, and such perception is pleasant in itself. He needs, therefore, to be conscious of the existence of his friend as well, and this will be realized in their living together and sharing in discussion and thought; for this is what living together would seem to mean in the case of man, and not, as in the case of cattle, feeding in the same place.

If, then, being is in itself desirable for the supremely happy man (since it is by its nature good and pleasant), and that of his friend is very much the same, a friend will be one of the things that are desirable. Now that which is desirable for him he must have, or he will be deficient in this respect. The man who is to be happy will therefore need virtuous friends.[1]

---

[1] The argument in 1170ᵃ14–ᵇ19 is admirably analysed by Professor Burnet, whom I follow, with variations:—

Pro-syllogism A (1170ᵃ16–19):

    Capacity is defined by reference to activity.

    Human life is defined by the capacity of perception or thought.

    ∴ Human life is defined by the activity of perception or thought.

                               [*cont. overleaf.*]

The limit to the number of friends

10. Should we, then, make as many friends as possible, or—as in the case of hospitality it is thought to be suitable advice, that one should be 'neither a man of many guests nor a man with none'[1]—will that apply to friendship as well; should a man neither be friendless nor have an excessive number of friends?

To friends made with a view to *utility* this saying would seem thoroughly applicable; for to do services to many people in return is a laborious task and life is not long enough for its performance. Therefore friends in excess of those who are sufficient for our own life are superfluous, and hindrances to the noble life; so that we have no need of them. Of friends made with a view to *pleasure*, also, few are enough, as a little seasoning in food is enough.

But as regards *good* friends, should we have as many

Pro-syllogism B (^a19–21):
　The determinate is good by nature.
　Life is determinate.
　∴ Life is good by nature.
Pro-syllogism C (implied):
　What is good by nature is good and pleasant for the good man (^a14–16, 21–22).
　Life is good by nature (conclusion of B).
　∴ Life is good and pleasant for the good man.
Pro-syllogism D (implied):
　Life is good and pleasant for the good man (conclusion of C).
　Perception and thought are life (conclusion of A).
　∴ Perception and thought are good and pleasant for the good man.
Pro-syllogism E (^a25–29):
　What is desired by all men and particularly by the good and supremely happy man is good in itself.
　Life is so desired.
　∴ Life is good in itself.
Lemma (^a29–32):
　Perception and thought are accompanied by consciousness of themselves.
Argument F (^a32–^b1):
　Perception and thought are life (conclusion of A).
　∴ Consciousness of perception and thought is consciousness of life.

---

[1] Hes. *Op.* 715 Rzach.

as possible, or is there a limit to the number of one's friends, as there is to the size of a city? You cannot make a city of ten men, and if there are a hundred thousand it is a city no longer. But the proper number is presumably not a single number, but anything that falls between certain fixed points. So for friends too there is a fixed number— | perhaps the largest number with whom one can live together (for that, we found,[1] is thought to be very characteristic of friendship); and that one cannot live with many people and divide oneself up among them is plain. Further, they too must be friends of one another, if they are all to spend their days together; and it is a hard business for this condition to be fulfilled with a large number. It is found difficult, too, to rejoice and to grieve in an intimate way with many people, for it may likely happen that

Argument G (ᵇ1-3):
    Consciousness of having something good is pleasant.
    Life is good in itself (conclusion of B and E).
    ∴ Consciousness of life is pleasant.
Argument H (implied):
    Consciousness of life is pleasant (conclusion of G).
    Consciousness of perception and thought is consciousness of life
        (conclusion of F).
    ∴ Consciousness of perception and thought is pleasant.
Lemma (ᵇ3-5):
    The existence of the good man is specially desirable because the
        activities of which he is conscious are good.
Argument I (ᵇ5-8):
    The good man is related to his friend as he is to himself (con-
        clusion of ch. 4).
    His own existence is desirable to him (conclusion of C).
    ∴ That of his friend is desirable to him.
Argument K (ᵇ8-14):
    His own existence is desirable because of his consciousness of his
        good activities (stated in ᵇ3-5).
    ∴ Consciousness of his friend's good activities is also desirable to him.
Summary (ᵇ14-17).
Argument L (ᵇ17-19):
    If a man is to be happy, he must have all that is desirable for him.
    Friends are desirable for a man (conclusion of I).
    ∴ If a man is to be happy, he must have friends.

[1] 1157ᵇ19, 1158ᵃ3, 10.

one has at once to be happy with one friend and to mourn with another. Presumably, then, it is well not to seek to have as many friends as possible, but as many as are enough for the purpose of living together; for it would seem actually impossible to be a great friend to many people. This is why one cannot love several people; love is ideally a sort of excess of friendship, and that can only be felt towards one person; therefore great friendship too can only be felt towards a few people. This seems to be confirmed in practice; for we do not find many people who are friends in the comradely way of friendship, and the famous friendships of this sort are always between two people. Those who have many friends and mix intimately with them all are thought to be no one's friend, except in the way proper to fellow citizens, and such people are also called obsequious. In the way proper to fellow citizens, indeed, it is possible to be the friend of many and yet not be obsequious but a genuinely good man; but one cannot have with many people the friendship based on virtue and on the character of our friends themselves, and we must be content if we find even a few such.

Are friends more needed in good or in bad fortune?

11. Do we need friends more in good fortune or in bad? They are sought after in both; for while men in adversity need help, in prosperity they need people to live with and to make the objects of their beneficence; for they wish to do well by others. Friendship, then, is more necessary in bad fortune, and so it is useful friends that one wants in this case; but it is more noble in good fortune, and so we also seek for good men as our friends, since it is more desirable to confer benefits on these and to live with these. For the very presence of friends is pleasant both in good fortune and also in bad, since

grief is lightened when friends sorrow with us. Hence
one might ask whether they share as it were our burden,
or—without that happening—their presence by its
pleasantness, and the thought of their grieving with us,
make our pain less. Whether it is for these reasons or
for some other that our grief is lightened, is a question
that may be dismissed; at all events what we have
described appears to take place.

But their presence seems to contain a mixture of
various factors. The very seeing of one's friends is plea-
sant | (especially if one is in adversity), and becomes a
safeguard against grief (for a friend tends to comfort us
both by the sight of him and by his words, if he is tactful, since he knows our character and the things that
please or pain us); but to see him pained at our misfortunes is painful; for every one shuns being a cause
of pain to his friends. For this reason people of a manly
nature guard against making their friends grieve with
them, and, unless he be exceptionally insensible to
pain, such a man cannot stand the pain that ensues
for his friends, and in general does not admit fellow
mourners because he is not himself given to mourning;
but women and womanly men enjoy sympathizers in
their grief, and love them as friends and companions
in sorrow. But in all things one obviously ought to
imitate the better type of person.

On the other hand, the presence of friends in our
prosperity implies both a pleasant passing of our time
and the pleasant thought of their pleasure at our own
good fortune. For this cause it would seem that we
ought to summon our friends readily to share our good
fortunes (for the beneficent character is a noble one),
but summon them to our bad fortunes with hesitation;
for we ought to give them as little a share as possible in
our evils—whence the saying 'Enough is *my* misfortune'.

We should summon friends to us most of all when they are likely by suffering a few inconveniences to do us a great service.

Conversely, it is fitting to go unasked and readily to the aid of those in adversity (for it is characteristic of a friend to render services, and especially to those who are in need and have not demanded them; such action is nobler and pleasanter for both persons); but when our friends are prosperous we should join readily in their activities (for they need friends for these too), but be tardy in coming forward to be the objects of their kindness; for it is not noble to be keen to receive benefits. Still, we must no doubt avoid getting the reputation of kill-joys by repulsing them; for that sometimes happens.

The presence of friends, then, seems desirable in all circumstances.

The essence of friendship is living together

12. Does it not follow, then, that, as for lovers the sight of the beloved is the thing they love most, and they prefer this sense to the others because on it love depends most for its being and for its origin, so for friends the most desirable thing is living together? For friendship is a partnership, and as a man is to himself, so is he to his friend; now in his own case the consciousness of his being is desirable, and so therefore is the consciousness of his friend's being, and the activity of this consciousness is produced when they live together, so that it is natural that they aim at this. | And whatever existence means for each class of men, whatever it is for whose sake they value life, in *that* they wish to occupy themselves with their friends; and so some drink together, others dice together, others join in athletic exercises and hunting, or in the study of philosophy, each class

spending their days together in whatever they love most in life; for since they wish to live with their friends, they do and share in those things which give them the sense of living together. Thus the friendship of bad men turns out an evil thing (for because of their instability they unite in bad pursuits, and besides they become evil by becoming like each other), while the friendship of good men is good, being augmented by their companionship; and they are thought to become better too by their activities and by improving each other; for from each other they take the mould of the characteristics they approve—whence the saying 'Noble deeds from noble men'.—So much, then, for friendship; our next task must be to discuss pleasure.

BOOK X · PLEASURE, HAPPINESS

PLEASURE

Two opposed views about pleasure

1. AFTER these matters we ought perhaps next to discuss pleasure. For it is thought to be most intimately connected with our human nature, which is the reason why in educating the young we steer them by the rudders of pleasure and pain; it is thought, too, that to enjoy the things we ought and to hate the things we ought has the greatest bearing on virtue of character. For these things extend right through life, with a weight and power of their own in respect both to virtue and to the happy life, since men choose what is pleasant and avoid what is painful; and such things, it will be thought, we should least of all omit to discuss, especially since they admit of much dispute. For some[1] say pleasure is the good, while others,[2] on the contrary, say it is thoroughly bad—some no doubt being persuaded that the facts are so, and others thinking it has a better effect on our life to exhibit pleasure as a bad thing even if it is not; for most people (they think) incline towards it and are the slaves of their pleasures, for which reason they ought to lead them in the opposite direction, since thus they will reach the middle state. But surely this is not correct. For arguments about matters concerned with feelings and actions are less reliable than facts: and so when they clash with the facts of perception they are despised, and discredit the truth as well; | if a man who runs down pleasure is once seen to be aiming at it, his inclining towards it is thought to imply

---

[1] The school of Eudoxus, cf. ᵇ9. Aristippus is perhaps also referred to.
[2] The school of Speusippus, cf. 1153ᵇ5.

that it is all worthy of being aimed at; for most people
are not good at drawing distinctions. True arguments
seem, then, most useful, not only with a view to knowledge but with a view to life also; for since they harmonize with the facts they are believed, and so they
stimulate those who understand them to live according
to them.—Enough of such questions; let us proceed to
review the opinions that have been expressed about
pleasure.

Discussion of the view that pleasure is the good

2. Eudoxus thought pleasure was the good because he
saw all things, both rational and irrational, aiming at
it, and because in all things that which is the object of
choice is what is excellent, and that which is most the
object of choice the greatest good; thus the fact that
all things moved towards the same object indicated
that this was for all things the chief good (for each
thing, he argued, finds its own good, as it finds its own
nourishment); and that which is good for all things
and at which all aim was the good. His arguments were
credited more because of the excellence of his character
than for their own sake; he was thought to be remark-
ably temperate, and therefore it was thought that he
was not saying what he did say as a friend of pleasure,
but that the facts really were so. He believed that the
same conclusion followed no less plainly from a
study of the contrary of pleasure: pain was in itself
an object of aversion to all things, and therefore its
contrary must be similarly an object of choice. And
again, that is most an object of choice which we choose
not because or for the sake of something else, and
pleasure is admittedly of this nature; for no one asks
to what end he is pleased, thus implying that pleasure
is in itself an object of choice. Further, he argued that

pleasure when added to any good, e.g. to just or temperate action, makes it more worthy of choice, and that it is only by itself that the good can be increased.

This argument seems to show it to be one of the goods, and no more a good than any other; for every good is more worthy of choice along with another good than taken alone. And so it is by an argument of this kind that Plato[1] proves the good *not* to be pleasure; he argues that the pleasant life is more desirable with wisdom than without, and that if the mixture is better, pleasure is not the good; for the good cannot become more desirable by the addition of anything to it. Now it is clear that nothing else, any more than pleasure, can be the good if it is made more desirable by the addition of any of the things that are good in themselves. What, then, is there that satisfies this criterion, which at the same time we can participate in? It is something of this sort that we are looking for.

Those who object that that at which all things aim is not necessarily good are, we may surmise, talking nonsense. For we say that that which everyone thinks really is so; and the man who attacks this conviction will hardly have anything more convincing to maintain instead. If it were irrational creatures that desired the things in question, there might be something in what is said; but if intelligent creatures do so as well, how can there be anything in it? But perhaps even in inferior creatures there is some natural good stronger than themselves which aims at their proper good.

Nor does the argument about the contrary of pleasure seem to be correct. They say that if pain is an evil it does not follow that pleasure is a good; for evil is opposed to evil and at the same time both are opposed to the neutral state—which is correct enough but does

[1] *Phil.* 60 B–E.

not apply to the things in question. For if both pleasure
and pain belonged to the class of evils they ought both to
be objects of aversion, while if they belonged to the class
of neutrals neither should be an object of aversion or
they should both be equally so; but in fact people
evidently avoid the one as evil and choose the other as
good; that then must be the nature of the opposition
between them.

Discussion of the view that pleasure is wholly bad

3. Nor again, if pleasure is not a quality, does it follow
that it is not a good; for the activities of virtue are not
qualities either, nor is happiness.

They say,[1] however, that the good is determinate,
while pleasure is indeterminate, because it admits of degrees. Now if it is from the feeling of pleasure that they
judge thus, the same will be true of justice and the other
virtues, in respect of which we plainly say that people of
a certain character are so more or less, and act more or
less in accordance with these virtues; for people may be
more or less just or brave, and it is possible also to act
justly or temperately more or less. But if their judgement is based on the various pleasures, surely they are
not stating the real cause,[2] if in fact some pleasures are
unmixed and others mixed. Again, just as health admits
of degrees without being indeterminate, why should
not pleasure? The same proportion is not found in all
things, nor a single proportion always in the same
thing, but it may be relaxed and yet persist up to a
point, and it may differ in degree. The case of pleasure
also may therefore be of this kind.

Again, they assume[3] that the good is perfect, while
movements and comings into being are imperfect, and

---

[1] Ibid. 24 B–25 A, 31 A.
[2] *Sc.*, of the badness of (some) pleasures.   [3] Pl. *Phil.* 53 C–54 D.

try to exhibit pleasure as being a movement and a coming into being. But they do not seem to be right even in saying that it is a movement. For speed and slowness are thought to be proper to every movement, and if a movement, e.g. that of the heavens, has not speed or slowness in itself, it has it in relation to something else; but of pleasure neither of these things is true. For while we may *become* pleased quickly, as we may become angry quickly, | we cannot *be* pleased quickly, not even in relation to someone else, while we *can* walk, or grow, or the like, quickly. While, then, we can change quickly or slowly into a state of pleasure, we cannot quickly exhibit the activity of pleasure, i.e. be pleased. Again, how can it be a coming into being? It is not thought that any chance thing can come out of any chance thing, but that a thing is dissolved into that out of which it comes into being; and pain would be the destruction of that of which pleasure is the coming into being.

They say, too,[1] that pain is the lack of that which is according to nature, and pleasure is replenishment. But these experiences are bodily. If then pleasure is replenishment with that which is according to nature, that which feels pleasure will be that in which the replenishment takes place, i.e. the body; but that is not thought to be the case; therefore the replenishment is not pleasure, though one would be pleased when replenishment was taking place, just as one would be pained if one was being operated on.[2] This opinion seems to be based on the pains and pleasures connected with nutrition: on the fact that when people have been short of food and have felt pain beforehand they are pleased by

---

[1] Pl. *Phil.* 31 ᴇ-32 ʙ, 42 ᴄ-ᴅ.

[2] The point being that the being replenished no more *is* pleasure than the being operated on *is* pain. For the instance, cf. Pl. *Tim.* 65 ʙ.

the replenishment. But this does not happen with all pleasures; for the pleasures of learning and, among the sensuous pleasures, those of smell, and also many sounds and sights, and memories and hopes, do not presuppose pain. Of what then will these be the coming into being? There has not been lack of anything of which they could be the supplying anew.

In reply to those who bring forward the disgraceful pleasures one may say that these are not pleasant; if things are pleasant to people of vicious constitution, we must not suppose that they are also pleasant to others than these, just as we do not reason so about the things that are wholesome or sweet or bitter to sick people, or ascribe whiteness to the things that seem white to those suffering from a disease of the eye. Or one might answer thus—that the pleasures are desirable, but not from *these* sources, as wealth is desirable, but not as the reward of betrayal, and health, but not at the cost o eating anything and everything. Or perhaps pleasures differ in kind; for those derived from noble sources are different from those derived from base sources, and one cannot get the pleasure of the just man without being just, nor that of the musical man without being musical, and so on.

The fact, too, that a friend is different from a flatterer seems to make it plain that pleasure is not a good, or that pleasures are different in kind; for the one is thought to consort with us with a view to the good, the other with a view to our pleasure, and the one is reproached for his conduct while the other is praised on the ground that he consorts with us for different ends.| And no one would choose to live with the intellect of a child throughout his life, however much he were to be pleased at the things that children are pleased at, nor to get enjoyment by doing some most disgraceful deed, though he were never to feel any pain in consequence. And there are many things we should be keen about even if they brought no pleasure, e.g. seeing, remembering, knowing, possessing the virtues. If pleasures necessarily do accompany these, that makes no odds; we should choose these even if no pleasure resulted. It seems to be clear, then, that neither is pleasure the good nor is all pleasure desirable, and that some pleasures *are* desirable in themselves, differing in kind or in their sources from the others. So much for the things that are said about pleasure and pain.

Definition of pleasure

4. What pleasure is, or what kind of thing it is, will become plainer if we take up the question again from the beginning. Seeing seems to be at any moment complete, for it does not lack anything whose coming into being later will complete its form; and pleasure also seems to be of this nature. For it is a whole, and at no time can one find a pleasure whose form will be completed if the pleasure lasts longer. For this reason, too, it is not a movement. For every movement (e.g. that of building) takes time and is for the sake of an end, and is complete when it has made what it aims at. It is complete, therefore, only in the whole time or at that final moment. In their parts and during the time they occupy, all movements are incomplete, and are different in kind from the whole movement and from each other. For the fitting together of the stones is different from the fluting of the column, and these are both different from the making of the temple; and the making of the temple is complete (for it lacks nothing with a view to the end proposed), but the making of the base or of the triglyph is incomplete; for each is the making

of only a part. They differ in kind, then, and it is not possible to find at any and every time a movement complete in form, but if at all, only in the whole time. So, too, in the case of walking and all other movements. For if locomotion is a movement from here to there, it, too, has differences in kind—flying, walking, leaping, and so on. And not only so, but in walking itself there are such differences; for the whence and whither are not the same in the whole race-course and in a part of it, nor in one part and in another, nor is it the same thing to traverse this line and that; | for one traverses not only a line but one which is in a place, and this one is in a different place from that. We have discussed movement with precision in another work,[1] but it seems that it is not complete at any and every time, but that the many movements are incomplete and different in kind, since the whence and whither give them their form. But of pleasure the form is complete at any and every time. Plainly, then, pleasure and movement must be different from each other, and pleasure must be one of the things that are whole and complete. This would seem to be the case, too, from the fact that it is not possible to move otherwise than in time, but it *is* possible to be pleased; for that which takes place in a moment is a whole.

From these considerations it is clear, too, that these thinkers are not right in saying there is a movement or a coming into being *of* pleasure. For these cannot be ascribed to all things, but only to those that are divisible and not wholes; there is no coming into being of seeing nor of a point nor of a unit, nor is any of these a movement or coming into being; therefore there is no movement or coming into being of pleasure either; for it is a whole.

---

[1] *Phys.* vi–viii.

Since every sense is active in relation to its object, and a sense which is in good condition acts perfectly in relation to the most beautiful of its objects (for perfect activity seems to be ideally of this nature; whether we say that *it* is active, or the organ in which it resides, may be assumed to be immaterial), it follows that in the case of each sense the best activity is that of the best-conditioned organ in relation to the finest of its objects. And this activity will be the most complete and pleasant. For, while there is pleasure in respect of any sense, and in respect of thought and contemplation no less, the most complete is pleasant, and that of a well-conditioned organ in relation to the worthiest of its objects is the most complete; and the pleasure completes the activity. But the pleasure does not complete it in the same way as the combination of object and sense, both good, just as health and the doctor are not in the same way the cause of a man's being healthy. (That pleasure is produced in respect to each sense is plain; for we speak of sights and sounds as pleasant. It is also plain that it arises most of all when both the sense is at its best and it is active in reference to an object which corresponds; when both object and perceiver are of the best there will always be pleasure, since the requisite agent and patient are both present.) Pleasure completes the activity not as the corresponding permanent state does, by its immanence, but as an end which supervenes as the bloom of youth does on those in the flower of their age. So long, then, as both the intelligible or sensible object and the discriminating or contemplative faculty are as they should be, the pleasure will be involved in the activity; | for when both the passive and the active factor are unchanged and are related to each other in the same way, the same result naturally follows.

How, then, is it that no one is continuously pleased?

Is it that we grow weary? Certainly all human things are incapable of continuous activity. Therefore pleasure also is not continuous; for it accompanies activity. Some things delight us when they are new, but later do so less, for the same reason; for at first the mind is in a state of stimulation and intensely active about them, as people are with respect to their vision when they look hard at a thing, but afterwards our activity is not of this kind, but has grown relaxed; for which reason the pleasure also is dulled.

One might think that all men desire pleasure because they all aim at life; life is an activity, and each man is active about those things and with those faculties that he loves most; e.g. the musician is active with his hearing in reference to tunes, the student with his mind in reference to theoretical questions, and so on in each case; now pleasure completes the activities, and therefore life, which they desire. It is with good reason, then, that they aim at pleasure too, since for every one it completes life, which is desirable. But whether we choose life for the sake of pleasure or pleasure for the sake of life is a question we may dismiss for the present. For they seem to be bound up together and not to admit of separation, since without activity pleasure does not arise, and every activity is completed by the attendant pleasure.

Pleasures differ with the activities which they accompany and complete: criterion of the value of pleasures

5. For this reason pleasures seem, too, to differ in kind. For things different in kind are, we think, completed by different things (we see this to be true both of natural objects and of things produced by art, e.g. animals, trees, a painting, a sculpture, a house, an implement);

and, similarly, we think that activities differing in kind are completed by things differing in kind. Now the activities of thought differ from those of the senses, and both differ among themselves, in kind; so, therefore, do the pleasures that complete them.

This may be seen, too, from the fact that each of the pleasures is bound up with the activity it completes. For an activity is intensified by its proper pleasure, since each class of things is better judged of and brought to precision by those who engage in the activity with pleasure; e.g. it is those who enjoy geometrical thinking that become geometers and grasp the various propositions better, and, similarly, those who are fond of music or of building, and so on, make progress in their proper function by enjoying it; so the pleasures intensify the activities, and what intensifies a thing is proper to it, but things different in kind have properties different in kind.|

This will be even more apparent from the fact that activities are hindered by pleasures arising from other sources. For people who are fond of playing the flute are incapable of attending to arguments if they overhear someone playing the flute, since they enjoy flute-playing more than the activity in hand; so the pleasure connected with flute-playing destroys the activity concerned with argument. This happens, similarly, in all other cases, when one is active about two things at once; the more pleasant activity drives out the other, and if it is much more pleasant does so all the more, so that one even ceases from the other. This is why when we enjoy anything very much we do not throw ourselves into anything else, and do one thing only when we are not much pleased by another; e.g. in the theatre the people who eat sweets do so most when the actors are poor. Now since activities are made precise and more en-

during and better by their proper pleasure, and injured
by alien pleasures, evidently the two kinds of pleasure
are far apart. For alien pleasures do pretty much what
proper pains do, since activities are destroyed by their
proper pains; e.g. if a man finds writing or doing sums
unpleasant and painful, he does not write, or does not
do sums, because the activity is painful. So an activity
suffers contrary effects from its proper pleasures and
pains, i.e. from those that supervene on it in virtue of
its own nature. And alien pleasures have been stated
to do much the same as pain; they destroy the activity,
only not to the same degree.

Now since activities differ in respect of goodness and
badness, and some are worthy to be chosen, others to
be avoided, and others neutral, so, too, are the pleasures; for to each activity there is a proper pleasure.
The pleasure proper to a worthy activity is good and
that proper to an unworthy activity bad; just as the
appetites for noble objects are laudable, those for base
objects culpable. But the pleasures involved in activities are more proper to them than the desires; for
the latter are separated both in time and in nature,
while the former are close to the activities, and so hard to
distinguish from them that it admits of dispute whether
the activity is not the same as the pleasure. (Still, pleasure does not seem to *be* thought or perception—that
would be strange; but because they are not found apart
they appear to some people the same.) As activities are
different, then, so are the corresponding pleasures.
Now sight is superior to touch in purity, | and hearing
and smell to taste; the pleasures, therefore, are similarly
superior, and those of thought superior to these, and
within each of the two kinds some are superior to
others.

Each animal is thought to have a proper pleasure, as

it has a proper function; viz. that which corresponds to its activity. If we survey then species by species, too, this will be evident; horse, dog, and man have different pleasures, as Heraclitus says 'asses would prefer sweepings to gold'; for food is pleasanter than gold to asses. So the pleasures of creatures different in kind differ in kind, and it is plausible to suppose that those of a single species do not differ. But they vary to no small extent, in the case of men at least; the same things delight some people and pain others, and are painful and odious to some, and pleasant to and liked by others. This happens, too, in the case of sweet things; the same things do not seem sweet to a man in a fever and a healthy man—nor hot to a weak man and one in good condition. The same happens in other cases. But in all such matters that which appears to the good man is thought to be really so. If this is correct, as it seems to be, and virtue and the good man as such are the measure of each thing, those also will be pleasures which appear so to him, and those things pleasant which he enjoys. If the things he finds tiresome seem pleasant to someone, that is nothing surprising; for men may be ruined and spoilt in many ways; but the things are not pleasant, but only pleasant to these people and to people in this condition. Those which are admittedly disgraceful plainly should not be said to be pleasures, except to a perverted taste; but of those that are thought to be good what kind of pleasure or what pleasure should be said to be that proper to man? Is it not plain from the corresponding activities? The pleasures follow these. Whether, then, the perfect and supremely happy man has one or more activities, the pleasures that perfect these will be said in the strict sense to be pleasures proper to man, and the rest will be so in a secondary and fractional way, as are the activities.

HAPPINESS

Happiness is good activity, not amusement

6. Now that we have spoken of the virtues, the forms of
friendship, and the varieties of pleasure, what remains
is to discuss in outline the nature of happiness, since
this is what we state the end of human affairs to be.
Our discussion will be the more concise if we first sum
up what we have said already. We said,[1] then, that it
is not a state; for if it were it might belong to someone
who was asleep throughout his life, living the life of
a plant, or, again, to someone who was suffering the
greatest misfortunes. If these implications are unaccept-
able, | and we must rather class happiness as an activity,
as we have said before,[2] and if some activities are necessary, and desirable for the sake of something else, while
others are so in themselves, evidently happiness must
be placed among those desirable in themselves, not
among those desirable for the sake of something else;
for happiness does not lack anything, but is self-sufficient. Now those activities are desirable in themselves
from which nothing is sought beyond the activity. And
of this nature virtuous actions are thought to be; for to
do noble and good deeds is a thing desirable for its own
sake.

Pleasant amusements also are thought to be of this
nature: we choose them not for the sake of other things;
for we are injured rather than benefited by them, since
we are led to neglect our bodies and our property. But
most of the people who are deemed happy take refuge
in such pastimes, which is the reason why those who are
ready-witted at them are highly esteemed at the courts
of tyrants; they make themselves pleasant companions

---

[1] 1095ᵇ31–1096ᵃ2, 1098ᵇ31–1099ᵃ7.   [2] 1098ᵃ5–7.

in the tyrants' favourite pursuits, and that is the sort
of man they want. Now these things are thought to be
of the nature of happiness because people in despotic positions spend their leisure in them, but perhaps
such people prove nothing; for virtue and reason, from
which good activities flow, do not depend on despotic
position; nor, if these people, who have never tasted
pure and generous pleasure, take refuge in the bodily
pleasures, should these for that reason be thought more
desirable; for boys, too, think the things that are valued
among themselves are the best. It is to be expected,
then, that, as different things seem valuable to boys and
to men, so they should to bad men and to good. Now,
as we have often maintained,[1] those things are both
valuable and pleasant which are such to the good man;
and to each man the activity in accordance with
his own state is most desirable, and therefore to
the good man that which is in accordance with virtue.
Happiness, therefore, does not lie in amusement; it
would, indeed, be strange if the end were amusement,
and one were to take trouble and suffer hardship all
one's life in order to amuse oneself. For, in a word, everything that we choose we choose for the sake of something
else—except happiness, which is an end. Now to exert
oneself and work for the sake of amusement seems silly
and utterly childish. But to amuse oneself in order that
one may exert oneself, as Anacharsis[2] puts it, seems
right; for amusement is a sort of relaxation, and we
need relaxation because we cannot work continuously.
Relaxation, then, is not an end; for it is taken for the
sake of activity.|

The happy life is thought to be virtuous; now a

---

[1] 1099ᵃ13, 1113ᵃ22–33, 1166ᵃ12, 1170ᵃ14-16, 1176ᵃ15–22.
[2] A Scythian prince who was believed to have travelled in Greece,
and to have been the author of many aphorisms.

virtuous life requires exertion, and does not consist in amusement. And we say that serious things are better than laughable things and those connected with amusement, and that the activity of the better of any two things—whether it be two elements of our being or two men—is the more serious; but the activity of the better is *ipso facto* superior and more of the nature of happiness. And any chance person—even a slave—can enjoy the bodily pleasures no less than the best man; but no one assigns to a slave a share in happiness—unless he assigns to him also a share in human life. For happiness does not lie in such occupations, but, as we have said before,[1] in virtuous activities.

Happiness in the highest sense is the contemplative life

7. If happiness is activity in accordance with virtue, it is reasonable that it should be in accordance with the highest virtue; and this will be that of the best thing in us. Whether it be reason or something else that is this element which is thought to be our natural ruler and guide and to take thought of things noble and divine, whether it be itself also divine or only the most divine element in us, the activity of this in accordance with its proper virtue will be perfect happiness. That this activity is contemplative we have already said.[2]

Now this would seem to be in agreement both with what we said before[3] and with the truth. For, firstly, this activity is the best (since not only is reason the best thing in us, but the objects of reason are the best of knowable objects); and, secondly, it is the most continuous, since we can contemplate truth more

---

[1] 1098ᵃ16, 1176ᵃ35–ᵇ9.

[2] This has not been said, but cf. 1095ᵇ14–1096ᵃ5, 1141ᵃ18–ᵇ3, 1143ᵇ33–1144ᵃ6, 1145ᵃ6–11.

[3] 1097ᵃ25–ᵇ21, 1099ᵃ7–21, 1173ᵇ15–19, 1174ᵇ20–23, 1175ᵇ36–1176ᵃ3.

continuously than we can *do* anything. And we think
happiness ought to have pleasure mingled with it, but
the activity of philosophic wisdom is admittedly the
pleasantest of virtuous activities; at all events the pursuit of it is thought to offer pleasures marvellous for
their purity and their enduringness, and it is to be
expected that those who know will pass their time more
pleasantly than those who inquire. And the self-sufficiency that is spoken of must belong most to the contemplative activity. For while a philosopher, as well as
a just man or one possessing any other virtue, needs the
necessaries of life, when they are sufficiently equipped
with things of that sort the just man needs people towards whom and with whom he shall act justly, and the
temperate man, the brave man, and each of the others
is in the same case, but the philosopher, even when by
himself, can contemplate truth, and the better the wiser
he is; he can perhaps do so better if he has fellow
workers, but still he is the most self-sufficient. | And this
activity alone would seem to be loved for its own sake;
for nothing arises from it apart from the contemplating,
while from practical activities we gain more or less apart
from the action. And happiness is thought to depend
on leisure; for we are busy that we may have leisure,
and make war that we may live in peace. Now the
activity of the practical virtues is exhibited in political
or military affairs, but the actions concerned with these
seem to be unleisurely. Warlike actions are completely
so (for no one chooses to be at war, or provokes war, for
the sake of being at war; anyone would seem absolutely
murderous if he were to make enemies of his friends
in order to bring about battle and slaughter); but the
action of the statesman also is unleisurely, and aims—
beyond the political action itself—at despotic power
and honours, or at all events happiness, for him and

his fellow citizens—a happiness different from political action, and evidently sought as being different. So if among virtuous actions political and military actions are distinguished by nobility and greatness, and these are unleisurely and aim at an end and are not desirable for their own sake, but the activity of reason, which is contemplative, seems both to be superior in serious worth and to aim at no end beyond itself, and to have its pleasure proper to itself (and this augments the activity), and the self-sufficiency, leisureliness, un-weariedness (so far as this is possible for man), and all the other attributes ascribed to the supremely happy man are evidently those connected with this activity, it follows that this will be the complete happiness of man, if it be allowed a complete term of life (for none of the attributes of happiness is *in*complete).

But such a life would be too high for man; for it is not in so far as he is man that he will live so, but in so far as something divine is present in him; and by so much as this is superior to our composite nature is its activity superior to that which is the exercise of the other kind of virtue. If reason is divine, then, in comparison with man, the life according to it is divine in comparison with human life. But we must not follow those who advise us, being men, to think of human things, and, being mortal, of mortal things, but must, so far as we can, make ourselves immortal, and strain every nerve to live in accordance with the best thing in us; for even if it be small in bulk, | much more does it in power and worth surpass everything. And this would seem actually to *be* each man, since it is the authoritative and better part of him. It would be strange, then, if he were to choose not the life of himself but that of some-thing else. And what we said before[1] will apply now:

[1] 1169^{b}33, 1176^{b}26.

that which is proper to each thing is by nature best and most pleasant for each thing; for man, therefore, the life according to reason is best and pleasantest, since reason more than anything else *is* man. This life therefore is also the happiest.

Superiority of the contemplative life further considered

8. But in a secondary degree the life in accordance with the other kind of virtue is happy; for the activities in accordance with this befit our human estate. Just and brave acts, and other virtuous acts, we do in relation to each other, observing our respective duties with regard to contracts and services and all manner of actions and with regard to passions; and all of these seem to be typically human. Some of them seem even to arise from the body, and virtue of character to be in many ways bound up with the passions. Practical wisdom, too, is linked to virtue of character, and this to practical wisdom, since the principles of practical wisdom are in accordance with the moral virtues and rightness in morals is in accordance with practical wisdom. Being connected with the passions also, the moral virtues must belong to our composite nature; and the virtues of our composite nature are human; so, therefore, are the life and the happiness which correspond to these. The excellence of the reason is a thing apart: we must be content to say this much about it, for to describe it precisely is a task greater than our purpose requires. It would seem, however, also to need external equipment but little, or less than moral virtue does. Grant that both need the necessaries, and do so equally, even if the statesman's work is the more concerned with the body and things of that sort; for there will be little difference there; but in what they need for the exercise of their activities there will be much difference. The

liberal man will need money for the doing of his liberal
deeds, and the just man too will need it for the return-
ing of services (for wishes are hard to discern, and even
people who are not just *pretend* to wish to act justly);
and the brave man will need power if he is to accom-
plish any of the acts that correspond to his virtue, and
the temperate man will need opportunity; for how
else is either he or any of the others to be recognized?
It is debated, too, whether the will or the deed is more
essential to virtue, which is assumed to involve both;
it is surely clear that its perfection involves both; |
but for deeds many things are needed, and more, the
greater and nobler the deeds are. But the man who is
contemplating the truth needs no such thing, at least
with a view to the exercise of his activity; indeed they
are, one may say, even hindrances, at all events to his
contemplation; but in so far as he is a man and lives
with a number of people, he chooses to do virtuous acts;
he will therefore need such aids to living a human life.

But that perfect happiness is a contemplative activity
will appear from the following consideration as well.
We assume the gods to be above all other beings blessed
and happy; but what sort of actions must we assign to
them? Acts of justice? Will not the gods seem absurd
if they make contracts and return deposits, and so on?
Acts of a brave man, then, confronting dangers and
running risks because it is noble to do so? Or liberal
acts? To whom will they give? It will be strange if they
are really to have money or anything of the kind. And
what would their temperate acts be? Is not such praise
tasteless, since they have no bad appetites? If we were
to run through them all, the circumstances of action
would be found trivial and unworthy of gods. Still,
everyone supposes that they *live* and therefore that
they are active; we cannot suppose them to sleep like

Endymion. Now if you take away from a living being
action, and still more production, what is left but contemplation? Therefore the activity of God, which surpasses all others in blessedness, must be contemplative;
and of human activities, therefore, that which is most
akin to this must be most of the nature of happiness.

This is indicated, too, by the fact that the other
animals have no share in happiness, being completely
deprived of such activity. For while the whole life of
the gods is blessed, and that of men too in so far as some
likeness of such activity belongs to them, none of the
other animals is happy, since they in no way share in
contemplation. Happiness extends, then, just so far as
contemplation does, and those to whom contemplation
more fully belongs are more truly happy, not as a mere
concomitant but in virtue of the contemplation; for
this is in itself precious. Happiness, therefore, must be
some form of contemplation.

But, being a man, one will also need external prosperity; for our nature is not self-sufficient for the
purpose of contemplation, but our body also must be
healthy and must have food and other attention. | Still,
we must not think that the man who is to be happy will
need many things or great things, merely because he
cannot be supremely happy without external goods;
for self-sufficiency and action do not involve excess, and
we can do noble acts without ruling earth and sea; for
even with moderate advantages one can act virtuously
(this is manifest enough; for private persons are
thought to do worthy acts no less than despots—indeed
even more); and it is enough that we should have so
much as that; for the life of the man who is active in
accordance with virtue will be happy. Solon, too, was
perhaps sketching well the happy man when he described him as moderately furnished with externals but

as having done (as Solon thought) the noblest acts, and
lived temperately; for one can with but moderate possessions do what one ought. Anaxagoras also seems to
have supposed the happy man not to be rich nor a des-
pot, when he said that he would not be surprised if the
happy man were to seem to most people a strange person; for they judge by externals, since these are all they
perceive. The opinions of the wise seem, then, to harmonize with our arguments. But while even such things
carry some conviction, the truth in practical matters is
discerned from the facts of life; for these are the decisive
factor. We must therefore survey what we have already
said, bringing it to the test of the facts of life, and if it
harmonizes with the facts we must accept it, but if it
clashes with them we must suppose it to be mere theory.
Now he who exercises his reason and cultivates it seems
to be both in the best state of mind and most dear to the
gods. For if the gods have any care for human affairs, as
they are thought to have, it would be reasonable both
that they should delight in that which was best and
most akin to them (i.e. reason) and that they should
reward those who love and honour this most, as caring
for the things that are dear to them and acting both
rightly and nobly. And that all these attributes belong
most of all to the philosopher is manifest. He, therefore,
is the dearest to the gods. And he who is that will presumably be also the happiest; so that in this way too the
philosopher will more than any other be happy.

*Legislation is needed if the end is to be attained: transition to
the* Politics

9. If these matters and the virtues, and also friendship
and pleasure, have been dealt with sufficiently in outline, are we to suppose that our programme has reached
its end? Surely, as the saying goes, where there are

things to be done the end is not to survey and recognize
the various things, | but rather to do them; with regard
to virtue, then, it is not enough to know, but we must
try to have and use it, or try any other way there may be
of becoming good. Now if arguments were in themselves enough to make men good, they would justly, as
Theognis says, have won very great rewards, and such
rewards should have been provided; but as things are,
while they seem to have power to encourage and stimulate the generous-minded among our youth, and to
make a character which is gently born, and a true
lover of what is noble, ready to be possessed by virtue,
they are not able to encourage the *many* to nobility and
goodness. For these do not by nature obey the sense of
shame, but only fear, and do not abstain from bad acts
because of their baseness but through fear of punishment; living by passion they pursue their own pleasures and the means to them, and avoid the opposite
pains, and have not even a conception of what is noble
and truly pleasant, since they have never tasted it.
What argument would remould such people? It is hard,
if not impossible, to remove by argument the traits that
have long since been incorporated in the character;
and perhaps we must be content if, when all the influences by which we are thought to become good are
present, we get some tincture of virtue.

Now some think that we are made good by nature,
others by habituation, others by teaching. Nature's
part evidently does not depend on us, but as a result
of some divine causes is present in those who are truly
fortunate; while argument and teaching, we may
suspect, are not powerful with all men, but the soul of
the student must first have been cultivated by means
of habits for noble joy and noble hatred, like earth
which is to nourish the seed. For he who lives as passion

directs will not hear argument that dissuades him, nor
understand it if he does; and how can we persuade one
in such a state to change his ways? And in general
passion seems to yield not to argument but to force.
The character, then, must somehow be there already
with a kinship to virtue, loving what is noble and hating
what is base.

But it is difficult to get from youth up a right training
for virtue if one has not been brought up under right
laws; for to live temperately and hardily is not pleasant
to most people, especially when they are young. For
this reason their nurture and occupations should be
fixed by law; for they will not be painful when they
have become customary. | But it is surely not enough
that when they are young they should get the right
nurture and attention: since they must, even when they
are grown up, practise and be habituated to them, we
shall need laws for this as well, and generally speaking
to cover the whole of life; for most people obey necessity
rather than argument, and punishments rather than
the sense of what is noble.

This is why some think that legislators ought to
stimulate men to virtue and urge them forward by the
motive of the noble, on the assumption that those who
have been well advanced by the formation of habits
will attend to such influences; and that punishments
and penalties should be imposed on those who disobey and are of inferior nature, while the incurably
bad should be completely banished. A good man (they
think), since he lives with his mind fixed on what is
noble, will submit to argument, while a bad man,
whose desire is for pleasure, is corrected by pain like
a beast of burden. This is, too, why they say the pains
inflicted should be those that are most opposed to the
pleasures such men love.

However that may be, if (as we have said)[1] the man who is to be good must be well trained and habituated, and go on to spend his time in worthy occupations and neither willingly nor unwillingly do bad actions, and if this can be brought about if men live in accordance with a sort of reason and right order, provided this has force—if this be so, the paternal command indeed has not the required force or compulsive power (nor in general has the command of one man, unless he be a king or something similar), but the law *has* compulsive power, while it is at the same time a rule proceeding from a sort of practical wisdom and reason. And while people hate *men* who oppose their impulses, even if they oppose them rightly, the law in its ordaining of what is good is not burdensome.

In the Spartan state alone, or almost alone, the legislator seems to have paid attention to questions of nurture and occupation; in most states such matters have been neglected, and each man lives as he pleases, Cyclops-fashion, 'to his own wife and children dealing law'.[2] Now it is best that there should be a public and proper care for such matters; but if they are neglected by the community it would seem right for each man to help his children and friends towards virtue, and that they should have the power, or at least the will, to do this.

It would seem from what has been said that he can do this better if he makes himself capable of legislating. For public control is plainly effected by laws, and good control by good laws; whether written or unwritten would seem to make no difference, | nor whether they are laws providing for the education of individuals or of groups—any more than it does in the case of music or gymnastics and other such pursuits. For as in cities laws

[1] 1179ᵇ31–1180ᵃ5.   [2] *Od.* ix. 114 f.

and prevailing types of character have force, so in households do the injunctions and the habits of the father, and these have even more because of the tie of blood and the benefits he confers; for the children start with a natural affection and disposition to obey. Further, private education has an advantage over public, as private medical treatment has; for while in general rest and abstinence from food are good for a man in a fever, for a particular man they may not be; and a boxer presumably does not prescribe the same style of fighting to all his pupils. It would seem, then, that the detail is worked out with more precision if the control is private; for each person is more likely to get what suits his case.

But the details can be best looked after, one by one, by a doctor or gymnastic instructor or anyone else who has the general knowledge of what is good for everyone or for people of a certain kind (for the sciences both are said to be, and are, concerned with what is universal); not but what some particular detail may perhaps be well looked after by an unscientific person, if he has studied accurately in the light of experience what happens in each case, just as some people seem to be their own best doctors, though they could give no help to anyone else. None the less, it will perhaps be agreed that if a man does wish to become master of an art or science he must go to the universal, and come to know it as well as possible; for, as we have said, it is with this that the sciences are concerned.

And surely he who wants to make men, whether many or few, better by his care must try to become capable of legislating, if it is through laws that we can become good. For to get anyone whatever—anyone who is put before us—into the right condition is not for the first chance comer; if anyone can do it, it is the man

who knows, just as in medicine and all other matters
which give scope for care and prudence.

Must we not, then, next examine whence or how one
can learn how to legislate? Is it, as in all other cases,
from statesmen? Certainly it was thought to be a part
of statesmanship.[1] Or is a difference apparent between
statesmanship and the other sciences and arts? In the
others the same people are found offering to teach the
arts and practising them, e.g. doctors or painters; but
while the sophists profess to teach politics, | it is prac-
tised not by any of them but by the politicians, who
would seem to do so by dint of a certain skill and experience rather than of thought; for they are not found
either writing or speaking about such matters (though
it were a nobler occupation perhaps than composing
speeches for the law-courts and the assembly), nor
again are they found to have made statesmen of their
own sons or any other of their friends. But it was to be
expected that they should if they could; for there is
nothing better than such a skill that they could have
left to their cities, or could prefer to have for themselves, or, therefore, for those dearest to them. Still,
experience seems to contribute not a little; else they
could not have become politicians by familiarity with
politics; and so it seems that those who aim at knowing
about the art of politics need experience as well.

But those of the sophists who profess the art seem to
be very far from teaching it. For, to put the matter
generally, they do not even know what kind of thing it
is nor what kinds of things it is about; otherwise they
would not have classed it as identical with rhetoric or
even inferior to it, nor have thought it easy to legislate
by collecting the laws that are thought well of; they say
it is possible to select the best laws, as though even the

[1] 1141^b24.

selection did not demand intelligence and as though
right judgement were not the greatest thing, as in
matters of music. For while people experienced in any
department judge rightly the works produced in it, and
understand by what means or how they are achieved,
and what harmonizes with what, the inexperienced
must be content if they do not fail to see whether the
work has been well or ill made—as in the case of painting. Now laws are as it were the 'works' of the political
art; | how then can one learn from them to be a legis-
lator, or judge which are best? Even medical men do
not seem to be made by a study of text-books. Yet people
try, at any rate, to state not only the treatments, but
also how particular classes of people can be cured and
should be treated—distinguishing the various habits
of body; but while this seems useful to experienced
people, to the inexperienced it is valueless. Surely,
then, while collections of laws, and of constitutions
also, may be serviceable to those who can study them
and judge what is good or bad and what enactments
suit what circumstances, those who go through such
collections without a practised faculty will not have
right judgement (unless it be as a spontaneous gift of
nature), though they may perhaps become more intelligent in such matters.

Now our predecessors have left the subject of legislation to us unexamined; it is perhaps best, therefore,
that we should ourselves study it, and in general study
the question of the constitution, in order to complete to
the best of our ability the philosophy of human nature.
First, then, if anything has been said well in detail by
earlier thinkers, let us try to review it; then in the light
of the constitutions we have collected let us study what
sorts of influence preserve and destroy states, and
what sorts preserve or destroy the particular kinds of

constitution, and to what causes it is due that some are well and others ill administered. When these matters have been studied we shall perhaps be more likely to see with a comprehensive view which constitution is best, and how each must be ordered, and what laws and customs it must use, if it is to be at its best.[1] Let us make a beginning of our discussion.

[1] 1181^b12–23 is a programme for the *Politics*, agreeing to a large extent with the existing contents of that work.

INDEX

Action, always particular, 50, cf.
146; and making, 1, 141 f.; and
the gods, 267; involuntary, 48
ff., its final cause, 179; its ori-
gins, 60, 138 f., 156; political,
264; voluntary, 105.

Activity, and products, 1; and
potentiality, 28, 240; and process, 186; and state of mind,
character, 13, 16, 29, cf. 261,
199; best, 17, cf. 268; comes
into being, 239; good and bad,
259; its end; 65; necessary and
desirable, 261; of God, 268;
of immobility, 191; of soul,
13, cf. 15; of reason, 265; perfect, 256; unimpeded, 187; virtuous, 20, 59, 263 f., cf. 21, 266.

Advantageous, the, 33, 100, 108,
142, 208, 209, 234; apparently,
236; ignorance of, 51, 146; relation to justice, 108, 124.

Aeschylus, 51.

Agamemnon, 211.

Agathon, 139, 141.

Age, 19, 84.

Alope, 177.

Ambition, 41, 95, 205.

Amusement, 42, 102 ff., 177, 261 ff.

Anacharsis, 262.

Anaxagoras, 146, 269.

Anaxandrides, 182.

Anger, 29, 33, 35, 41, 53, 69 f.,
96 ff., 110, 127, 134, 165, 173 f.;
acts done in, 52 f., 127; incontinence in, 160, 168 f., 170;
restraint of, 97.

Aphrodite, 174.

Appetite, lust, 29, 35, 53, 69, 75,
77, 169; acts due to, 52 f., 166;
bad and good, 162, 267; differences of, 174; for noble and
base objects, 169, 259; natural
and peculiar, 74 f., 173; weak
and strong, 161 f.

Appetitive element, 27, 78.

Argives, 71.

Aristocracy, 113, 209 ff.

Aristotle, reff. to other works:
An. Post., 140, 141; *Phys.*, 255;
? *Pol.*, 111, 125; ? *Rhet.*, 43.

Art, 11, 14, 30, 118, 141 f., 144;
and nature, 18, 28, 38, 257;
and practical wisdom, 142,
144; and science, 1, 56, 142,
144; and virtue, 28, 29, 33, 34,
38; excellence in, 143 f., product
of, 184, 186.

Association, 117, 208 ff., 212, cf.
Society.

Athenians, 93.

Athlete, 54, 68.

Barbarians, 159, 172.

Bashful man, 43.

Bias, 108.

Black Sea, 171.

Blessed, 19 ff.

Boastfulness, 42, 66, 100 f.

Body, 105, 252; and mind, 72;
and soul, 24, 212; pains of, 176;
pleasures of, 32, 72, 73, 168,
174, 179, 182, 187, 188, 189 f.,
235, 262, 263; vices of, 61.

Boorishness, 31, 42, 103, 104.

Brasidas, 124.

Brute, i.e. animal, 69, 138, 145,
157, 159, 174, 184, 187; opp.
to man, 175, 190.

Brutishness, 74, 159, 171 f., 174 f.

Buffoonery, 42, 103 f.

Calypso, 46.

Cannibalism, 171.

Carcinus, 177.

Category, 8.

Celts, 66.

Chance, 17 ff., 21, 55 f., 81, 188;
and art, 34, 141.

Character, 4, 53, 83, 84, 100, 102,
104, 138, 156, 193, 225 f., 248,
266, 270, 271, 273; its essential
element, 218; love of, 220.

Child, 12, 17, 19, 48, 59, 77, 170,
171, 172, 184, 187, 203, 210,
213, 214, 227, 233, 272; cp. to
chattel, 123; intellect of, 253.

277

INDEX

Exchange, 117 ff.
Experience, 65, 68, 148, 153, 201, 273, 274.
Eye of the soul, 156, cf. 153.

Fact, and reason, 5, 14; and argument, 235, 248, 249, 269.
Faculty, capacity, 23; and activity, 28, 233, 240; and happiness, 23; and purpose, 102; and state of character, 35 f., 102; as disposition, 152; as part, 25; calculative, 138; of soul, 25.
Father, 27, 126, 170, 173, 203, 207, 210 f., 219, 223 f.; justice of, 123; friendship of, 211.
Fear, 35, 48, 68, 84, 104 f., 126, 270; defined, 63; and confidence, 40, 63, 71.
Fearlessness, 40, 64, 70.
Flatterer, 42, 84, 93, 100, 205, 253.
Fortune, good, prosperity, 15, 17, 91, 93, 188, 192, 238, 244 f., 270; goods of, 107.
Friend(s), agency of, 57; and fellow citizens, 12; another self, 228; in prosperity and adversity, 244 ff., 238; not flatterer, 253; number of, 243 f.; should live together, 199 f., 246.
Friendly feeling, love, 35, 194, 195, 200, 204, 230, 233, 234.
Friendship, 99, 192–247; analogy in state and home, 210 ff.; and equality, 204 ff.; and goodwill, 194 ff., 201, 230 ff.; and self-love, 227 ff.; as virtue, 192; between equals, 194 f., 203, 215 ff.; likes, 193, 197, 226; unequals, 203 f., 215, 218 f.; unlikes, 220; childish, 226; claims of, 223 ff., ending of, 225 ff.; greatest external good, 238; happy man's need of, 238 ff.; legal and moral, 216; natural, 219; of goodness, 196 f., 200 f.; of utility and pleasure, 195 f., 201 ff.; perfect, 196 f., 201; political, 207 ff., 209 ff., 218, 232, 244; with gods, 213;

companions, 200, 207, 211, 213 f., 220, 244; relations, 213 ff.; problems of, 193.

Gain, 117, 218.
Geometer, 14, 148, 258.
Geometry, 151.
Glaucus, 129.
God, 8, 24, 159, 204, 228, 268; single pleasure of, 191; gods, 23, 87, 88, 90, 124, 132, 159, 204, 208, 213, 222, 267 f., 269; gift of, 18.
Good, the, 6, 12, 14, 24, 248, 249 f., 251, 254; and pleasant, useful, 194, 253; apparent, 58, 62, 194; another's, 108, 123; as many senses as being, 8; defined, 1, 11, 249; chief, 2, 11, 12, 16, 184, 187 f.; divided into activity and state, 185; final, 12, 62, 157; Idea of, 5, 7 ff.; natural, 250; goods, absolutely and relatively, 9, 185, cf. 10, 107, 194, 195, 196; achievable by action, 4, 10, 11, 146; bodily, 15, 189; column of, 9; external, 15, 90, 188, 238; human, 2, 14, 25, 143, 146; obj. of competition, 237, cf. 235; universal, 7.
Good temper, 27, 29, 41, 46, 96 f., 98, 108.
Goodwill, 194, 230 f.
Graces, 118.
Gymnastics, &c., 8, 30, 37, 56, 71, 135, 154, 273.

Habit, 5, 28, 171, 190, 271, 273, 275; and nature, 183, 271.
Habituation, 14, 17, 77, 179, 183.
Happiness, 5–25, 155, 183, 261–9; after death, 19 f., 22 f.; and amusement, 262 f.; and external goods, 268 f., and feeling, 251; components of, 108; defined, 5–17; how acquired, 17 ff.; human, 25; impossible for animals, 268, slaves, 263; in intellectual and moral activity, 263–7; no man called happy while

279